Haunted

ISSUES OF GLOBALIZATION
Case Studies in Contemporary Anthropology
Series Editors: Carla Freeman and Li Zhang

The Native World-System:
An Ethnography of Bolivian Aymara Traders
in the Global Economy
Nico Tassi

Sacred Rice:
An Ethnography of Identity, Environment,
and Development in Rural West Africa
Joanna Davidson

City of Flowers:
An Ethnography of Social and Economic Change
in Costa Rica's Central Valley
Susan E. Mannon

Labor and Legality:
An Ethnography of a Mexican Immigrant Network
Ruth Gomberg-Muñoz

Listen, Here Is a Story:
Ethnographic Life Narratives from Aka
and Ngandu Women of the Congo Basin
Bonnie L. Hewlett

Cuban Color in Tourism and La Lucha:
An Ethnography of Racial Meanings
L. Kaifa Roland

Gangsters Without Borders:
An Ethnography of a Salvadoran Street Gang
T. W. Ward

Haunted

An Ethnography of the Hollywood and
Hong Kong Media Industries

SYLVIA J. MARTIN

New York   Oxford
OXFORD UNIVERSITY PRESS

Oxford University Press is a department of the University of Oxford.
It furthers the University's objective of excellence in research, scholarship,
and education by publishing worldwide. Oxford is a registered trade mark
of Oxford University Press in the UK and certain other countries.

Published in the United States of America by Oxford University Press
198 Madison Avenue, New York, NY 10016, United States of America.

© 2017 by Oxford University Press

Library of Congress Cataloging-in-Publication Data

CIP data is on file at the Library of Congress
ISBN number: 978-0-19-046446-2

9 8 7 6 5 4 3 2 1

Printed by R.R. Donnelley, United States of America

This book is dedicated to
Barbara Rebecca Martin and Jeffery Martin.

TABLE OF CONTENTS

....

LIST OF ILLUSTRATIONS
....

ACKNOWLEDGMENTS

First and foremost, I offer my deepest gratitude to my parents Barbara R. Martin and Jeffery Martin. Their unwavering support has meant everything to me.

I thank all the media workers in Los Angeles and Hong Kong who so generously shared their time and thoughts with me for this project. From their experiences and stories I hope I am able to convey some of the complexities of their labor. I am grateful for their participation, and I cherish the friendships that have grown out of this research.

I am indebted to Victoria Bernal for her guidance and warm encouragement of my work; I have learned much from her vision of anthropology. The conceptual insights and concrete advice she brings to this and other projects continue to inspire me. Tom Boellstorff has indefatigably offered creative ways of working through ideas as well as wonderfully practical perspectives. Bill Maurer has been a rich source of intellectual acuity and a staunch advocate. These three scholars have taught me so much, and generously provided exciting and invaluable ways to participate in the academic community.

Other scholars played vital roles at various stages of this project, many of whom who read earlier sections of this book. In anthropology, I particularly appreciate the insights of Mei Zhan, Tejaswini Ganti, Faye Ginsburg, Sherry Ortner, Clare Wilkinson-Weber, and Michael Fischer. I am grateful for the enthusiasm and feedback over the years, whether it be through book projects or conferences, from: Toby Miller, Vicki Mayer, Gina Marchetti, David Hesmondhalgh, Mette Hjort, Lo Kwai Cheung, Laikwan Pang, Michael Curtin, John Caldwell, Tom Gunning, and Poshek Fu.

At the University of California, Irvine, I enjoyed the support of many people, including Mike Burton, Leo Chavez, Karen Leonard, Michael Montoya, and Dorothy Solinger. My dissertation writing group—Neha Vora, Jennifer Chase, and Judith Pajo—was a crucial source of sustenance and camaraderie. Other friends from the UCI community who shared this experience include Janaki Parikh, Vickie Luong, Selim Shahine, Kiki Papageorgiou, Rosie Conley-Estrada, Roberto Gonzalez, Karen Robinson, Duy Nguyen, Nanao Akanuma, Caroline Melly, Tom Douglas, Justine Hanson, and Jenny Fan.

I thank all my colleagues at The University of Hong Kong. They have been very welcoming, and offer a vibrant intellectual community. I appreciate their support of this endeavor, particularly David Palmer and Travis Kong. Other friends and colleagues who have been an invaluable part of this journey include Yael Warshel, Dennis Lopez, Nicki Cole, and Pardis Mahdavi. I have also had many enthusiastic students along the way who inspired me with their passion for anthropology and all things media.Heartfelt thanks to Jennifer D., Shana Hagan, Lotti Pharriss Knowles, John Knowles, Mark Tapio Kines, Boris Cheung, Kyoko Tochikawa, Oliver Hurtter, Rebecca Schott, Jill, Gail, and Kevin.

This material is based upon work supported by the Fulbright Postdoctoral Research in the Social Sciences program at The University of Hong Kong. I also benefitted from the generous assistance of the University of California Pacific Rim Research Program as well as the Labor Studies Group and Center for Asian Studies at the University of California, Irvine. Any findings, opinions, or conclusions expressed in this material do not necessarily reflect the views of those entities. Any errors are my own. I am grateful to the Hong Kong Film Archives and Hong Kong Film Services Office for their helpful assistance.

I thank the journal *Visual Anthropology Review* for permission to publish a slightly revised version of my article "Of Ghosts and Gangsters: Capitalist Cultural Production and the Hong Kong Film Industry" Volume 28, Issue 1, Pages 32–49, May 2012. I also thank the journal *Critical Studies in Media Communication* for their permission to publish a slightly revised version of my article "The Death Narratives of Revitalization: Colonial Governance, China, and the Reconfiguration of the Hong Kong Film Industry" Volume 32, Issue 5, Pages 318–332, December 2015.

This book would not have been possible without the kind support and enthusiasm of Carla Freeman, Li Zhang, Sherith Pankratz, Meredith Keffer, and Roxanne Klaas at Oxford University Press. I also deeply thank the reviewers for their time, careful attention, and detailed feedback for my manuscript: Allan C. Dawson, Drew University; Sherry B. Ortner, University of California, Los Angeles; Robin Conley, Marshall University; Cynthia Jenzen, Schoolcraft Community College; and Leila Rodriguez, University of Cincinnati.

Paul, Carol, David, and Kelly have all lent a hand with life outside of academia and provided laughs over the years for which I am grateful. I deeply appreciate the warmth and unceasing kindnesses of all my in-laws who have made the world a smaller place.

Finally, of my beloved husband Ah Kit—the person with whom I have shared this journey the most—I shall say the least, as he wishes.

"The End"

"You're playing a dead body." It was 2003, and I had decided to seek work as an extra[1] at a network television show at a major studio in Los Angeles, California, as a way to immerse myself in an ethnographic study of media production. I wanted to better understand how media personnel,[2] from actors to electricians, forge social relationships around the camera. When I called Central Casting (the company to whom the process of finding extras was subcontracted by studios and production companies) to find out what stage I was to report to the next day, I was a little taken aback to hear I was to play a corpse. What would performing death entail? In the meantime, I was told that as a non-union extra I would be paid $50 for the eight-hour shift and the overtime rate for any remaining hours, with a 12-hour shift expected. Breakfast, lunch, and dinner would be provided by the production company, which I discovered generally spent $3 million to $4 million per episode to produce (a sum that included the salaries of the entire production). However, when I checked in the next morning at 6 to the wardrobe station on the studio lot, I had been reassigned to the role of a bystander. I was relieved, as it would have been challenging to observe the filming activity if my/the corpse's eyes were supposed to be closed. Also, as other extras confirmed while we were getting into costume in the studio restrooms, while it could be interesting to play a corpse, it could also be slightly <u>macabre</u> given the blood and disfiguring prosthetics.

disturbing and
horrifying

1

Several years later, across the Pacific Ocean in Hong Kong, I again encountered the prospect of participating in a spectacle of death. One of my informants, Shirley, a Hong Kong filmmaker, was about to start production on her film. Her script called for a "Western woman" to be brutally stabbed. I'd helped Shirley edit the English in the script and attended a few preproduction meetings. Filming with a small budget, Shirley wanted to work with people she knew who could be prevailed upon to work for low wages, such as the anthropologist who had been peppering her with questions. But when Shirley asked me to play the role, I hesitated. I was eager to repay my debt to her, and interested in participating in the spectacle, but I knew that I'd have to leave Hong Kong shortly, and filming might not conclude before then. I also couldn't help but note that I was yet again confronting the labor of performing death. By this point, I'd been made aware by media workers in both Hollywood and Hong Kong that filming a death scene (especially one's own) can raise ontological and cosmological issues for those involved. The script in fact called for the woman to die a very bloody death. After discussing the scheduling conflict, Shirley acknowledged the enactment of death within the context of Hong Kong media production, which is shaped by Chinese popular religion and folk beliefs about the inappropriateness of photographing the dead. Shirley told me that she would pay me the *lai see* ("lucky money," or ritual payment of actual money put into small red envelopes) after filming my death scene.

In Hong Kong film and television production, *lai see* is often paid by producers or directors to actors or stunt workers who perform scenes in which violence or death is enacted, in addition to their formal salary. *Lai see* in Hong Kong is typically dispensed by family members at holidays and birthdays, and sometimes by employers to staff for services rendered. Yet its disbursement in the entertainment industry also indicates an appreciation for a risky job well done. The token payment is interpreted as a form of protection to the performer, as well as the rest of the production team, to appease any *gwei* ("spirits") who may be drawn to the spectacle of death and violence—a holdover from Cantonese opera troupes who acknowledged that spectral viewers may make mischief for performers. Some informants saw the disbursement of *lai see* as merely a courtesy and a cultural custom. Some were matter of fact about filming death scenes and did not believe there was any merit to the idea of spirits. Yet many people I spoke to acknowledged that filming death scenes is considered risk-prone and spiritually provocative. When Hong Kong actor Law Lok Sam died an apparently unprecedented five times on five different Hong Kong TV programs within 24 hours in 2011, it made headlines around the world. His fans were upset at this spate of deaths, and even news reports such as the one posted in the *Sydney Morning Herald* on April 11, 2011 explained to readers that Law was given *lai see* by his colleagues for "good fortune." Various actors, stunt workers, and production personnel have been alleged to be plagued or possessed by spirits during filming; the payment of *lai see* in this context underscores that media workers labor between the worlds of life and death.[3]

I nearly brushed off Shirley's offer of *lai see*, but I realized that since this was a common (albeit casual) custom in Hong Kong production culture, I should follow their convention. However, shortly after I consented to play the role in Shirley's film, the start of filming was delayed until close to the time of my departure from Hong Kong. Because I would be unable to complete the film shoot, Shirley hired a professional actress instead. Yet it had become evident to me by that point in my research that filming death scenes was fairly common in narrative film and scripted television production—I had observed and heard about quite a few such scenes. In fact, the volume of death scenes was unsurprising given the spectacular "shock and awe" genres and storylines that commercial media industries in North and South America, Asia, and Europe launch onto regional and global markets. Love and death are considered universally legible and marketable themes, transcending language barriers. Many film and television genres (such as action, crime, romance, horror, and thriller) utilize death and dying as a key threat upon which the plot pivots. But what kind of labor is involved in creating these spectacles? How do cultural ideas about death, and the process of filming it, manifest in our very "modern" media industries in different parts of the world? In contrast to managerial acknowledgment in Hong Kong, ontological concerns about filming such content in Hollywood, I found, were usually handled privately and informally by the individual involved, which some personnel did through private prayer, or intentionally wearing a religious symbol under one's costume, or even keeping a statue or icon of St. Clare of Assisi (the Catholic Church's patron saint of television) near one's person. Drawing on various religious and cosmological practices to protect oneself from a liminal state, staged though it might be, raises questions about supposedly rationalistic industrial production processes. They also accentuate specific commonalities and contrasts between Eastern and Western media production.

This book examines the experiences of the women and men who create narrative film and scripted television in two commercial production centers, Los Angeles (Hollywood) and Hong Kong (what some media practitioners and scholars have called the "Hollywood of the East").[4] My behind-the-scenes perspective is acquired from ethnographic fieldwork of film and television industries in Hollywood and Hong Kong between 2003 and 2007. I attempt to convey media workers' views about their day-to-day work as well as their broader concerns about job insecurity as production work has declined in both Hollywood and Hong Kong, moving to other locales. Looking at the culture(s) of the production process (or, "production culture," as John Caldwell terms it [Caldwell 2008: 7]) entails identifying patterns within and between the two sites from an anthropological perspective. Therefore, it is not just media personnel's observable behavior that is of interest to me, but their reflections and concerns about their work that they shared with me. I conducted research at production companies and studio offices in Hollywood and Hong Kong; however, I focus on the activity and attitudes on the production floor, the immediate site where filming occurs. The production floor, or set, can be an indoors and enclosed space on a sound stage at a studio,[5] or outside on the studio's backlot, or it can be at an off-studio site, at another location. The same sound stage or backlot may be used for both film and television shows, and since many informants work in both film and television, or "entertainment," in Hollywood and Hong Kong, my analysis retains that fluidity.

Many media personnel described their work—its processes, its performances, and its conditions—as "all-consuming", and an indelible experience; in many ways, it seemed to haunt them. The set is a transformative space: strangers play lovers, healthy individuals become invalids, dark stages turn into bright wonderlands, and one's embodied age, nationality, race, and gender can be altered in the process (sometimes problematically). These transformations involve the affective labor of teams of people including set designers, camera operators, lighting technicians, prop masters, makeup artists, stunt workers, and actors, many of whom draw upon a combination of precise technical skills, intense emotionality and empathy as well as physicality to create these evocative images. Yet setwork, as intense and concentrated as it is, is not untouched by global dynamics. Indeed, globalization studies have shown us that daily activities in specific localities are "contingent on globally extensive social processes" (Inda and Rosaldo 2007: 7). An overarching concern that emerged during my research was this: what does it mean to work in an industry where, on the set, time and space is transformed in order to create fantastic visual spectacle, while the very conditions for the work on the set are impacted by turbulent global processes and government policies such as free-trade agreements (Hong Kong and China) and state legislation for tax credits (California)? While production personnel build, destroy, and rebuild entire worlds on a film set, they grapple with outsourcing, offshoring and border-crossing—issues of globalization that setwork is not removed from. This book attempts to help fill in what media scholar Vicki Mayer refers to as the "connection between macro and micro that is so frequently lost in the efforts to describe the current media landscape, its interconnected industries, and its networks of professionals" (Mayer 2009: 15).

From the work involved in filming death scenes to the decline of place-based production in both Hollywood and Hong Kong, this book presents an account of loss experienced at multiple levels. I argue that despite the rationalization and corporatization of film and television production in Hollywood and Hong Kong, risk is also avoided in both sites through "irrational" means such as religion and the supernatural. In fact, the risks that emerge, and some of the ways in which they are addressed, reveal practices of spirituality and spectrality that are enfolded within ostensibly secular, industrial work sites. For instance, a Hollywood stunt worker tucks both padding *and* quotes from the Bible under his clothing for protection moments before he performs a dangerous stunt, and a Hollywood producer consults tarot cards and psychics for professional guidance; a Hong Kong film crew burns incense to appease any lurking ghosts on set. The ways in which risks are understood and addressed reveal locally specific cultural practices as well as the broad commonality of the concerns that drive them. Evidently, nonsecular approaches for avoiding industrial risk are to be found in Western contexts and not restricted to Eastern and exotically "Other" ones.

Following the multisited mode of ethnography (Marcus 1995), this book is a connective study as much as it is a comparative one as I explore the thematic links between the two commercial production centers, with attention to localized practices. As Boellstorff, Nardi, Pearce, and Taylor point out, "Moving across cultures to expand and deepen research is not always aimed at finding difference; commonalities and linkages are just as important" (Boellstorff et al. 2012: 63). Undoubtedly, there is a lack of equivalency between the two entertainment industries: one is based within an established global superpower and the other within a former British colony that is now a Special Administrative Region of a rising global player. The disparities are discussed in subsequent chapters, yet I want to point out here that for many decades, there have been transnational flows of genres, capital, and people between these two sites, such as U.S.-born, Hong Kong-raised Bruce Lee, who traversed between Hollywood and Hong Kong in the 1970s, and Hollywood-based filmmakers Christopher Nolan and Michael Bay filming in Hong Kong in the 21st century. Even though certain production practices can be attributed to local cultural attitudes, the flows of technology, labor, and genres mean that no one media production site is completely self-contained and separable. In looking at the "cross-cultural and relational dynamics" in what Lieba Faier and Lisa Rofel refer to as ethnographies of encounter (Faier and Rofel 2014: 364), I demonstrate that connections also emerge between Hollywood and Hong Kong through similar concerns and fears embedded in the industrial process of creating spectacular images, such as the risks of stunt work. Convergences also emerge through film co-productions and collaborations, forming what I refer to as media assemblages (see also Govil 2009). Examining the connections and commonalities, as well as the contrasts, between the Hollywood and Hong Kong production centers also offers a perspective on changing American and Chinese entertainment business relationships with each other, which is addressed in the Epilogue.

Studying a non-Western media industry such as Hong Kong's may at first glance seem more "anthropological" than America's, especially given the Euro-American–based discipline's lengthy fascination for "Other" regions. But as Laura Nader called for (1972), anthropologists must also "study up" within the United States to learn how American power is created and maintained. According to a California state legislature study released in April 2014, in terms of gross output, the American motion picture industry (which includes film, TV, commercials, and music videos) is larger than the automotive repair and maintenance industry, the former calculated at $120 billion, the latter at $112 billion (Taylor 2014). Nader named the communication industries as one of the arenas of power that anthropologists should strive to understand better, to which I would add the film and television industries in their global reach in production and distribution, and film's lengthy involvement with the U.S. government, which I discuss further in Chapter 1.

My work builds from other anthropological studies of film and television production (Abu-Lughod 1995; Dornfeld 1998; Ganti 2002, 2004, 2012a; Ortner 2009, 2013; Pandian 2015; Wilkinson-Weber 2004, 2012). In 1946 Hortense Powdermaker was the first anthropologist to conduct an ethnographic study of a film industry: Hollywood. A student of Bronislaw Malinowski, Powdermaker examined the links between the social relations of the Hollywood studios, the content of films, and American society, detecting the rampant uncertainty and insecurity in the industry that persists today. Also attuned to industry insecurity, Sherry Ortner's perceptive analysis of the contemporary American independent film community that defines itself as "Not Hollywood" reveals the class tensions and social attitudes of creative labor within an unstable, neoliberal economy. Ortner insightfully analyzes the work of filmmakers who came of age during a time of increasing state rollbacks and debt. Providing a rich foundation for ethnographic scholarship of commercial film production particularly in a postcolonial, non-Western context, Tejaswini Ganti has generated an extensive body of work examining the Hindi-language film industry and its "social worlds." Ganti also focuses on the instability of the industry, and her comparison of the Bollywood film industry's rituals for managing uncertainty to Malinowski's discussion of magic in *Magic, Science, and Religion* recalls the claims of Powdermaker (Malinowski's mentee) of Hollywood as a system steeped in magic (Ganti 2012a: 247–251). As Ganti observed, "the everyday life of Hindi filmmaking is marked by a variety of Hindu ritual practices" (Ganti 2012a: 247); these include prayers to the god Ganesh and the placement of images of a Hindu and Muslim saintly figure on film sets that Ganti glosses as "Malinowskian manifestations of magic" in their aim to confer success in the face of extreme uncertainty. Given Ganti's and my findings, and the decades-long engagement with psychics, tarot card readers, and New Age religions by Hollywood personnel, Powdermaker's assertion that Hollywood members attributed success to "the supernatural sphere" merits serious reconsideration (Powdermaker 1967: 284). Cultural expressions of religion and enchantment have generally been considered beyond the scope of recent Western media industry or organizational studies, yet looking at how they play a salient role in the production process is compatible with anthropology's commitment to focusing on what Ganti, citing Fred Myers, refers to as "meaning-making" within "commercially oriented cultural production" (Ganti 2012a: 6; Myers 2002: 7).

By including the rarely accessed vantage points from below-the-line as an extra and an intern, as well as observing filming and stunt work in Hong Kong, I hope to provide a more diverse picture of media personnel (cf. Abu-Lughod 1995, 2005; Dornfeld 1998). It was also through my fieldwork of working as an extra that I realized the degree to which the labor of acting—from principal cast to stunt workers to "extras"—structures much of the production culture. Actors in particular are the visible face of commercial media productions, with public stakes and risks that should be recognized (see Martin 2012).[6] Claire Wilkinson-Weber points out that in ethnographies of performance, anthropologists have participated in the field as musicians or dancers but rarely as actors, even in ethnographies of film and television (Wilkinson-Weber 2012). She suggests that "[p]articipant observation as an extra would be one means to learn more about the range of everyday practices that make up the life of the set"

(Wilkinson-Weber 2012: 14). My work as an extra in Hollywood contributes to the growing recognition that media personnel in fact often favor their immediate audience of co-workers on set over "the audience" in the abstract as they strive to meet the physical and emotional challenges of their labor, impress their colleagues, and leverage their professional reputation on the production floor (see also Ganti 2012b; Hesmondhalgh and Baker 2013).

Media production ethnography is a growing field that has emerged from other disciplines as well. Anglo-American media industry studies have yielded invaluable accounts of production, influenced by the disciplines of sociology of media, cultural studies, political economy, and organizational studies (D'Acci 1994; Gitlin 1983; Levine 2001; Miller et al. 2005). Leo Rosten's pioneering analysis of Hollywood in 1941 provided an abundance of astute observations, guided by his sociology training (Sullivan 2009: 40). In observations that resonate today, Rosten pointed out the "morbidity" and "threatening future" that the Hollywood community fostered as an expression of its extreme insecurity and anxiety (Rosten 1941: 39). He also reflected on the industry's "notoriously superstitious" character, with its "astrologers and horoscopists" (Rosten 1941: 225, 227). More recently, David Hesmondhalgh and Sarah Baker's work is particularly attuned to the constraints of creative labor in television in England (2008, 2013). Media studies scholar John Caldwell has called for ethnographic studies of "production cultures" as "social communities in their own right" composed of diverse individuals and work practices (Caldwell 2008: 2). Critical media studies have produced penetrating accounts of Western media production that finely delineate the complicated power relations of organizational hierarchies (Caldwell 2008; Grindstaff 2002; Hesmondhalgh and Baker 2008; Lotz 2009; Mayer 2008, 2011; Mayer, Banks, and Caldwell 2009).

Production processes of the Hong Kong film and television industry have been discussed to varying degrees by film studies, cultural studies, communications, and sociology scholars with a growing body of fascinating ethnographic work that illustrates the impact of cross-border work on media professionals (see Chow and Ma 2008; Szeto and Chen 2013). In a study that included ethnographic research of the Hong Kong television industry, Eric Kit-wai Ma noted the force of commercialism driving creative decisions of his TVB interviewees (Ma 1999: 137). Laikwan Pang, Joseph M. Chan, Anthony Y. H. Fung, and Chun Hung Ng, Michael Curtin, Esther M. K. Cheung, Gina Marchetti, and Tan See-Kam, Steve Fore, and Lisa Odham Stokes and Mike Hoover have all conducted highly valuable interviews with Hong Kong film industry participants. Other rich discussions of production processes in Hong Kong film scholarship access the information from a combination of archival materials, oral histories, studio documents, print media interviews, film festivals, and industry events (see Bordwell 2000; Curtin 1999; Davis and Yeh 2008; Fu 2000; Jarvie 1977; Kar 2000; Morris et al 2005; Rodriguez 1999; Teo 2008; Yeh and Davis 2002).

The Risks of Filming Death

While working as an extra on a network television drama, I witnessed the emotional risk that comes with performing death. In one particular episode in which I was walking in the background, the scene revolved around a character who in the script had been recently widowed. The scene was choreographed to include what in the production process is referred to as a "walk and talk," a shot in which the principal actors walk and speak their lines while the extras fill the background, the Steadicam camera operator swirling about the production floor, capturing the activity with the Steadicam's handheld perspective.

At a cue from the director, the first assistant director shouted for us all to get into our places for the shot. He was anxious to get the shot since, in addition to needing to meet a delivery date for the episode, filming delays could push up many personnel's daily and weekly rate, costing the production company even more money. After his command was issued, the second assistant directors positioned themselves at various locations throughout the set, a few even crouching below camera level within the frame of the shot. In these positions, the second assistant directors were able to silently coordinate the flow of foot traffic by peering into their miniature Sony monitors that were hardwired to the main TV playback monitor so that they could observe the composition of the shot while it was being filmed. Final adjustments were made as the Steadicam operator was secured into his body-mounted camera harness by his assistant. The scopic regime of the television set was in full force.

At this moment the actress who played the widow (I shall call her Susan) arrived on set from the hair and makeup trailer, looking somber. After exchanging a few whispers with the director, Susan was escorted to her mark by the first assistant director.[7] "This is her first scene since her husband died," another extra whispered to me. The extra was referring to the actress' on-screen husband. After the director yelled "Action!" I started to walk in my assigned direction, mimicking the rest of the extras attempting to resemble busy employees while we tried not to bump into each other. We also had to avoid colliding with the roving Steadicam operator and stumbling over the wires snaking along the ground.

Susan spoke her first lines, and after one of the characters responded to her with another line of dialogue, she suddenly burst into unscripted tears. As the director yelled "Cut!" and took Susan aside, sounds of impatience from the extras and the crew were audible, as the filming schedule would be pushed back. "I'm so sorry, I just can't help it," the actress sobbed to the director. The first assistant director awaited instructions since he was responsible for regulating the set and the daily progression of the production schedule. The crew were uncertain how long this break would last. The makeup artist assigned to Susan hovered near her, hoping to fix the actress' complexion. Yet instead of subsiding after a few moments, Susan's weeping continued, with members of the production openly gawking at this spontaneous display of grief unfolding before us.

After a few more moments and a nod from the director, the first assistant director called out, "OK, background artists, please return to the holding area! Everybody else, please await further instructions." The extras coordinator, dressed in his pseudo-military outfit of camouflage pants and combat boots, bellowed at our group of approximately 40 extras through his bullhorn to return to what he called our "holding pen" between shots, a designated waiting area on the soundstage, away from the behind-the-camera drama.

"I guess it got to her," another extra commented to me. As we shuffled over to the holding pen, I wondered what exactly "it" was that got to her. A principal actor on the show, Susan would cancel the interview that I had scheduled with her for later that day, so it was not until several weeks later that I learned more. Sitting in her trailer on her lunch break between filming, Susan earnestly responded to my queries about what had prompted her weeping. Susan said,

> Just recently, with Sam, we were married on the show, and I was actually completely unprepared for how Sam's character's dying was going to affect me. And in a funny sort of way, it wasn't, well I don't know if it was my character or me, it was almost like I felt, I knew he was leaving, and . . . but I realized I had a fear of death, and all of my own personal fears were suddenly being brought out into the open and I was having to cope with them while I was acting. And almost every single day, I would just burst into tears. And the poor makeup people had to keep blotting my face and I was like, "Sorry, I'm so sorry," but it was overwhelming. And uh, I

got very angry with Sam, like, "Why are you doing this to me?" and it went on and on and on. I was bawling my eyes out all the time. And even, it sort of hasn't ended. Because I was doing a show at the end of last year and I was in a taxi going home from filming with two girls I was working with and they were talking about that particular episode where Sam's character died and asking me how it was and so I started talking to them about it and I burst into tears. And it was a huge emotional journey. And it was just something I couldn't control at all. And so my own very raw fears came into play, without me asking them to. And without me being able to cope with them . . . from a tragedy point of view I was completely enveloped. And it's hard, because at the end of the day, you're crying and everything and they yell "Wrap!" and "Time to go home!," and then you've got to be [real-life] Mom.

The extra had guessed right: the hectic production schedule, subject to the budget, does not accommodate the affective labor involved in creating the spectacle that "got" to Susan and that can haunt a person. I would find that this type of blurring between fiction and reality and triggering of real-life fears—of feeling "completely enveloped" as Susan put it—afflicts other personnel on the set besides actors such as directors and camera operators, demonstrating that this was not just a matter of actors "going Method."[8]

Themes of the Book

Although the specific forces driving decline in local production in Hollywood and Hong Kong varied, and took differing forms, a theme of loss was overarching. The loss reflected economic and political changes (such as Hollywood's "runaway production" and its 2007 Writers Guild strike, and Hong Kong's declining film industry, which started in the 1990s and accelerated after the 1997 Asian financial crisis and the territory's return to China). The body count on screen seemed to reflect the fewer occupational opportunities for many media personnel in both sites. Downsizing in the workplace has in fact become a nearly universal storyline, with many workers feeling it across industries and around the world. In their 2010 report, the Milken Institute found that California "lost 10,600 entertainment industry jobs, more than 25,000 related jobs, $2.4 billion in wages and $4.2 billion in total economic output since 1997 as film and TV production has moved to other states and countries" (Klowden, Chatterjee, and Hynek 2010). As Bob Strauss reported in the *Los Angeles Daily News* on January 4, 2014, the Milken Institute estimated that between 2005 and

2012, the number of film production jobs in California decreased by about 4,500, and California's "market share of one-hour network series . . . shrunk from 65 percent in 2005 to just 36 percent in 2012." Hollywood media personnel are among those working- and middle-class Americans who have been experiencing the economic downturn—but something more, as well. As Ortner notes, "Surrounding the fears about jobs are the fears about larger forms of social loss—loss of home, loss of social identity" (Ortner 258). Similar fears have been felt in Hong Kong. In the past several years, before the 2014 "Umbrella Uprising," Hong Kong nativist activists flew the former British colonial flag at marches to protest the loss of a local Hong Kong identity—a loss that Hong Kong film and television personnel also expressed to me when I started this research a decade ago, and that was fueled by a growing sense of helplessness over enormous socioeconomic disparity and an encompassing mainland Chinese presence.

In filmed entertainment, the stakes for on-screen characters are often a matter of life or death; off screen, similar stakes were often sounded by the people I came to know at both the level of their career and the survival of local production. Therefore, throughout the book I argue that media personnel's accounts of death scenes, deadlines, terminations, strikes, industrial decline, and the expiration of a territory come to represent a pervasive, multifaceted sense of demise that haunts media workers. Paradoxically, for industries renowned for churning out escapist fare, not-so-happy endings posed a definite hazard. I have identified three key themes that, in various configurations, concerned personnel in both sites: risk, death, and enchantment.

Risk

Risk is endemic to the industrial production of media (see also Ganti 2012a: 245), and the entrepreneurialism expected of personnel in commercial media means that risk is simultaneously avoided and embraced. Jittery investors and the threat of financial loss are a common preoccupation. There are other forms of risk: physical dangers can emerge from heavy-handed management that coerces personnel into various projects and productions, which I explore in Chapter 6. Some people also see the camera as a risk object; it is, after all, the material and symbolic force around which film and television production revolves. I found that the camera serves as an active entity: a provocateur of questionable practices and a device that "captures" one's soul. Risks of a supernatural nature are also thought to occur, including spirit possessions.

Then there are risks of a socioprofessional nature, such as trying to meet production deadlines while extracting the best job performance from all involved. Amid the seemingly impersonal throb of rationalized, capitalist work practices, actors, camera operators, carpenters, directors, sound engineers, and others are impacted by the content of what they film and must adapt to provocative material; this can take a heavy toll on their personal lives. Susan, for instance, found filming some storylines enjoyable and even liberating; death scenes, however, lingered with her, causing emotional stress, until she ultimately overcame her fears about mortality. In fact, I found that many personnel such as stunt workers, camera operators, and directors welcomed the opportunity to be transported by the themes and images that make up the spectacle. Some were even quite drawn to the physical and emotional risks that occur on set, such as the opportunity to "blow shit up" or temporarily immerse themselves in emotionally vulnerable situations. They saw these situations not only as "challenges" that could propel their individual career trajectories forward, but, in some cases, as fodder for immediate thrills and chills during a long workday. Given the popularity of role playing that venues from Disney amusement parks to Renaissance Fairs and Civil War reenactments to online gaming offer people all over the world, as well as our capacity for identity formation through work (Kondo 1990), anthropologists and media scholars should be attuned to the set as an evocative site of identity transformation and transition. Social risks in the form of public shaming through scornful reviews and reception also haunt actors and directors. The loss of respectability can also pose a risk; from Hollywood to Hong Kong to Bollywood, there is a long history of illicit financing and sexual exploitation of women that taints the image of entertainment industries, and, particularly in Hong Kong, these stigmas linger.

Industrial uncertainty is pervasive in both sites, especially given post-Fordist, flexible production with subcontracting, offshoring, and outsourcing heightening job insecurity (Harvey 1991: 151).[9] During my research in Hong Kong and Los Angeles, film and television personnel faced a growing sense of uprootedness and insecurity. For Los Angeles–based media personnel, offshoring, or "runaway production" as many in Hollywood call it, has led to a shortage of local jobs and the risk of local unemployment. Tax incentives offered by other U.S. states and cheaper labor supplied for overseas filming have offered Hollywood studios a way to cut costs and disempower the unions while limiting Los Angeles-based production employment. "Hollywood North" and "Hollywood South" have become premier destinations for Los Angeles-based film and television production (Mayer and Goldman 2010; Tinic 2005). After Hong Kong's 1997 return to China, the decline in local production was due to not only the 1997 Asian financial crisis and piracy, but also Hollywood's increasingly forceful entry into Hong Kong through marketing and distribution channels (see Chan et al. 2010; Scott 2005: 9). China's liberalization policies and efforts to promote cross-border trade relations and economic integration through film and television co-productions have not reinvigorated local production in Hong Kong (Chow and Ma 2008). Thus, one of the biggest risks media personnel in both sites face is that of decline, even, as some described it, death.

Death

I have described a few instances of the complexities of performing death. Off screen, labor management issues of downsizing, offshoring, and project and contract termination are also pervasive, compounded by fickle executives and investors. "The opportunities are just dying out," actors, camera operators, and production personnel in Los Angeles would repeatedly tell me, referring to individual career decline from the plummeting production jobs. According to FilmL.A., in 1997 "the majority of large-budget studio features were produced in California, with many in L.A. By 2013, most high-value feature projects were made elsewhere" (FilmL.A. Research, 2014, p. 3). In researching the "primary production location of the top 25 live-action feature-length films determined by the highest worldwide box-office," FilmL.A. found that the number of these films for which California was the location of principal photography declined from 11 in 2003 to six in 2006. The recent trend in "local" feature film production has been toward small, independent films with low-paying, short-term work. "Never know when I'll get my next gig" was another common refrain from media personnel in the project-to-project, independent contractor and subcontracted conditions. "You think there aren't many parts for black actresses? Imagine what that means for black stunt women. We're a dying breed," a black stunt woman told me. The Hong Kong I stepped into early in my fieldwork had experienced a collective sense of loss. The deadly disease SARS had quickly claimed lives, the 1997 Asian Financial Crisis had depleted the film industry of many of its investors, and two major entertainment stars, Leslie Cheung and Anita Mui, had died premature deaths within months of each other, diminishing the pool of Hong Kong talent. "Our industry is dead," numerous Hong Kong media personnel would tell me over and over. The industry's decline, noted by scholars as well as practitioners (Marchetti 2000; Pang 2001, 2007), reflected what Ackbar Abbas referred to as Hong Kong's "culture of disappearance" as the city returned to China (Abbas 1997: 14).

Laikwan Pang observes that Hong Kong's film industry has been attempting to "shift from the more traditional place-based industrial model to become a deft coordinator in the new economy" (Pang 2007: 423). Change and transition are endemic to capitalism's "innovative self-destruction" cycle (Berman 1982), particularly flexible specialization with its pursuit of "permanent innovation" (Piore and Sabel 1984: 17). Yet the risk of finality—and imagery of it—haunts media personnel in these two industrial production centers situated across the Pacific Rim. It is important to think critically about this dramatic industry discourse while recognizing that an industry or production cycle may be depressed but not dead. Remakes, reboots, and revitalization efforts are made in Los Angeles and Hong Kong, and local production reconfigures into regional production (as with Hong Kong's cross-border co-productions and "pan-Asian" ventures). Yet as Sherry Ortner explains in her ethnography of Los Angeles independent filmmakers, her interviews and fieldnotes served as "texts to be taken apart in order to understand the language, the discourse, and the modes of self-expression of the world of independent film," noting that she listened closely to "the ways in which people spontaneously seem to say or write the same things in many different contexts" (Ortner 2013: 400, 437; see also Boellstorff et al. 2012: 97 on cultural logics). Similarly, the sheer repetition of complaints I heard from informants in both Hollywood and Hong Kong about fears of death and decline led me to consider that theme as central in their subjective perspective.

Thus, I contend that many people in these lively production sites, who are commonly regarded as churning out "escapist" entertainment, face grave concerns. From grappling with dangerous filming conditions and performing death scenes as well as industrial decline, offshoring, and downsizing, media workers struggle to stay alive, retain their livelihood, and rejuvenate their industries. The commercial context of production in Hollywood and Hong Kong breeds an infinite stream of finalities such as project failures, cancellations, and killed-off characters. From production assistants to actors, "this job could be my last" is a common refrain resulting from the project-oriented flexible labor arrangements for many sub-contract workers in both Hollywood and Hong Kong. Many of my fellow extras on the set of a long-running network television program, referred to as "family" by other long-term production personnel and actors, were contracted week to week with no guarantee of renewal. Even when filming romantic comedies or sitcom TV shows, contract termination, downsizing, and accidents on set are an issue. Industrial and geopolitical decline also contributed to an ethos of demise. On a Hong Kong film set, a producer expressed her sadness at the lack of films being made in Hong Kong. Indeed, 2047, the projected year of complete convergence between Hong Kong and China, looms in the not-too-distant future, signaling the diminishing of a particular local sensibility and sovereignty. Currently, tensions continue to escalate for China and Hong Kong's "one country, two systems."

The overarching theme of death also should not be surprising given that much of the commercial film and television content that media workers work long hours on revolves around dark subject matter. American medical and crime television dramas as well as films such as *Contagion, Interstellar, San Andreas, District 9, Surrogates, Eagle Eye*, and *I, Robot* summon up the technological, financial, and creative resources of Hollywood personnel to present the masses with dystopic visions of disease, disasters, cloning, and surveillance. As Slavoj Zizek notes, Hollywood's capabilities to imagine dystopias has even been tapped by the state; after 9/11, Hollywood filmmakers were summoned to Washington, DC to help security experts "brainstorm" various disaster scenarios (Zizek 2002: 16). In 2004, for instance, a year when I was conducting fieldwork, out of the top 20 U.S. feature films, there were six action films, three dramas, three adventure films, one crime, and one thriller, according to IMDb. Films such as *The Bourne Supremacy, Spider Man 2, The Day After Tomorrow, I, Robot, Van Helsing*, and *The Grudge* contain scenes of death, dying, or extreme violence. In 2004 in Hong Kong, films such as *Three Extremes: Dumplings, The Eye 2, New Police Story, Moving Targets, Jiang Hu*, and *Breaking News* also featured a lot of violence and dying. Ghost and gangsters films are popular Hong Kong genres that have done well in overseas markets; the specter of death haunts both of these underworlds. Some of the most prevalent, potent, and profitable images that commercial film and television in Hollywood and Hong Kong generate are those surrounding death and dying, particularly in action, science fiction, horror, drama, and romance genres; even in comedies, loss and death are not uncommon plot devices. Creating so many dystopic visions and contending with issues of mortality, it is therefore not surprising that production personnel in these mass production sites become susceptible to the imagery and themes that they film.

Death, after all, has been a key narrative device and source of spectacle since the inception of the motion picture. Early film capitalized on "sensational melodrama" (Singer 2001), driven in part by fears about the real world: a violent, visceral industrial modernity that would see the invention of machines overtake the humans who created them. The classic 1917 silent film image in *Teddy at the Throttle* of a damsel in distress tied to railroad tracks with an oncoming train in the distance, played to comedic effect, nevertheless hinges on the threat of death from the rush of the modern, industrializing world. We continue to be bombarded with images of impending death a century later—fantasy fodder for, arguably, that most profound of human experiences: the end of the life course. As anthropology's interest in the life course and religion has shown us, a significant part of the human condition lies in tackling the prospect of our mortality, and the imagery depicted in narrative films and scripted television reflects that challenge. These films and TV programs *show* audiences how to live and, just as importantly, how to die—providing us, in a Geertzian fashion, "a kind of sentimental education" (Geertz 1973: 449). It is these visions of grappling with mortality that become immortalized on the screen.

These deaths, deadlines, and declines also signify the risks and uncertainties and shifting geopolitical circumstances that influence production and markets. They shape many of the human frailties pervading the production process. Thus, I reveal the stakes for media workers who create spectacle in how they contend with the sociocultural, physical, political, and ontological complexity of staging death and violence. Concerns about death, decline, and the possibility of renewal are not restricted to commercial film and television industries, but, heightened in these contexts, they bring to the fore the risks and dramas that are part of the contemporary human experience.

Enchantment

"In Hollywood, however, there appears to be a greater use of magical thinking on a conscious level and as a tool for achieving success than elsewhere in the modern world."

—Hortense Powdermaker, *Hollywood the Dream Factory: An Anthropologist Looks at the Movie-Makers*, 1951, p. 284

"We were filming on location and someone recommended a local shaman come bless the whole production. I thought it was a good idea. You always want to protect yourself."

—Hollywood network television producer and writer, 2005, interview

The third theme, related to the themes of risk and death, is enchantment. The industry's public-relations spin of the "magic" of moviemaking and "enchantment" of dazzling illusions is a tired trope. But we shouldn't dismiss media workers' accounts of cameras becoming haunted and actors "possessed" by the melodramatic storylines and images they create. I use the term "enchantment" to encompass everything from official religion to folk beliefs, and to signal Weber's mistaken prediction. I contend that religion and the supernatural manifest in ostensibly secular, rationalized media production practices.

Interest in the supernatural and divination has long been pursued by Hollywood personnel; as Rosten observed of Hollywood in 1941, "clairvoyants, palm readers, astrologers, and the seers of ludicrous cults flourish in the movie colony" (Rosten 1941: 225). However, rather than ascertaining an empirical basis for claims of spectral interference, I take seriously people's discourse and deployment of them in order to understand what media production means to them. Joseph Bosco's argument about the anthropological necessity of studying the supernatural is relevant here. He writes that "the phenomenon needs to be analyzed at a different level from the instrumental level; it is socially, symbolically or experientially special, and may or may not be instrumentally valid or significant" (Bosco 2003: 145). He points out that the Chinese ghost stories that his students at Chinese University of Hong Kong tell deserve study because they are "true at a cultural level," with "real effects" of evoking emotions and changed behaviors even if the ghosts do not act (Bosco 2003: 145).

Historically, actors and performers across cultures (including Cantonese Opera performers) have been seen as mediumistic, vulnerable to episodes of possession by a supernatural force or entering into a trance state of some kind (Liu 2003; Schechner 2002; Turner 1985; Zhen 2005). Anthropologist Barbara Ward noted that when Cantonese Opera troupes in Hong Kong were hired to perform operas in honor of temple openings in the New Territories, they would also occasionally be called upon to make ritual offerings of incense and even perform exorcisms, similar to priests, illustrating the connection between performance and religion (Chan 1993; Ward 1979). Ritualized or spontaneous, such transportations attest to the uncanny experience of performance and production (which I extend to media workers such as directors, camera operators, and makeup artists, among others, who help create such settings).

In Hong Kong, I was invited to attend a producer's consultation with a Chinese astrologer to determine the most auspicious time to start a new project; it is not uncommon there to seek astrological forecasts in order to ensure a fortuitous shoot, along with other, more economistic methods. The Thai mystic of Chinese descent known as Bak Lung Wong (whose name means "White Dragon King") was a popular astrological consultant for numerous prominent Hong Kong film directors, producers, and celebrities until he died in 2013. Media personnel would fly to the White Dragon King's temple in Thailand, where he divined auspicious film titles, forecast the cast's horoscopes, and scheduled movie opening dates. A Hong Kong producer I interviewed attributed his film's commercial and critical success to his team's hard work and strong script, but also partly to the White Dragon King's blessing and technical suggestions.

Holidays such as *Yue Laan Jit* (Ghost Festival) in Hong Kong serve as public acknowledgment that ghosts intermingle with the living. However, the film/TV community is considered by many Hong Kong people, and within the media industries themselves, as overtly concerned with spiritual protection and assistance in financial success. I was invited by producers, directors, and a stunt worker to visit Daoist temples and Chinese astrologists to forecast success. Attendance at the *hoih geng laih* ("opening lens" ceremony), in which paper money and incense are burned to gods and ghosts for protection and success, is expected of production members before filming for a project starts, as much for tradition as for the publicity it garners. At such ceremonies, even casual ones, there is an overlap of the ritual economy with the secular economy: special-purpose votive money is burned to the God of Fortune for actual financial success. Elements of the ceremony come from Buddhism and Daoism, while the filmmakers are sometimes casual or practicing Christians, reflecting local syncretistic culture and religion. These kinds of rituals are found in other media industries: as Ganti notes, in Bollywood, members of upcoming film productions gather for the *mahurat*, a ceremony that marks an "astrologically calculated auspicious date and time" in which to start the film venture (Ganti 2012a: 248).[10]

Yet Hollywood is not closed off from the kinds of cosmological concerns and consultations that are especially prevalent in southern California, which has long attracted alternative, Eastern, and New Age religions. For instance, the Warner Bros. studio website informs visitors who sign up for studio tours, "In common with most studios, the number 13 is considered unlucky, so there is no Stage 13." At Universal Studios, there is no Stage 13 on its front lot, nor, its website for studio tours explains, any multiple of 13 such as 26 or 39. During his initial research in Hollywood in 1939, Leo Rosten also found reports of industry members' avoidance of unlucky number 13 (Rosten 1941: 225, 227). Illustrating that financial decisions in Hollywood are not devoid of the divining found more explicitly in Hong Kong, 20th Century Fox Studios in Los Angeles kept an official astrologer, Joyce Jillson, on its payroll for decades. According to a report from the Associated Press on October 8, 2004, in the *Boston Globe,* Jillson advised on auspicious dates for films to open, including the opening date for *Star Wars* in 1977. Numerous interlocutors in Hollywood also spoke of consulting tarot card readers to provide additional information as to the best choices to make regarding career and project decisions. It should not be overlooked that Hollywood's film industry, from its inception, imported (and continues to import) theater actors whose profession is full of superstitions as well (such as the longtime tradition of wishing an actor "break a leg" before a performance instead of "good luck" as the oppositional logic is supposed to help one avoid tempting fate). This is a workforce whose members have been primed to ponder ritual and the relationship between reality and fiction, cause and effect.

As early as the 1930s Paramahansa Yogananda started to build his Self-Realization Fellowship Temple in Hollywood with donations made by followers he had accrued in the 1920s, and by 1950 the Lake Shrine temple opened in Pacific Palisades, both areas home to thousands of entertainment professionals. For the past several decades, the international religious organizations Church of Scientology, Soka Gakkai International, and the Kabbalah Center have owned major centers in Los Angeles, and all three boast Hollywood celebrity members. These organizations claim members who have reportedly received spiritual and social support (particularly members of Japanese and Jewish diasporas for the latter two), yet these organizations have also courted controversy for some of their methods and beliefs.

Hollywood's first controversial and charismatic Christian figure was famed faith healer and evangelist preacher Aimee Semple McPherson. McPherson dazzled churchgoers in 1920s Los Angeles with her spectacularly designed sermons, and reportedly drew upon the resources of Hollywood studios and stars to decorate her Los Angeles church, Angelus Temple (Sutton 2009: 73). According to historian Matthew Avery Sutton, McPherson befriended silent film star Charlie Chaplin, who had attended her sermons and told her that part of her success was due to her use of "props and lights. Oh yes, whether you like it or not, you're an actress" (Sutton 2009: 76). Already famous for her savvy use of radio, McPherson even founded a movie production company, Angelus Productions (Sutton 2009: 154). (Incidentally, McPherson had traveled to Hong Kong as a missionary in 1910, another connection between the two production sites.) Given this history of religious organizations and figures and New Age movements in Los Angeles, it shouldn't be surprising that religious and mystical practices are embedded in Hollywood industrial relations (see also Rosten 1941: 19).

Cameras are also implicated in the enchantment process, filming the spectacular images in these commercial industries. The camera—still and motion picture—represents an ambivalent force, as historical, cross-cultural, and contemporary beliefs and claims about it "capturing" something, an essence, of who or what is being filmed, attest (Gunning 1995b; Zhen 2005: 159). Since the 19th century, camera technologies have been used to document war, death, and even the afterlife, as with postmortem and spirit photography (Gunning 1995b; Ruby 1999). As Hong Kong still photographer Ho Fan explains, cultural attitudes about cameras in 1950s Hong Kong included the recognition of their ability to seize one's spirit. The local subject of one of Ho's photographs responded with anger after Ho took his photo. In an August 10, 2014, interview with the *South China Morning Post*, Ho told journalist Amy Nip, "'With a knife in his hand, a pig butcher said he would chop me. He wanted his spirit back,' explaining that superstition had it that a person would have his spirit captured by the camera." In fact, the Chinese term for film is "electric shadows" (*dihn yang* in Cantonese); shadows on screen were understood in early 20th-century China as representing the soul, thus connoting life and death (Zhen 2005: 159). From early 20th-century Hong Kong to contemporary media workers in Hollywood who also speak of the "soul capture" aspect of cameras, people have expressed astonishment and unease about the camera's ability to capture some perceived core or essence of a person. The work practices such as the *lai see* mentioned earlier incorporate some of these concerns.

Modernity

That ontological risks exist for media personnel, and that they are addressed and avoided in part through religion and the supernatural, reveal that such "modern" and ostensibly secular commercial industries are not entirely "disenchanted," as Max Weber claimed capitalist industry would become. In exploring media personnel's interstitial experiences, this book goes beyond media production to contribute a broader perspective on how capitalist production in the 21st century remains enchanted. It contributes to the anthropology of modernity and its position that modern rationality is not as dominant or straightforward as assumed.[11] The notion of progress trumpeted by the European Enlightenment predicted that science and secularity would overtake superstition. Yet centuries later, on the eve of the new millennium, Comaroff and Comaroff noted the "new spirit" of capitalism: the magical increase of money through frequently divine and legally dubious means with "the use of the bodies of some for the empowerment of others" (Comaroff and Comaroff 1999: 281–282). The unevenness and uncertainty of labor systems under market reform in postcolonial, postsocialist, and postrevolutionary societies, combined with neoliberalism's invocation to privatization and entrepreneurship, has resulted in instances of witchcraft, zombie labor, and spirit possession in Africa and Asia, confirming that such enchantments are an indelible part of our modern world.[12]

Comaroff and Comaroff have emphasized that what they refer to as occult economies rely upon "power/knowledge that transgress *the conventional, the rational, the moral*" (Comaroff and Comaroff 2000: 316, italics added). Politics and statecraft are not separable from the occult; according to Isak Niehaus, who has demonstrated that the South African ANC used witchcraft beliefs as part of their liberation tactics for the post-apartheid regime, anthropological research has revealed that witchcraft beliefs continue to be found in nearly all continents (Niehaus 2002: 225). In his ethnography of IsiZulu-speaking members of a settlement in Durban, South Africa, Jason Hickel found that suspicions about the economic success of foreigners in Durban is attributed to witchcraft; migration, poverty, and unemployment associated with neoliberal policies there are a direct result of globalization (Hickel 2014).[13]

In their overview of the prevalence of magic, Henrietta L. Moore and Todd Sanders argue that the occult and enchantments are "neither a return to 'traditional' practices nor a sign of backwardness or lack of progress; they are instead *thoroughly modern manifestations of uncertainties, moral disquiet, and unequal rewards and aspirations in the contemporary moment*" (Moore and Sanders 2002: 3, italics added). As markets open up in Vietnam, for instance, "re-enchantments" in the form of ancestor worship and mediumship return to that society, with Thai migrant workers propitiating spirits as a way to exert control over their precarious labor (Johnson 2012: 768). The inseparability of cosmology from contemporary, industrial media production demonstrates that Western and Eastern media production does not necessarily occur in a de-sacralized modernity. This is particularly the case in industries in which people are expected to work long hours yet see little prospect of job security or long-term reward—even industries that revolve around market rationality and capitalist calculation. As I emphasize throughout, authority and labor control operate beyond conventional managerial forces and corporate structures. Studio psychics and ghost appeasement signal the risks of film and television production and are expressions of the diverse economic and cultural practices and pressures that make up late capitalist production, thus offering, as Hickel suggests in his work on witchcraft, a critique of capitalist modes of accumulation (Hickel 2014).

Cosmological and religious expressions are commonly found among cultural groups and individuals, so it should not be surprising that people who toil at the heart of film and television industries in practically any location hold heterogeneous and hybridic worldviews (see also Ganti 2012a). From formal religion to informal rituals, people cope with increasing inequalities and structural adjustments with an array of responses. Political-economic and organizational studies of media production rarely address these cultural dynamics. When I began fieldwork, I did not expect people to talk about religion or the supernatural in the entertainment industries, but it kept cropping up in various conversations and contexts, in both sites (see also Strauss 2014). Yet it should actually not be astonishing at all that in the Los Angeles-based and Hong Kong-based entertainment industries, local and regional beliefs and practices (evangelical Christianity, Buddhism, Daoism, New Ageism, alternative religions, and spirit possession and exorcism) proliferate. The divine and the mystical have never left us, particularly in industrial production.

Framing: The Multisited and Multisighted

The focus of this book is on the media personnel and the production processes within the film and television industries of Hollywood and Hong Kong, as well as between them. I chose these two industrial centers because I wanted to update Hortense Powdermaker's 1951 ethnography of America's commercial film industry (see also Ortner 2013). Hollywood has for nearly a century been a source of American soft power, representing American culture and values overseas, and generating revenue in the billions. Yet Powdermaker's pioneering ethnography of Hollywood, conducted in 1946–1947, was intended to shed light on American society and was restricted within the boundaries of the United States, before the intensification of global flows that started in the early 1970s. Powdermaker's U.S.-based study also requires updating as television has since emerged, and is integrated with film and other entertainment media. Finally, for over half a century Hollywood has been connected to Hong Kong's highly commercial film industry. Hollywood has utilized Hong Kong as one of its offshore production sites, or "satellites" (Scott 2005: 53), for its cheap labor and stunning scenery; it is Hollywood's stepping stone into business in China, including film co-productions, and as I discuss in the Epilogue, Hong Kong has become an alternative to China as the location for Hollywood red-carpet film premieres. Hollywood has also been a stepping stone for Hong Kong producers, directors, actors and stunt workers for many decades.

The relationship between the Hollywood and Hong Kong media industries has evolved into a veritable object of study in transnational film studies, cultural studies, and Asian studies, reflecting academia's increasing attention to such processes.[14] There is a symbiotic relationship in their lengthy exchange of creative ideas, finance, talent, technology, and staging techniques, aided by diasporic migrations of people from China's Guangdong province and Hong Kong as well as overseas markets for Cantonese-language films. In the 1910s and 1920s, Moon Kwan Man-ching and Joe Chiu both worked in early Hollywood cinema, Moon as an extra and a consultant to D. W. Griffith on his film *Broken Blossoms* (1919), before they established Grandview Film Company, the "first big film studio in Hong Kong modeled along Hollywood lines" (Kar 2000: 50). As film historian Law Kar notes of their time in America, "that exposure touched their psyches and, indirectly, the cinema in its earliest formation" (Kar 2000: 44). Decades later, in 1973, Bruce Lee's film *Enter the Dragon* was a co-production between Hong Kong's Golden Harvest studio and Hollywood's Warner Bros. Stunt colleagues of Bruce Lee I spoke to in Hong Kong recalled safety measures for filming that Lee had brought over with him from the United States. Golden Harvest would continue to co-produce films in Hollywood such as *Cannonball Run* and *Teenage Mutant Ninja Turtles*. Producers, directors, stunt choreographers, and actors such as Raymond Chow, Sammo Hung, Jackie Chan, John Woo, Yuen Woo Ping, and Chow Yun Fat have over the past several decades worked in both places. Hollywood blockbusters have been filmed in Hong Kong, and Hong Kong media personnel I interviewed spoke of film and television projects they worked on in Hollywood from decades ago. Encounters to this degree have only recently started to exist between Hollywood and Bollywood (see Ganti 2012a: 14), and Hollywood and China. I use the concept of media assemblage in Chapter 1 to explain convergences between Hollywood and Hong Kong media production. Drawing from Aihwa Ong's use of assemblage, which refers to heterogeneous and contingent ensembles and "nonlinear dynamics" in the formation of Southeast Asian knowledge societies (Ong 2005: 339), media assemblage describes the interconnected relationships between Hollywood and Hong Kong industries. In looking at the growing relationship between Hollywood and India, media studies scholar Nitin Govil also proposes using assemblage to "more effectively capture the texture and spirit of dynamic associations created by the material, discursive, and symbolic itineraries of commodity exchange" (Govil 2009: 64).

While I do consider differences between the two industrial sites, I also emphasize thematic commonalities and points of connection between Hollywood and Hong Kong.[15] Looking at media assemblages situates this research in transnational studies, which emphasize interactivity (Zhan 2001)[16] and connections (Grewal and Kaplan 2005; Morris et al. 2005) to understand the relationships and encounters as they are experienced by media personnel. It is hard to fully understand one industry without seeing how it intersects with the other given the global dynamics that shape them. Just as an industry or a nation-state is defined not solely by its physical boundaries and internal dynamics but also by its "far-flung" relationships and associations (Bernal 2005: 660), so my fieldsite was constructed through the social relationships and trajectories of individuals and loose communities of media workers, some of whom were rooted in one industrial site but some of whom routinely crossed borders, the latter typical of workers in post-Fordist economies.

Situated in large industrial centers near ports, surrounded by waves of immigrant populations, neither the Hollywood nor Hong Kong media industries are self-contained, bounded entities. To some media workers, the industries of Hollywood and Hong Kong (and China) were clearly linked through ideas, networking, and material resources, whereas for others the connections were not so obvious (the latter were mostly American informants who knew that Hollywood has "satellites" but were not very aware of Hong Kong's industries, although they cited China as a vague threat). The question of permeable boundaries and border crossing was an overwhelming feature in terms of both the informants' ability to work in different sites and adapting to changing work conditions given the decline in historic place-based production. The movements of media workers from both sites have been shaped by the transnational yet uneven shift from Fordist to post-Fordist production in the form of offshoring, and working in both film and television formats was a frequent tactic for Hollywood and Hong Kong informants. Political shifts such as Hong Kong's 1997 return to mainland China have also triggered new career trajectories (Ong 1999, 2005). Border crossing was a more common phenomenon for Hong Kong informants, who were becoming resigned to working in Beijing or elsewhere in China—relocating or commuting regularly. Southern California–based Hollywood informants were willing to work temporarily on American films shooting overseas or out of state, but permanently relocating was far less desirable.

Sets in both sites were male-dominated spaces, particularly for key positions such as director, cinematographer, and executive producer as well as the traditionally male domains such as carpentry, lights, and transportation, especially in Hong Kong. The striking disparities on set result from decades-long biased and discriminatory hiring decisions on the part of predominantly male studio executives, investors, directors, cinematographers, stunt directors, and technical department heads, based on gender norms in both sites. This is discussed further in Chapter 3. Filming entails a whole economy of looks and stares, which is partly understandable as everyone needs to assess how things will look on camera, but it also provides an excuse for people to leer at one another; despite a general level of professionalism, actresses and female extras and stunt workers can at times be particularly vulnerable to this kind of scrutiny, especially if they are skimpily costumed. The set I spent the most time on in Hollywood was the most respectful one in terms of work environment; it was also the most diverse one in terms of gender, race, and ethnicity, including producers and directors. However, the majority of the key creative and technical positions were held by men of white, Euro-American descent. In general, I observed more women working across all production departments on set in Hollywood than in Hong Kong, particularly in television, and in Hollywood, the majority of those women were white.

The industries in both sites are fairly racially and ethnically homogenous (white in Hollywood, Chinese in Hong Kong), and that was reflected on the sets I observed. The overwhelmingly Euro-American white productions of Hollywood, however, do not accurately reflect the racial diversity within the United States, a disparity that was rarely commented on by informants there.[17] Several Hong Kong informants described occasional encounters with white Hollywood executives and directors in which they felt they were expected to conform to racial stereotypes. Within Hong Kong itself, there is a long history of racist colonialism. As film scholar Poshek Fu describes the early part of the 20th century: "Racism was rampant in the colony, where social life was racially segregated. For example not only were the natives not allowed to live in certain residential areas like the Peak, which was 'reserved' for Europeans, they were paid less than the Europeans for the same work on the grounds of race" (Fu 2000: 202). This history is crucial for understanding Hong Kong, and for when contemporary Hong Kong filmmakers complain that Hollywood productions receive preferential treatment from the government when filming in Hong Kong. However, local media workers I interviewed rarely framed tensions in terms of race, but as local versus foreigner, and Hong Kong government officials continuing the British colonial policy of marginalizing local interests in favor of foreign ones, especially given Hong Kong's "global city" status (this is discussed more in Chapter 4). Foreigners can be "Westerners,"[18] often described with the slang term "*gwei lo*" (ghost man), but, as several informants explained, members of other Asian productions that film in Hong Kong, such as Japanese or Indian, can also be considered outsiders. Yet in Hong Kong, the tensions that surfaced the most in production processes were cultural ones, as what Mirana M. Szeto and Yun-chung Chen call the perceived "mainlandization" of the local Hong Kong industries increased after Hong Kong's 1997 return to China through the rise in mainland Chinese personnel, language, censorship, and investment via cross-border co-productions (Szeto and Chen 2013). The political construct of "one government, two systems" that China uses to describe its governance over the mainland and the Special Administrative Region of Hong Kong hovered uncomfortably over the city's film industry in particular.

I was fortunate to be able to spend time with several interlocutors in both sites (film shoots and meetings took several Hong Kong directors, producers, and actors to Hollywood). Yet conducting multisited fieldwork that spans the Pacific Rim is an inherently uneven experience. Cross-cultural fieldsites are not fully commensurable due to cultural specificities, and the racial, class, and gender identities of the ethnographer articulate in different ways in different sites (see Marcus 1995: 113). Consequently, the anthropologist's multisited fieldwork experiences lack equivalency, and subsequent ethnographic writing is an exercise in scale shifting (Strathern 1995). Thus, I discuss Hollywood and Hong Kong media production as a transnationally occurring practice that is grounded in locally specific contexts. Within multiple chapters I tack between Hollywood and Hong Kong to talk about overarching and overlapping themes of risk, death, and enchantment that articulate on the local level. At times I analyze production practices at the scale of the set, at other times at the scale of the industry, and at yet other times at the scale of the transnational.

By "commercial" film and television in Hollywood, I mean for-profit projects aimed at mass audiences, as opposed to "independent" and avant-garde projects made outside of (or in intended opposition to) the studio system (see Ortner 2013: 4), or educational or exclusively state-funded media. In Hong Kong, however, even low-budget films made by independent production companies were commonly referred to as the English-language term "commercial" by many filmmakers and production personnel as they seek mass audiences in Hong Kong and Chinese diasporic communities for maximum profit. I also use the term "commercial" to invoke ethnographic analyses of capitalist work discipline on factory floors—or, in this case, film and television sets (see also Freeman 2000; Lee 1998; Ong 1987). Examining media production as *work* allows us to see issues of power and hierarchy within commercial production and the drive for profit accumulation. The set is indeed a production site in which people (similar to workers in electronics factories, confectionaries, physics labs, informatics, and stock markets) create and shape their social and professional identities in large part through their relation to technology and each other amid issues of power relations, capitalist discipline, and market relations (Freeman 2000; Kondo 1990; Mayer 2011; Ong 1987; Traweek 1988; Zaloom 2006). It is also important to note that while some media personnel may be privileged in terms of class background and education, the physical risks of the job, and the emotional stress that comes from inconsistent work, impacts them too.

For a little background, Hollywood studios were taken over by media conglomerates in the 1980s through to the early 2000s (e.g., 20th Century Fox was acquired by News Corporation in 1985 and Universal was bought by Vivendi in 1997). According to Sherry Ortner, "the conglomerization of the studios ratcheted up the need for studio divisions to show a particularly strong bottom line and thus reinforced the blockbuster tendency that had started in the 1970s" (Ortner 2013: 97). Blockbuster and "tentpole" films, the latter intended by a studio to generate the maximum profits by spawning a variety of other media and merchandise in order to cover losses from less successful films (Davidson 2010: 9), are quite rightly derided by film critics and scholars for their emphasis on simplistic storylines, reductive characterizations, and problematic gender and race representations. Yet they also feature "shock and awe" visuals that harken back to Western and Chinese stage entertainments that strove to dazzle audiences. Thus I want to consider the style of "commercial" film and television with its mass-market, wide appeal, as opposed to "high art." Whereas Adorno and Horkheimer (2002) compellingly condemned the "cultural industry" of the American film industry as too commodified and superficial and thus repressive—a view shared by Hortense Powdermaker—contemporary anthropology must reconsider the appeal of mass-produced spectacle from urban centers that have been so globally pervasive (see also Ganti 2000, 2012b). This entails recalling early cinema's exhibition roots in fairgrounds, amusement parks, vaudeville, peep shows, and burlesque (in China and Hong Kong as well as the United States). One of the main points of connection and commonality between the Hollywood and Hong Kong media industries is their emphasis on producing images, or spectacle.

From the inception of this project in both sites I observed that the production processes in film and television are deeply intertwined with one another, so I have not partitioned them into separate strands of study (see also Caldwell 2008: 9, 376–377). For instance, a studio production company at which I interned in Los Angeles was a film *and* television production company. Production company executives made hiring and logistical decisions that drew from their experiences in both mediums. Financial and creative information and strategies employed for films were adapted for television projects, and vice versa. The Hollywood studio soundstages on which I observed are used for filming both television shows and films. Hong Kong's film and television industries also retain a "symbiotic" relationship, as Eric Kit-wai Ma explains, with "strong institutional ties with each other" (Ma 1999: 2). In both locations, people often worked in both mediums (especially camera operators, sound engineers, makeup artists, and production assistants), drawing upon the same equipment and resources for both. One of the executives of the Hollywood film/TV production company utilized his former contacts at the television production office housed at the same studio and was able to use the television program's set to shoot his film, as well as some of the TV show's crew and equipment. Film and television, or "entertainment," evolve out of and bolster one another, and this is evident in Hong Kong as well, with actors and stunt workers in particular working in both mediums. In their production of television dramas, Hong Kong's commercial television station TVB, owned by Sir Run Run Shaw, drew from the resources offered by Shaw's preexisting film studio (Curtin 2007: 110). TVB also operated a renowned training program in the 1970s and 1980s for actors and directors, and many of those people were hired by film production companies in the late 1970s because of their training in the fast-paced world of television production (Teo 2000: 102). These social and professional networks formed at TVB's training program would serve as a springboard for future collaborations at film companies such as Golden Harvest and Cinema City. Contacts between Hong Kong film and television continue among directors, producers, stunt workers, actors, and writers as a strategy to increase employability.

Access

Access to sets in Hollywood and Hong Kong was very challenging due to confidentiality agreements (this was formalized only in Hollywood), and fears of tabloid exposure and internet leaks. From Hortense Powdermaker's attempts at on-set observation in the 1940s to today, Hollywood producers have tightly controlled access to the site of production there, making entrée very difficult for outsiders (see Caldwell 2008: 375; Ortner 2009, 2013; Powdermaker 1967). Prior to my fieldwork, several actors' privacy had been violated in both Hollywood and Hong Kong by entertainment tabloids, so I tried to tread carefully. Entrée was a little easier and less formal in Hong Kong; certainly, access was a less common request there.

Given these conditions and Institutional Review Board regulations, I have followed anthropology's convention of maintaining the confidentiality of informants with pseudonyms, and, mindful of the sensitive nature of writing about people's professional experiences and political sentiments, I have also anonymized some production information. Snowball sampling was a frequent method for eliciting research participants in each site. Media industries can be quite volatile, and comprised of relationships that ebb and flow. Many thousands of people work in Hollywood film and television, although the numbers of employed people vary, especially given that part-time, short-term labor may or may not be counted by government and industry sources.[19] According to Hong Kong's Census and Statistics Department, the employment figures for "motion picture and other entertainment services" between 2004 and 2007 came to just under 20,000 people, although that covers more than the film and television industries (Hong Kong Employment and Statistics Section, 2004–2007). As numerous informants said, the actual number of those working regularly in the Hong Kong film and television industries was more approximately under a thousand, which meant "you can't say anything bad about anyone." In Hollywood, on the set of one television show in particular, there had been numerous breaches of trust by extras and tabloid reporters, so I was discouraged from taking photographs on set (and this was before the ubiquity of social media). There were repeated warnings at that time to everyone about copyright of behind-the-scenes footage and Internet leaks; initially there were fewer copyright concerns about my taking photographs on set in Hong Kong but that changed over time.

Conducting fieldwork in Hollywood and Hong Kong entailed long-term participant observation, interviews, archival research, and discourse analysis. In addition to interning for several years at a film and television production company in Hollywood, I spent hundreds of hours on Hollywood film and television sets and several dozens of hours on Hong Kong film and television sets (the latter site more difficult to access as there was a lower volume of production). I observed and spoke with individuals from extras to executives in both sites. I was an observer (and at times participant, as an extra) on the set of a Hollywood television drama. I was able to track several interlocutors between Hollywood and Hong Kong as they worked and lived in both places. My fieldwork in Hollywood was conducted one or two days a week over most of 2003 to June 2005 except during field trips to Hong Kong, and between April 2006 and August 2006, with follow-up visits in 2007. Fieldwork in Hong Kong was conducted over various fieldtrips: June to September 2004, July 2005 to March 2006, and December 2006 to February 2007. I interviewed 50 media workers in Hollywood and 50 in Hong Kong, to varying degrees of depth. I conducted interviews on sets, in production offices, on studio lots in canteens and trailers, at screenings, and in cafes. Interviewees included stunt workers in both sites as well as entertainment journalists and government employees in Hong Kong. I interviewed a few Anglo-American expatriates in Hong Kong and numerous Hong Kong personnel working in or visiting Hollywood, but these groups were not analogous, since the Euro-American expatriates in Hong Kong benefitted from the legacy of Hong Kong's colonial infrastructure and welcoming attitude toward "expat" professionals (which include myself), whereas most of the Hong Kong personnel in Hollywood, as racial minorities in a very different cultural context, experienced racial stereotyping or discrimination at some point in their time in Los Angeles.

My internship[20] in Hollywood at a film/TV production office at a studio provided entrée to other sites and sets, and the employees were very generous with sharing their thoughts, experiences, and connections. Some of my duties included reading scripts, helping to develop film projects, assisting in correspondence, and attending studio screenings and film premieres. I also analyzed industry materials such as budgets, production schedules, scripts, and trade magazines. In Hong Kong, I observed mostly on film sets on location throughout the city and for television production at a studio soundstage. Numerous directors, producers, production personnel, and stunt workers were magnanimous in helping me navigate the Hong Kong media industries and recounting their experiences to me. I also conducted archival research at the Hong Kong Film Archive, and assisted a little in editing English-language scripts. Fieldwork was costly in Hong Kong, one of the most expensive cities in the world, and challenging, as many people were more cautious to respond to me than in Hollywood (this was also in some cases because I am a Westerner and an industry outsider). When I started fieldwork there by cold-calling production companies, several members of family-run production companies were suspicious of a foreigner asking about financing and logistics, and admitted later that they had been fearful that I might sell their secrets to competitors. A few Hong Kong media workers also expressed astonishment at the notion of a scholarly study of film and television production, a reflection, partly, of the industries' socially marginal status (which I discuss later), while most Hollywood personnel, although protective of their production space, saw such an endeavor as a natural outcome of the industry's popularity and power.

Despite the common assumption that being on a set is "just a lot of waiting around," I found it in both sites to often be a very socially interactive experience full of networking, storytelling, competitive performance, gifting, and gossip. Each set had its own particular etiquette. In general, production crew and extras were easier to approach than principal actors, who in turn were more accessible in Hong Kong than in Hollywood as they had fewer intermediaries and worked in a less hierarchical and fragmented system.

Hollywood production personnel, especially several assistant directors and a few makeup artists, were very helpful with explanations and facilitating my time on set. Numerous extras also kindly took me under their wing and shared their stories, dreams, and fears with me. On Hong Kong sets and at production companies I was also offered generous support and assistance, and a few media workers became good friends, taking me under their wing. As a Westerner in Hong Kong—and specifically a white American female one—I was granted innumerable daily privileges in the city by Hong Kong locals that people visiting from other parts of the world, especially Southeast Asia and Africa sometimes are not, such as unsolicited offers of help while navigating public transportation, gracious service at shops, and seeming immunity from any law enforcement or immigration scrutiny; all of these privileges smoothed my experiences in Hong Kong. Regarding my fieldwork, as a white, American outsider who had spent time in Hollywood, some doors in Hong Kong opened easily to me as some people were interested in talking about Hollywood; sometimes, however, my outsider status was hard to overcome. A few Hong Kong informants initially seemed a little self-conscious that their industry may be compared unfavorably to Hollywood's, although I tried to reassure them that this was not a study that would compare which industry was "better" or more "advanced" but a cross-cultural exploration of filming in multiple sites that would acknowledge commonalities and connections as well as differences. In contrast, while some informants in Hollywood were interested in their Hong Kong counterparts, they never expressed self-consciousness about the status of their industry in relation to Hong Kong.

Structure of the Book

Each of the seven chapters represents varying combinations of the three themes—risk, death, and enchantment. Findings from Hollywood and Hong Kong are often combined, demonstrating the interconnectedness of media production practices, while local variations are specified. Although Chapter 1 does point out contrasts between the two industries, even chapters focused primarily on Hollywood or Hong Kong do not—cannot—entirely exclude the presence of the other. Therefore, the chapters are organized mostly as a collection of interconnected themes and topics, not sequentially partitioned by site. In this, the concept of assemblage acts as a stylistic device to convey the interlocking themes and topics of the book, working against the separability and attendant hierarchizing of the "West and the Rest" that can occur with comparative accounts.

Each of the three parts represents a different constellation of the three themes of risk, death, and enchantment. Thus, the first part on risk, death, and enchantment is called *The Assemblages of Spectacle*. In this part, Chapters 1 and 2 provide a brief overview of the Hollywood and Hong Kong media industries—their connections, commonalities, and contrasts—as well as the ways in which spectacle is produced on the production floor. Chapter 1 illustrates how the two industries have connected at specific junctures and the emergence of media assemblages. Chapter 2 demonstrates that setwork is itself a spectacle, creating a primary, interactive audience of media workers. I posit that the participatory element of production—especially with extras and crew who heckle and hail lead actors on set—is rooted in the live performance dynamic of variety shows, vaudeville and circus audiences, and early film's "cinema of attractions" (Gunning 1990).

In the second part, *Local Sets, Global Forces*, Chapters 3 and 4 look at the spatial configurations of these place-based industries. Chapter 3 looks at multiple forms of risk in Hollywood, with attention to how setwork dynamics should be seen in the context of globalization and offshoring. This chapter looks at issues of "runaway productions," the 2007 Writers Guild strike, and the experiences of a Hong Kong film director working on a Hollywood film set. Chapter 4 explores the impact of British colonial policy and Hollywood's aggressive marketing and distribution strategies on the Hong Kong film industry as it reconfigures after the territory's return to China, amid the discourse about the "death" of the Hong Kong film industry. Both of these chapters help us comprehend the disordered globalizing processes of cultural production.

The third part, *Performance and Possession*, looks at how media work-ers' labor of performance and working with camera technologies intersect with cosmology, challenging the notion of production occurring in a dis-enchanted modernity. Chapter 5 demonstrates that media production en-compasses a heterogeneous combination of social and economic forces by showing how ghosts and gangsters are pervasive as not only on-screen genres in Hong Kong film but also off screen as part of the production process. In Chapter 6, I use the concept of affective labor to discuss how the work of producing spectacle in Hollywood and Hong Kong entails the traversal between fiction and nonfiction for media workers, resulting in accounts of possession and feeling overtaken by the themes they are work-ing to convey amid the (ir)rationalized production processes. In Chapter 7, I turn to camera technology—the instrument to, and through, which all the activity on the set is directed, and various media workers' fears and fascinations with it, illustrating that premodern fears about "spirit cap-ture" are still with us in these technology-driven and seemingly secular, modern sites. The Epilogue looks at how the themes of the book manifest in Hollywood and Hong Kong today, with new iterations of demise—and rebirth—in current local, regional, and global configurations.

PART I

The Assemblages of Spectacle

CHAPTER 1

Contrasts, Commonalities, and Connections

Hollywood and Hong Kong

In this chapter I discuss key contrasts, commonalities, and connections between the Hollywood and Hong Kong entertainment industries, focusing on production processes. I provide a brief overview of the industries and look at how Fordism and flexible production and the role of unions play out in contemporary production processes. I also explore various convergences between people and projects in both sites. The two production sites have linked up at specific junctures over the past century and mutually informed each other. In exploring the contemporary relationship between the Hollywood and Hong Kong media industries, it becomes apparent that they are tethered together in contingent ways through organizational histories, migration, politics, and transnational co-productions. The varying configurations of local productions and transnational film ventures, with uprooted media workers, constitute what I refer to as media assemblages—formations that comprise diverse cultural and political entities. Yet I also show that globalization does not shut down specific, local practices. As Birgit Meyer and Peter Geschiere note of globalizing processes, "people's awareness of being involved in open-ended global flows seems to trigger a search for fixed orientation points and action frames, as well as determined efforts to affirm old and construct new boundaries" (Meyer and Geschiere 1999: 2).

Ideological Contrasts

A major contrast between Hollywood and Hong Kong is the way in which their governments regard the ideological potential of filmed entertainment. As early as the 1910s, the American government recognized Hollywood as a prime engine for promoting the United States overseas, through images of American life and goods, and the trade in American film itself. In addition to legally codifying American film as intellectual property, in 1916 the U.S. State Department established a motion-picture section to protect American interests (Miller et al. 2005: 60–61). In 1918, Congress passed the Webb–Pomerene Act, which granted immunity to American film companies regarding antitrust laws for overseas distribution, ostensibly to aid the war effort (Balio 1993). The Webb–Pomerene Act allowed U.S. studios to form a cartel for exports of American goods and attendant ideology. Miller et al. explain Hollywood's strategy for international dominance via feature films in the 1910s and 1920s: "Hollywood began to sell to Asia and Latin America, almost wiping out Brazilian production, for example, by purchasing local distributors" (Miller et al. 2005: 61). By the 1920s, in Hollywood's leading export sites of Britain, Australia, Argentina, and Brazil, "the Federal Government institutionalized commercial attachés in its embassies" (Miller et al. 2005: 61). Additionally, the major Hollywood studios enforced the profitable blind bidding and block booking of their films to independent exhibitors overseas, a practice that was endorsed by the Motion Picture Export Association of America (MPEAA) (this practice ended with the U.S. Supreme Court ruling in 1948) (Balio 1993). Hollywood was clearly regarded as a valuable resource for America's "soft power" (Nye 2004) by the U.S. government.

To this day the American commercial film and television industry continues to receive support from the U.S. government in the form of federal and state government subsidies and incentives, and through limits on foreign imports and foreign ownership, as well as the U.S. government's dominant role in GATT and WTO policies (Miller et al. 2005). What some refer to as "Washwood" connotes the entangled relations between federal and state forces and American entertainment, including the military–industrial complex. Further, American cultural values of innovation and entrepreneurship are enshrined in cinematic lore (e.g., "motion picture *arts and sciences*"), and American defense and security sectors have lauded American filmmakers Steven Spielberg and George Lucas for their roles as pioneers of American innovation and champions of galactic might, illuminating the vestiges of Cold War ideology couched within American entertainment. Spielberg received a medal from the U.S. Department of Defense (and is, incidentally, a Knight Commander of the British Empire), while Lucas was awarded the National Medal of Science and Technology by President George W. Bush. Events such as the Cold War and American involvement in Vietnam and Iraq have helped shape the off-screen trajectory and character of the American motion-picture and television industries (such as the House Un-American Activities Committee's blacklisting of several hundred Hollywood workers during 1947 and 1951) as well as film content since 9/11. Presidential administrations also endorse various productions and projects; for instance, in the 2014 email hack of Los Angeles–based Sony Pictures Entertainment, emails emerged that confirm that "at least two U.S. government officials screened a rough cut of the Kim Jong-Un assassination comedy *The Interview* in late June and gave the film—including a final scene that sees the dictator's head explode—their blessing."[1] In other words, the depiction of the killing of the leader of a long-standing Cold War enemy was sanctioned by the American government. Contemporary American television programs and blockbuster films showcase the research and development that the United States has pursued in its "war on terror," such as sophisticated weaponry and surveillance technologies (as seen on television shows *CSI* and *24*, and in films such as the *Bourne Identity* series and *Eagle Eye*). Indeed, Hollywood functions as a "military-entertainment complex" (Lenoir and Lowood 2005): the University of Southern California's Institute for Creative Technologies is a U.S. Department of Defense–sponsored University Affiliated Research Center working in collaboration with the U.S. Army Research Laboratory. The Institute for Creative Technologies uses Hollywood blockbuster and game-makers' CGI (computer-generated imagery) and storytelling capabilities to design virtual technologies for the Army to train soldiers deployed to Iraq and Afghanistan in "cultural sensitivity."

In contrast, for the past century the Hong Kong film industry has existed within a laissez-faire capitalist system that has offered little government support for its sustainability. Unlike Hollywood, Hong Kong's film industry is not a national one. A former colony of Britain, the city-state of Hong Kong has been, since its 1997 return to China, a Special Administrative Region (SAR) of China, under what is known as a "one country, two systems" form of governance. Hong Kong has historically been valued for its port: following its capture by the British after the Opium Wars between 1839 and 1860, the colonial government used Hong Kong's harbor (seen in Photo 1.1) to turn the colony into an entrepôt and thus to further British imperial interests in shipping, banking, and trade. Government officials

PHOTO **1.1** Hong Kong's Victoria Harbour *(Credit: Author)*.

and economists have for decades declared Hong Kong to be a haven of free-market practices with minimal government interference. A salient feature of Hong Kong's economy was "positive non-interventionism," a colonial policy pursued by Hong Kong in the 1960s to maintain an open and "free" economy with little government intervention (Castells 2000; Ngo 1999b; So 2004).

During Hong Kong's colonial era, working in the entertainment in-dustries was considered a source of revenue for individual studio heads in what were often family-based organizations, and not a way to deliberately advance the territory's soft power, particularly as Britain's own national film industry struggled to compete with Hollywood. Social attitudes in Hong Kong toward working in the film and television industries have also had some bearing on the trajectories of individual media workers and the general direction of the industry. Work in the media industries has been for many Hong Kong locals associated with *lo pin moon*: involve-ment in "slanted door" business—dubious work, as opposed to "straight door" business. While Hollywood shares a past filled with criminal figures and activities, Hollywood movie stars such as Ronald Reagan and Arnold Schwarzenegger became successful at the presidential and gubernatorial level; however, this kind of crossover has not happened yet in Hong Kong and would be unlikely, not just because of Hong Kong's lack of universal suf-frage but because of the film industry's history of socially marginal status. Yet in China, these societal distinctions are less important: Hong Kong movie star (and co-star of American blockbuster franchise *Rush Hour*) Jackie Chan was appointed to the National Committee of the Chinese Peo-ple's Political Consultative Conference, and Hong Kong actor and film-maker Stephen Chow was appointed to the Guangdong's Chinese People's Political Consultative Conference committee, both by the Chinese Com-munist Party. These are political advisory boards, and other celebrities and famous athletes serve on them as well. These Hong Kong–based tal-ents are thus recruited for China's soft power.

Neither production site has been left untouched by the sociopolitical dynamics of the regions in which they are embedded. Even with the grow-ing financial ties between Hollywood and China, and filming overseas, the development and ideological center of Hollywood remains in the United States and generally Los Angeles, and despite the large immigrant popula-tions and diverse languages of Los Angeles, the language of mainstream entertainment business is English, with its power base largely white and Euro-American. The shifts in governance that Hong Kong has endured have left their trace on the off-screen activities of its media industries, such as colonial censorship of on-screen representations and lack of support for the development of the Hong Kong film industry. Hong Kong's film in-dustry underwent a switch from Cantonese to Mandarin in the late 1960s and early 1970s, partly because it was dominated by mainland Chinese and Singaporean filmmakers and partly to target the Taiwanese market (Teo 2000: 91). A glutted Taiwanese market and a surge in popular local

Cantonese-language television programs in Hong Kong in the 1970s led to the Hong Kong film industry's reversion to Cantonese. Subsequently, Hong Kong's famed "identity crisis" of the 1990s as its return to China drew nearer (Lu 2000; Matthews, Ma, and Lui 2008) also manifested within the transnational, diasporic entertainment industry, and Mandarin has again become useful for Cantonese personnel to speak. During my fieldwork, numerous Hong Kong directors and producers complained to me about "primitive" or "unsophisticated" labor practices and aesthetics of mainland Chinese media workers. "Open" was an English term I commonly heard and read about in Hong Kong to describe its rule of law, political transparency, and free press in relation to China, which by contrast was seen as "closed." While Hong Kong and China have since 2003 seen an increase in fused economic relationships, tensions between the territory and the nation have expanded, evident in the growth in local political movements that, among some followers, call for the expulsion of Chinese from the city. These nativist sentiments combined with the desire to see the promise of universal suffrage and more equitable living conditions, culminating in the Umbrella Uprising in the fall of 2014, which continues to brew. The tensions between Hong Kong and China are further discussed in Chapter 4.

Industrial Overviews: Commonalities and Contrasts

There is a major commonality and a major contrast between the Hollywood and Hong Kong media production processes, both of which are embedded in their industries' histories.[2] There are of course many similarities and differences between these two production sites, but these two are the most striking. The key commonality is that both Hollywood and Hong Kong were organized along Fordist systems of production for commercial film.[3] Hollywood's Fordism was at its height between the 1930s and the 1950s, and Hong Kong's between the 1950s and the 1970s. During these times, major film studios in both sites churned out large quantities of predictable fare through established genres for domestic and overseas consumption. They accomplished this through rationalized production processes with stables of long-term, full-time employees. The key difference between Hollywood and Hong Kong is in the role of unions: for over 80 years, Hollywood has had strong unions shaping the conditions of much of the media labor, due in large part to their ability to collectively bargain (although there is a growing abundance of nonunion labor). In contrast,

Hong Kong's entertainment industry has a long history of weak unions and guilds, particularly for below-the-line workers, and this has been exacerbated by the lack of a collective bargaining law in the territory's history and the strong influence of pro-business investors who can easily replace activist crew members (see also Szeto and Chen 2013).

Fordism

Both film industries in the 20th century gained international acclaim as place-specific industrial sites with a very high output, such that those urban areas became entwined in the international recognition for their film industries.[4] Hollywood started out as what geographer Allen Scott calls a "branch-plant extension" of New York's motion-picture industry and became an "economically sustainable agglomeration in its own right" in southern California by 1915, with dozens of small production companies (Scott 2014: 33). Hollywood's agglomeration was aided by the lure of abundant sunshine and mild winters, a diversity of terrain and pretty locales (as seen in Photo 1.2), and a growing centralization of creative and technical services. By the 1930s, Hollywood boasted eight "majors" organized along Fordist lines and several smaller independent production companies. Until the early 1960s, the majors (the "Big Five" of MGM, Paramount, Warner Bros., 20th Century Fox, and RKO and the "Little Three" of Columbia, United Artists, and Universal) constituted a "concentrated oligopoly" (Storper 1994: 203).

Like Hollywood, Hong Kong's film industry began with small production companies; the American and former circus employee Benjamin Brodsky is credited by Hong Kong film historian Law Kar as central to jump-starting the organization of the local film industry, producing commercial film shorts in the territory in 1909 through his Asia Film Company, and screening those shorts back in Los Angeles in 1917 (Kar 2000: 45). Cantonese-language cinema was quite diffuse as it was also made in China during the early years, especially Shanghai and Guangzhou, and one of Hong Kong's biggest production companies, Grandview Film Company, originated in San Francisco, funded by Chinese Americans, moving to Hong Kong in 1935 (Fonoroff 1988: 297). By 1939, when members of the Shanghai film industry fled as war refugees to the British colony, there were more than 40 film studios in the colony (Fu 201). Yet it was in fact the Shanghai film industry in its prewar years that had modeled its production practices on Hollywood's classic Fordist example (Teo 2005: 193). By the 1950s, however, Hong Kong boasted two studios organized along

PHOTO **1.2** Lake Hollywood *(Credit: Author).*

Fordist lines: Shaw Brothers and Cathay Studios. The major studios in both places were also vertically integrated, meaning that those studios took over production, distribution, and exhibition divisions, and the star system flourished in both sites. Movietown, Shaw's studio facilities in the New Territories' Clearwater Bay, comprised sound and outdoor stages, a color laboratory, a training school, canteens, dormitories for workers, and apartments for performers and directors (Bordwell 2000). "The studio ran twenty-four hours a day, working 1,200 employees in ten-hour shifts" (Bordwell 2000: 63). Shaw Brothers productions were enormously successful not just in Hong Kong, but in overseas territories such as Taiwan and southeast Asia.

By the 1970s, the Fordist studio system of American film production had declined and moved into a flexible style of organization; the project-based work of filmmaking meant that there were "shifting, temporary teams of creative workers and associated technical workers engaging with one another in personalized, open-ended systems of interaction" (Scott 2005: 5). As the Hong Kong film industry shifted from a Fordist to a flexible mode of production in the 1970s, studios downsized, as with Golden Harvest and, later, Cinema City. In the 1980s the Hong Kong film industry became organized along a largely flexible, decentralized mode of production with other independent production companies that drew from a "casual workforce" (Curtin 2007: 60), its television industry less so.[5] The film industry was characterized by independent production companies headed by entrepreneurs who diversified into real estate and jewelry, and in some cases disbanded after production of a single film (see Curtin 2007; Fore 1994; Fu 2000; Rodriguez 1999; Stokes and Hoover 1999). As Szeto and Chen describe in their research on the Hong Kong film industry, the kind of "flexible independent system" that has emerged revolves around "highly networked individuals" who "organize around secured investment/funding in a very short period of time after a round of phone calls . . . a whole team can be assembled in two weeks" (Szeto and Chen 2013).

Hollywood currently features a combination of Fordist and flexible modes of production, retaining some of the assembly-line labor features yet exhibiting the niche production and outsourcing of flexible production, with a reduction in union power. John Caldwell sees this mix of modes of production in Hollywood as what gives the film and television industries their endurance (Caldwell 2008: 34). However, Allan Scott claims that despite Hollywood's rise in flexible production, the major studios remain key players (Scott 2005: 37, 46–47). Currently, there are six majors (Columbia, Disney, 20th Century Fox, Paramount, Warner Bros., and Universal), and they have become "fountainheads of financial and coordination services for independent producers in combination with overall marketing and distribution activities" (Scott 2005: 8). Studios and firms in Hollywood are "notably aggressive on the marketing front, and have built up an extensive system of distribution channels through which

their outputs flow smoothly to the rest of the world" (Scott 2005: 9)—
including Hong Kong. In the late 1980s to the early 2000s, Hollywood
studios were bought out by media conglomerates, and ancillary markets such as gaming have increasingly been where media conglomerates
make their money. Hollywood studios may continue to appear to be self-
contained units, worlds unto themselves: the Hollywood studio lot at
which I spent many months resembled a suburb, boasting its own fire
department, eateries, Starbucks, and gym. Yet for below-the-line personnel based in both Hollywood and Hong Kong, the post-Fordist shift from
permanent payroll work to part-time, project-to-project labor is felt more
strongly as site-specific and studio-based production work lessens. The
maintenance of social networks is crucial to individuals in their attempts
to find as consistent employment as possible.

From Leftist Film Activities to Grooming Rights: Unions and Labor in the Hong Kong and Hollywood Media Industries

Hollywood boasts a long history of a unionized labor force, with job segmentation and fixed pay scales. In contrast, Hong Kong offers guild associations for various segments of media labor; however, these tend to be
loose, informal, and not as devoted to professionalizing and credential-
izing its members through educational seminars, cold readings, scene
showcases, and industry events as is common in some of the Hollywood
unions and guilds, which also provide frequent networking opportunities.
Also, Hong Kong guild associations do not enforce fixed pay scales as the
Hollywood unions have. Contracts and legal enforcements are generally
less pervasive and formally applied in the Hong Kong film/TV industries
than in Hollywood, and salaries for celebrity actors and directors in Hong
Kong are much lower than their counterparts' in Hollywood. For instance,
between the years 2003 and 2006, principal actors on a Hollywood drama
I spent time on earned approximately US$3 million a season (one actor
earned more than double that amount a season), over multiple seasons,
whereas a Hong Kong TV star made approximately US$389,610 per TV
series (their income could be supplemented by advertising campaigns). On
Hollywood film studio projects, lead actors made anywhere from a couple
million dollars to US$20 million a film, whereas a Hong Kong film star
earned approximately US$1.29 million a film.

It is crucial to examine the history of unionized film labor in Hong
Kong, especially since many informants described the lack of strong
unions as a "natural" byproduct of the entrepreneurial environment of
filmmaking in Hong Kong. This byproduct is not natural but constructed

through deliberate colonial and capitalist policies, and this nexus of ideo-logical interests links Hong Kong's media industries with the American media industries' own history of profit maximization. The minimal union-ized film labor in Hong Kong is largely due to British colonial authorities' clampdown on collectivizing film practices, some of which were brought over from China. These efforts originated in Hong Kong during Japan's 1941–45 occupation of Hong Kong and continued after Britain's reoccu-pation of the city (Rodriguez 1999: 109). As Hector Rodriguez explicates in his discussion of the history of Hong Kong filmmaking, film activists from China encouraged Marxist study groups for Hong Kong film person-nel, cooperative screenwriting, and educational film content. The People's Republic of China (PRC) organizations such as the Xinhua news agency funded Hong Kong film collectivization efforts and agitation for better labor conditions through the attempted penetration of private film com-panies. Over decades, waves of labor strikes in Hong Kong were sparked by periods of anti-imperialism and pro-communism in mainland China (e.g., the 1949 creation of the PRC and later the 1967 Cultural Revolution). In fact, in 1952 (during an active phase of anticolonial, pro-China film-worker activity in Hong Kong), leftist Hong Kong film workers agitated for back payments and even incurred a strike against a privately owned film company. Citing Law Kar and Jay Leyda, Rodriguez notes that the response of the British colonial authorities was to deport over 20 strik-ing film workers who were "accused of plotting on behalf of the People's Republic" (Rodriguez 1999: 112). This event occurred during a volatile point in America's Cold War, underscoring the former Allied powers' battle against communism on multiple fronts and the intersection of Hong Kong's film industry with American ideological interests. As Rodriguez points out, when anticolonial riots broke out in Hong Kong in 1967, triggered by China's Cultural Revolution, leftist film workers in Hong Kong were seen aiding striking workers and forming communist groups such as the "All Circles Anti-British Persecution and Struggle Committee," which led to sev-eral stars being imprisoned in detention camps (Rodriguez 1999: 112).

In a move that would hold enormous repercussions for the Hong Kong film industry and its labor organization, colonial authorities encouraged the growth of "right-wing" private film companies run by entrepreneurs that disregarded leftist trade unions such as the Association of Cantonese Film Workers (Rodriguez 1999: 110, 115). Many of these private compa-nies, such as Shaw Brothers, established ties with Taiwan's Guamindang (and anticommunist) ministries, which offered funding, distribution licenses, and tax deductions for Hong Kong films that were anti-China.

As part of the "Red Movie Ban," the Guamindang induced pledges among Shaw Brothers and Cathay Studios employees to cease distributing or exhibiting movies in China. Thus, as Rodriguez claims, "despite their claim to political neutrality, colonial authorities had actually worked to enhance the power of capitalist management" (Rodriguez 1999: 111). As Rodriguez goes on to argue, these actions on the part of colonial authorities were intended to depoliticize not only film as a specifically Hong Kong industry but, more broadly, Hong Kong's public culture. These Anglo and anticommunist Chinese movements intersected with America's own alliances with "free" market economies and promotion of free enterprise. Weak labor laws in Hong Kong have discouraged unionization and collective bargaining, a clear division of film labor, and consistent regulation of worker safety, which has had a negative impact on media workers.

Although unions hold a lengthy history in Hollywood, they have been and remain a source of conflict, especially in an increasingly flexible and "precarious" industry (Curtain et al. 2016) and within a broader, national shift toward neoliberalism that supports union-busting. Job segmentation in Hollywood continues to be contentious, even in seemingly mundane tasks. For instance, I was nearly yelled at by a crew member on the set of a TV program for attempting to move a wire on the ground that I had nearly tripped on as "that could threaten someone's job." The crew member explained to me that tasks delineated for specific positions needed to be retained for the people filling those positions.

In another example, on the set of a Hollywood television show I observed a dispute between workers that represents the struggle to delineate job tasks in an industry that continues to retain elements of a Fordist organization of labor. In the hair and makeup trailer of this show, a fight erupted between a makeup artist and a hairstylist over who had grooming rights to a principal actor's eyebrows. The principal actor was being readied for his upcoming scene, and after styling his hair, the hairstylist had attempted to groom the actor's eyebrows. The makeup artist assigned to this actor, while working on another actor, happened to notice the hairstylist attending to the actor's eyebrows. A quarrel broke out between the hairstylist and makeup artist, centered on the conundrum that eyebrows are *hair* (the responsibility of the hair department), yet they are located on the *face* (the terrain of the makeup department). Shouts between makeup and hair escalated, threatening to hold up production, since tasks such as these are, in a Taylorist fashion, timed to the minute in the production schedule. Meanwhile, the actor whose brows were in question quietly leaned back, sipped his coffee, and stoically let the heated argument play out around him. The first assistant director was radioed over to the trailer to mediate this Solomon-like dispute, which had ground all work in the trailer to a halt. He entered the trailer, and, citing a guild policy on the spot, ruled in favor of the makeup artist, then quickly exited. The hairstylist burst into tears and refused to talk to the makeup artist in question for the rest of the day; indeed, relations between all of hair and makeup remained tense for a few days. At the end of the day, a senior makeup artist on set told me that the first assistant director's ruling was "a victory" for makeup departments. I was to find over the coming months that job protectionism fueled many of the on-set tensions between crew members in Hollywood. With nonunion productions in Los Angeles and the increase in runaway production, which draws largely from local, nonunionized labor, organized labor in Hollywood faces many challenges.

When I recounted these stories to industry workers in Hong Kong, they were shocked at the degree to which people's jobs are defined and protected in Hollywood, many of them citing the preferred "flexibility" of the Hong Kong film and television industry—in which, ostensibly, any group of people do "whatever it takes" to get things done—as a much more commonsensical and practical approach. They expressed that the integrity of the film or program becomes lost amid such claim-staking. A common theme among Hong Kong media workers (from producers to production assistants) was that while they envied the bigger budgets and higher pay of Hollywood, they disdained the task delineations that they understood Hollywood unions to reinforce. Yet Hollywood productions are increasingly nonunion and rely upon part-time, short-term, contracted workers who lack benefits and protections. It is not just blockbuster films that shoot overseas to bring production costs down, but also network and cable television fare (many workers' bread and butter), that film in Canada, what Serra Tinic calls "Hollywood North" (Tinic 2005: 29), or out of state. The increase in offshore production also means less regulation of union rules (and a rise in exploitation) for media workers. The struggle over job distinctions via eyebrows may at first glance appear quaint, yet such disputes signal the growing tensions surrounding job protection of specialized tasks, the dismantling of the unions, and the agitation for one's livelihood. As I pointed out to a few Hong Kong media personnel, there was no universal healthcare scheme in the United States as there was in Hong Kong, and union membership offers group health insurance plans as a result of labor contracts and collective bargaining. Most freelance and independent contractors in Hollywood, however, do without health insurance altogether in an industry whose work entails enormous physical risks.

Flexibility

In the post-Fordist era, flexibility is a general characteristic of global film labor, with its own local and regional characteristics. Shooting action films in Hong Kong, for instance, entails a more open-ended process, choreographed "with an eye towards adapting the performance to available resources and immediate constraints at the shooting location" (Curtin 2007: 59). Dialogue is more improvised in Hong Kong, particularly in film. For instance, on the set of a Hong Kong film I observed in 2006, the director hurriedly rewrote dialogue for principal characters in between shots. He kept the two writers on hand during filming in order to do this (and one of the writers also acted in the film). His producer told me that this kind of flexibility just isn't possible in Hollywood. While this doesn't happen on every set in Hong Kong, the role of the writer there is less formal, less delineated, and less valued than in Hollywood, so quick changes can and do occur on set. This was something I rarely observed on studio films and television in Hollywood, although it can happen in independent filmmaking. The environment of a Hollywood set is generally more controlled, particularly if filming is at a studio, with executives dropping by to keep an eye on things. Multiple Hong Kong directors and producers described their production style's flexibility as an advantage and distinctly "Hong Kong."

The tendency toward exterior filming in Hong Kong means that production personnel work within the constraints of the physical and social landscape of the territory. In the diminishing availability of large studio space and with the post-Fordist turn to downscaled and more flexible shooting, location filming for television and film means that production personnel have to be highly mobile, diplomatic, and creative. They must be able to deal with testy urban dwellers on Hong Kong Island and Kowloon, and angry villagers in the countryside areas of the New Territories, many of whom have expressed frustrations with disruptions to traffic, increased noise levels, or inadequate permission. In the New Territories, villagers have been known to demand payment for filming on privately owned land. Additionally, both police officers and triad members may disrupt film crews for, respectively, permits or "protection" payment. Film crews in Hong Kong are extremely sensitive to the physical and social environment in which they film, going to great lengths to not disrupt the pace of city or rural life (such as whispering and miming instructions to one another while filming near private homes, and literally running in to capture a shot and then running out). This differs from the imposition of many Hollywood productions on the cities of Los Angeles, Burbank, or Santa Monica when filming exteriors. Although Hollywood film productions pay hefty fees to acquire permits for filming exteriors, the space that some of these productions occupy during filming underscores the reverence that Hollywood fosters. The extensive police motorcades that accompany camera crews filming from cameras mounted on moving vehicles, the closure of streets and traffic detours, and the police officers stationed outside trailers and workstations on urban and residential streets highlight the amount of resources Hollywood productions devote to taming the physical and social environment.

The vaunted "flexibility" of production personnel that I frequently heard about in Hong Kong has also, I argue below, contributed to the contingent conditions of media workers' labor. Hong Kong informants almost always used the English-language term "flexibility" with a positive connotation. They embraced geographic mobility and linguistic versatility as key components of what the film industry defines as being flexible (see also Martin 2013). In doing so, they replicated the entrepreneurial bent for which the Hong Kong film industry has come to be known (Stokes and Hoover 1999). Those who celebrate flexibility often invoke Hong Kong's reputation as a free-trade haven of hardworking entrepreneurs who have embraced the market (Friedman 2006; Hong Kong Trade Development Council 2005). These attitudes stem from the British colonial policy of positive nonintervention, which instituted minimal market regulation, low taxation and tariffs, and loose labor laws. During my fieldwork, many members of the Hong Kong film industry attributed the industry's success to its "openness" and its colonial economic policies of laissez-faire, especially when contending with vague and restrictive stipulations imposed by Chinese authorities and ministries. Yet the flexibility of the film industry and of its members is partly a result of, and response to, deliberate colonial policies that scourged leftist, anticolonial elements and promoted the interests of right-wing companies. It should also be noted that the flexibility celebrated by some is partly a result of a colonial administration that did not foster local industrial development (Castells 2000; Chiu, Ho, and Lui 1997).

Hong Kong media workers frequently proclaimed that flexibility—a prominent element of production processes in Hong Kong (Fore 1994)—is crucial to their careers and to the survival of the industry. In many parts of the world, the threat of outsourcing and of casualization means that workers within a labor segment must "innovate" in order to perform multiple tasks that were previously outside the scope of their labor roles. Whether workers commute across the border for jobs in Beijing or work on foreign productions in Hong Kong, their adjustments require new languages and dialects and increasingly itinerant lifestyles and new kinship arrangements (see also Martin 2013). These flexible characteristics have resulted in a production culture that heavily touts mobility and adaptability. Yet flexibility also includes avoiding political uncertainty or embracing political and economic shifts, such as Hong Kong's trade agreement with China. Thus flexibility is not without risk, as it entails sudden geographic moves, ideological transitions, and new business and social practices. Risk taking is espoused by the Hong Kong SAR government for its residents. Flexibility, after all, is not merely an economic behavior; it has become a cultural attitude, an identity, an ethos to be embraced (Martin 1995; Ong 1999). Citing Colin Gordon, Aihwa Ong emphasizes that under neoliberal governmentality, individuals cannot be reliant on the state; they must be "self-enterprising" and are "obligated to become an 'entrepreneur of himself or herself'" (Gordon 1991: 43–44; Ong 2006: 14). Additionally, the notion of flexibility is not without historical and political connotations in the region, given the steady migrations of the Cantonese-speaking population between southern China and Hong Kong. Many of these Hong Kong transnational media personnel shared an education level that included finishing high school, some English-language education in Hong Kong, and in some cases, overseas education. While some Hong Kong informants were "flexible citizens" who had acquired overseas education in places such as Australia, Canada, England, and the United States, prepared by English-language education in the British colony of Hong Kong (Ong 1999), others, especially some of the (largely male) technical workers, grew up in government housing, and numerous stunt workers had left secondary school to help support their families.

The working-class background of some people in the Hong Kong entertainment media, especially the more physical labor, is also evident in Hollywood. Among the below-the-line workers there who revealed their education level to me, most had completed high school (a few had dropped out) and some had pursued college or an associate degree; others had instead obtained vocational training for their craft, such as electrician or carpentry work. In Hollywood, although technical craftspeople such as the mostly white male electricians and carpenters are often described as working class, and some of those I knew were not college educated, those who were union members, while sporting a blue-collar style of presentation, earned what many would consider a middle-class income if they worked regularly, ranging between $40,000 and $70,000 a year. However, some of them shared that they came from what they described as working class backgrounds (lower income with little autonomy) and had to support a multi-person household on their single income in a very expensive city. In both sites, people (including actors) told me that production held an appeal because higher education is not required, yet there is always the dream of "making it" financially. The path to making it, though, can incur many expenses (such as head-shots).

The production of television in Hong Kong offers an example of how Fordist and flexible production systems are combined. As Eric Kit-wai Ma noted in his comparative ethnographic study of the production of commercial and noncommercial Hong Kong television dramas, the process for a TV drama "comes about less as a rational organization and more as loosely coupled collectivity functioning in a 'satisficing' manner: decisions are made not by exploring all options but by selecting between 'handy' alternatives" (Ma 1999: 134). In Ma and Chow's 2004 observations of Hong Kong television production across the border in China, production is "flexible yet routinized" with a Chinese production crew hired on a project basis and supervised by visiting Hong Kong experts who can take advantage of more diverse landscapes and cheaper production support than in Hong Kong (Chow and Ma 2004: 205–6). Commercial terrestrial television was first launched in 1967 in Hong Kong as Television Broadcast Ltd (TVB), after the anticolonial riots (Ma 1999: 24). Through television, and particularly melodrama serials, images and storylines of local Hong Kong life came into people's homes, a shift from the more abstract and less specific content of Hong Kong–produced films (Ma 1999: 29). A commercial broadcaster, TVB has avoided controversial topics over the years, especially since it courts overseas audiences, whereas Radio Television Hong Kong (RTHK) is a radio broadcaster and government department of Hong Kong that has offered "non-commercial, alternative, and diversified" television programming, similar to a public broadcaster (Ma 1999: 12). As Ma notes, in the 1980s and early 1990s some RTHK programming was critical of both the colonial government and communist China (Ma 1999: 120).

In 2005 in Hong Kong I visited the set of a television drama at TVB studios. An informant who took me on set had a pass for the studio; its security was less extensive and pervasive than that of a Hollywood studio. We arrived for the nighttime shoot that had just begun at 10:30 p.m. Unlike Hollywood, the stars of the show were not given their own trailers; instead, there was a general resting room for all the actors. Overall, there are fewer divisions between the stars and the rest of the cast in Hong Kong, and the meals on this show were usually brought in by everyone, potluck style, not catered by the production company as is the case in Hollywood. Similarly, there were no special hair and makeup rooms for the stars of the show as there are in Hollywood. A well-known Hong Kong actor who had worked on a Hollywood blockbuster film told me of his loneliness at being assigned to a trailer, preferring the more "social" style of Hong Kong productions. In the large makeup and wardrobe room used by everyone I observed an altar dedicated to General Guan (a popular Taoist and Buddhist deity) at which a few actors lit incense; "TV is a dangerous business," the producer explained to me later, especially given the death scenes filmed for the show.

A nearly hour-long program, each episode took approximately six days to shoot, with six different directors who worked in shifts. The production schedule was as follows: all exterior shots were filmed during the day, and all interior shots filmed throughout the night. So, for example, when we arrived on set at 11:30 p.m., they had only been filming that scene for an hour and would continue to do so till about 6 a.m. Many of the actors worked day and night, with only a few hours of sleep in between "shifts," and a day off every fourth day or so. This differed from network dramas filming at the studios in Hollywood, which, as per union rules, stipulate mandatory hours off between shifts. However, Hollywood single-camera, one-hour network dramas film approximately 35 to 38 weeks a year; on those sets I visited, the physical and emotional exhaustion of the cast and crew was also quite palpable as 16-hour days were very common. The Hong Kong sound stage was smaller than what I observed in Hollywood, with a smaller crew than the Hollywood network shows.

After being introduced to some of the lead actors, they greeted me in English in an assortment of British, Australian, and Canadian accents, several of them mentioning their overseas background without my asking, as my appearance indicated my "Westerner" status. As we chatted, I asked the actors how the episode retained continuity in tone if there are six different directors. They all grinned and suggested I watch the show myself to decide; another informant told me later that this is an aspect of factory-style shooting they don't like. However, given the team of producer-writers involved in Hollywood network dramas, not to mention all the guest directors cycled in and out, continuous tone is also an issue in Hollywood television production. Long noted for its strict control over actors, TVB's contracts for actors were full-time and exclusive. However, during my fieldwork, flexible contracts became available to featured actors; in the case of a couple of informants, they could work overseas on other film and television projects between this program, but they also could not count on consistent employment. The producer for this program had worked at TVB for many years, and said he often worked up to 22 hours a day. Visiting the set after midnight, he asked me if his set was smaller than the TV sets I'd been on in the United States. I replied, "A bit." He laughed and told our mutual friend, "They [Hollywood] think of us how we think of the mainland." A year later when I met this producer again, he was gloomily planning his retirement in Australia, telling me that with viewership declining, because "cable television ruins local taste," and with the company laying off employees, "We will never be like before 1997 . . . the best is gone."

Media Assemblages: Joint Productions and Collaborations

In the fall of 2006 in Hong Kong, while watching television, I saw an ad on Hong Kong television in English with Chinese subtitles that featured Arnold Schwarzenegger, the governor of California and former "Terminator" celebrity, and Jackie Chan, the ubiquitous Hong Kong action star in both Hong Kong and Hollywood films and a spokesperson for Hong Kong's film industry. In the commercial, Schwarzenegger and Chan rode motorcycles side by side and announced that they are joining forces to call on people to "terminate" the criminal activity of film piracy such as illegal downloading. Filmed in Los Angeles in 2005 by the director of *Terminator 3: The Rise of the Machines*, the commercial was the product of a joint decision between Hong Kong, SAR's Intellectual Property Department, and the California Commission for Jobs and Economic Growth to promote awareness about the protection of intellectual property rights and the evils of piracy in Hong Kong and California. These two icons of masculine strength, law, and governance riding side by side illustrated the conjoining of state interests and market forces to battle legal issues as well as individual trajectories. I refer to this and other such convergences between the two industrial sites as "media assemblages."

Aihwa Ong's use of the term "assemblage" is useful to understand the diverse collection of practices and personnel that make up commercial media production. In her analysis of Southeast Asian "ecologies of expertise," Ong's interpretation of Deleuze and Guattari's notion of assemblage refers to the merging of disparate elements to produce heterogeneous meanings and spaces. Ong argues against Manuel Castells' claim that developmental regions are excluded from global networks by positing instead that new technologies link emergent combinations of institutions, social actors, and values that transcend discrete "regional" or "global" networks, as in Singapore and Malaysia (Castells 1996; Ong 2005).[6] The new "ecologies" there produce innovative forms of information and territorial engagement, with "expatriates" from developed and developing nations mixing with local populations and becoming linked into elite universities (Ong 2005: 338–339). The notion of assemblage is relevant here because it conceptualizes the relationship between production sites with differing, yet linked, social, economic, and technological histories.

The media landscape of Hollywood and Hong Kong can be seen as comprising a diverse combination of practices, ideas, and individuals that come together at particular times and under specific circumstances in formations that destabilize simple stratification between regions and industries. Media assemblages represent uneven and contingent collaborations at the project or industry level, such as an international film co-production or a Hollywood adaptation of an Asian film, as I will discuss in Chapter 3. It is also important to note that the interests that spur such ensembles are not always uniform. As Ong and Collier point out, "An assemblage is the product of multiple determinations that are not reducible to a single logic" (Ong and Collier 2005: 12).

The notion of assemblage to provide a more "textured" understanding of current production configurations is becoming more apparent in media studies. Nitin Govil describes the increasing number of "co-ventures" between Indian entertainment conglomerates such as Reliance ADA Group with the American DreamWorks studio and independent U.S. production houses as an example of assemblage (Govil 2009: 63–64).[7] Similar to Govil, my use of assemblage further directs attention to the actual geopolitical differences and tensions that characterize such ensembles, which are less discernible in Arjun Appadurai's broad description of "mediascape," which refers to electronic perspectives of cultural flows. Assemblage, as Ong and Govil use it and I develop it here and elsewhere, underscores the on-the-ground interactivity of diverse players; it helps us recognize those points of connection between ostensibly separate entities and distinct processes, and the contingencies that arise. For instance, reflecting the geopolitical distinctions that emerge in media production, the TVB television producer described the Hong Kong actors he strove to cast in his show: "I hired actors who look like they are from an open society. They don't look like they speak *Putonghua* [Mandarin]."

There are multiple scales of interactivity between the two sites of Hollywood and Hong Kong. Interaction occurs at the scale of flexible individuals who shuttle between the two sites (and sometimes other sites in between) for films such as *Kill Bill*, *Face/Off*, and *Mission: Impossible*. In the 1990s, the political and economic concerns of Hong Kong media workers during the city's "countdown" to its 1997 return to China converged with the global profit-accumulation strategies of the American entertainment industry. A number of high-profile Hong Kong film personnel such as actor Chow Yun Fat, director John Woo, stunt director Yuen Woo Ping, director, actor, and martial arts director Sammo Hung, and director Peter Chan (among others), worked on Hollywood film and television. Historically, Hollywood has been quick to poach the most commercially successful media workers from overseas media industries (Miller et al. 2005), and at this specific time Hollywood was eager to capitalize upon the ingathering of a Chinese sensibility and pool of talent and (capitalist) know-how with an eye to China's emerging market potential. Yet Hollywood and Hong Kong interactivity also operates at the scale of transnational co-productions such as *Kung Fu Hustle* (a Hong Kong/China/Hollywood production) and Hong Kong films that use international casts (e.g., *Teenage Mutant Ninja Turtles III*). These connections also occur at the scale of place-specific projects that film on location in the other site (usually Hollywood films in Hong Kong, such as Hollywood's *The Dark Knight* and *Transformers: Age of Extinction*).

Media assemblage that encompasses capital interests and operations between state and industry becomes especially evident when an American tentpole film uses an international location for its backdrop. For instance, in 2007, the production team behind the Batman franchise *The Dark Knight* chose to film several scenes in Hong Kong to help proffer a dazzling array of vistas to audiences around the world. The American-based production team's desire to showcase Hong Kong's famed skyline (a breathtaking vista of neon signs earmarking the real estate owned by multinational corporations in the city's financial center) articulated neatly with the Hong Kong SAR's government initiative to beam its global-city status to the rest of the world. In other words, corporate and state interests of Hollywood and Hong Kong merged through film production to perpetuate their survival as they understand it: for the former, a transnational franchise, and for the latter, the "global" status of its post-1997 city, a priority given the city's competition with Shanghai for international film locales and "Asia hub" status. Yet the operation of this ensemble was not entirely smooth: the eight-day film shoot in Hong Kong entailed long filming hours that disrupted residents and businesses in the busy area of filming, with ensuing complaints, and there were disputed accounts of the government of Hong Kong SAR pocketing a large fee for the arrangement (see more on this in Chapter 4). However, several Hong Kong personnel described to me individual career benefits of this collaboration: one of the production assistants on this shoot was able to parlay this experience into working in Hollywood a year later, while a production manager told me of the transferable skills he and his colleagues gained by working on an American film of this magnitude (such as coordinating helicopter-camera teams) that would be put to use on future shoots in Hong Kong and across the border in China on China/Hong Kong co-productions. While the low cost of media labor in Hong Kong and the preferential treatment for an American production by government authorities led to some local outcry, my point here is that such combinations increasingly comprise diverse yet interrelated motivations and processes for individuals and entities involved.

Yet a century prior, there were encounters between the two industrial centers through the migrations and sojourns of entertainers such as Cantonese Opera troupes and director/stunt choreographer teams to California. As early as the 1850s, Cantonese Opera troupes traveled from Hong Kong (and the southern Chinese Guangdong province) to perform for goldmine workers during the California Gold Rush (Kar 2000: 60). According to Hong Kong film historian Law Kar, Cantonese Opera troupes regularly performed for the overseas Chinese communities throughout the West Coast up through the 1930s (Kar 2000: 60–61). It was during these later tours that Cantonese opera troupe members watched Hollywood films. Inspired by the American silent and sound films they saw on screen, Cantonese opera performers introduced elements of Hollywood films into the production of Cantonese opera, including "special effects, makeup techniques, settings, costumes, and mise-en-scene," and Western musical instruments (Kar 2000: 61). There were more direct interactions as well. A Cantonese opera star received an invitation from Douglas Fairbanks, Sr. to tour the major Hollywood film studios (Kar 2000: 61). In addition to Opera players, other individuals worked in early Hollywood film. Moon Kwan Man-Ching, for instance, came from Cantonese-speaking Guangzhou in China to work as an extra in Hollywood in the 1910s, where he learned about film techniques. In 1919 D. W. Griffith hired him to work as a consultant on "Chinese culture" for his film *Broken Blossoms*. Kwan then went to Hong Kong, integrating what he had learned in Hollywood, and directed films in the colony; in 1924 he returned to Hollywood to work as a consultant on a Lon Chaney film before returning to Hong Kong again

(Kar 2000: 50–61). These early encounters heralded the assemblages evident today.

This fusion of Hollywood and Cantonese opera would surface again in Hollywood in the 1970s, emerging from the spectacle of Cantonese opera: some of the martial arts and stunts performed on stage such as the styles of jumps and work with swords and sticks appeared in Hollywood film and television. The Hollywood/Hong Kong encounter came to be literally embodied in the person of Bruce Lee. Lee was born in San Francisco's Chinatown in 1940 while his father was touring in a Cantonese opera troupe in California. Lee appeared on stage in Cantonese opera as a baby. The family then returned to Hong Kong, and as a child, Lee starred in Cantonese movies. After studying martial arts in Hong Kong, he traveled to the United States to attend college, and taught martial arts. Situated in Los Angeles, he later appeared in the Hollywood TV series *The Green Hornet* and worked on the film *The Chinese Connection*. Lee later was contracted by the Hong Kong production company Golden Harvest, and he went on to make several Hong Kong martial-arts films that became successful around the world, including the United States. Hong Kong's Avenue of the Stars on the promenade at Victoria Harbour features a statue of Lee (Photo 1.3).

PHOTO **1.3** Bruce Lee Statue at Hong Kong's Avenue of the Stars at Victoria Harbour *(Credit: Author).*

There has been a steady stream of flexible citizens between the United States and Hong Kong who help form these ensembles. These individuals are afforded higher levels of political, legal, and financial acceptance and privilege by state agencies and are assisted by industry executives because of their perceived ability to maximize capital accumulation. Numerous media personnel, propelled by political economic fears or potentials, have been able to work in both sites, such as Chow Yun Fat and John Woo. Yet for many actors from Hong Kong seeking on-camera work in Hollywood, there have been fewer casting opportunities given the dearth of roles there for Asians and Asian-Americans and, for Hong Kong directors and producers, studio assumptions about genre expertise (e.g., martial arts and horror). Most of the traffic in labor in the early 2000s flowed from Hong Kong to Hollywood, although some Anglo-American individuals based out of Hollywood were able to instrumentalize the preferential conditions for expatriates in Hong Kong and launch projects there, opening film production companies in Hong Kong and, through the Closer Economic Partnership Arrangement (CEPA), becoming involved in productions with China. Many people I spoke with who work in both sites used the clichéd English-language term "bridge" to describe their role between Hong Kong and Hollywood, and Hong Kong and the Anglo-European West.

One such individual is a Hong Kong producer who regularly travels between San Francisco, Los Angeles, New York, Hong Kong, China, and southeast Asia, seeking financiers and production deals and attending to production logistics. With his British education and Cantonese and Mandarin language skills, as well as his far-flung kinship and socioprofessional ties, this producer represents the cultural diversity of Hong Kong, a diversity that has aided his flexible work practices and his participation in co-productions. Another Hong Kong director and writer, based in Hong Kong, visits Hollywood for meetings on potential projects at least once a year. His films have been screened at film festivals in Los Angeles, which serve as a launching pad for meetings with Hollywood production executives. His family and social networks are strung across the Pacific Rim (encompassing Hong Kong, China, Canada, and California) and help to activate his multistranded career. One of his films was a co-production with a European company. Yet another person, a Hong Kong actor, joined her husband when he was able to immigrate to the United States from Hong Kong for his work several decades ago and acquired U.S. passports for them both. Dividing her time between Hong Kong and Los Angeles, Rachel was able to find short-term film and television work in both Hong Kong and Hollywood. Other media workers have similar trajectories that crosscut the production sites of Hollywood and Hong Kong, and other places as well, demonstrating not only the mobility of such individuals and the utility of diasporic populations for these sojourners, but also the interconnections of variously located production sites.

Since the 1990s, subsidiaries of American-based multinational media corporations have increasingly staked their East Asian headquarters or satellite and distribution offices in Hong Kong, including, during the time of my fieldwork, Columbia TriStar (owned by Sony Corp.) and The Weinstein Company. Post-1997 Hong Kong, with its laissez-faire capitalism and Western-style banking services, constitutes a space of political and economic "exception" into which these foreign companies can venture into China (Ong 2006). These collaborations are the result of convergences between market forces and the city-state, which continues the colonial policy of welcoming Euro-American business and investment. The uneven arrangements between American-based corporate entities and Hong Kong SAR governance (and, by extension, Chinese media workers, financiers, and government authorities) form an assemblage with involvement from Westerners. Several Hong Kong media workers who worked in these offices in Hong Kong saw the managerial staff and executives as introducing Western-style business practices and standards (such as contracts and IP concerns). Some Hong Kong studios had ties to American distributors, such as Miramax and Disney. Co-productions between Hong Kong and Hollywood films such as *Kung Fu Hustle* and *Kung Fu Hustle 2* are also combinants of diverse elements in financing, labor, and geographic filming sites. For instance, a director I observed on set in Hong Kong was later hired to work on a Chinese-language remake of a South Korean film; the original South Korean film producers were also financing (and maintaining creative input on) the Hong Kong remake in a joint production between the Hong Kong and South Korea production companies.

The notion of assemblage is also instructive because with CEPA, for instance, it becomes apparent how the Hong Kong film industry can be understood as a key player in a combination of projects that crosscut discrete "regional" or "global" networks. CEPA is a 2003 treaty between China and Hong Kong that is designed to bolster Hong Kong industries with investment and access while facilitating China's integration with liberalization. Under the various stages of CEPA, the audiovisual industries have received the dual benefits of mainland government financing as well as the profits from distribution to mainland audiences, since CEPA "domestic" products are not subject to import quotas. In return, Hong

Kong film and television scripts must receive censors' approval (China does not yet have a film rating system), and a certain percentage of the film/TV projects are required to be filmed in China and use mainland media workers. Thus, through CEPA, Hong Kong industry members with multiple passports and dual citizenships create linkages with film workers in a nominally communist society that has undergone market reform, as well as with other, diversely positioned territories throughout Asia and the rest of the world, including personnel from the United States, Australia, Thailand, South Korea, Japan, and Canada. In fact, since my fieldwork in Hong Kong, there has been a growing number of pan-Asian productions that bring together Taiwan, South Korea, Japan, Hong Kong, and China in finance, production, marketing, and distribution (see Yeh and Davis 2008) for regional *and* global audiences, with influences from American and European cinema and production techniques and involvement with Westerners. These regional productions also bring together diverse East Asian practices and expertise.

Nevertheless, cross-border media projects between Hong Kong and mainland China are instrumentalized in the nation-building enterprise of "Greater China," which entail not only films but also television soap operas intended for Hong Kong and overseas Chinese audiences; many informants commuted or relocated to China to work on these co-productions. The creation of Warner Bros. Hengdian in China (in which an American media conglomerate merges with Chinese private and state-run companies) and the University of Southern California's Institute of Creative Technologies' collaboration with the Chinese Academy of Sciences illustrates the emerging clusters of American and Chinese corporate and government operations and interests. Yet as Ong points out with the "state-university-firm" clusters in Singapore and Malaysia (Ong 2005: 340), heterogeneous knowledge production does not emerge without (re) inscribing "tensions." Such tensions emerge from the recurring pattern of expatriates benefitting from the state's preferential economic policies toward them while local Malays, for instance, serve as the second tier of labor, finding themselves in the rehearsed position of sustaining a neo-colonial order. Similarly, while the "multiple determinants" that generate these media assemblages between Hollywood and Hong Kong (and other territories to which they are linked) "are not reducible to a single logic" (Ong and Collier 2005:12), the resulting cultural dynamics of such ensembles can fall into the familiar cultural order of things, as will be shown through the example of a Hollywood production filmed in Los Angeles and directed by a Hong Kong director in Chapter 3. In the next chapter, however, we zoom in on the space of the set.

CHAPTER 2

....

The Production of Spectacle/ The Spectacle of Production

The Set

As Walter Benjamin noted in 1936, "The shooting of a film, especially of a sound film, affords a spectacle unimaginable anywhere at any time before this" (Benjamin 1968: 232). Today, film and television sets remain a spectacle to behold.

Film and television sets are generally a busy and hectic space that resemble an obstacle course at times, with wires snaking along the floor and light stands and camera equipment that personnel can easily bump into. Intricate camera technologies such as Steadicam sometimes demand as much attention and prep time as the actors. The set is also a sound stage upon which emotional themes are played out by media workers, who themselves form a preliminary audience in the production process. As I argue throughout this chapter, there are many times that workers on the production floor of commercial film and television consider the conventional "audience" to be secondary to themselves as spectators. The more immediate audience of media workers is in fact a highly participatory one. The ways in which people perform their jobs on set are socially mediated, with lots of conferring and competing. There is also a very social *display* of skills for the sake of each other: as fellow entertainers, illusionists, and tricksters; as future employers; as rivals. Thus, decisions about how imagery and performance are created and conveyed are shaped by not only directors or producers or studio and corporate executives but also by individuals below the line such as extras and production assistants. This dynamic and interactive process recalls the heckling and hailing interplay between stage performers and audiences in the variety theater tradition that influenced early film, and which also produced spectacular images, or what film historian and theorist Tom Gunning refers to as the "cinema of attractions" (Gunning 1990: 59).

Learning to Walk

On my first day of being an extra on a network television drama in Hollywood, I had to quite literally learn how to walk in a shot. In doing so, I learned how to work in the narrative, single-camera, commercial style common to many Hollywood films and television programs. I received a crash course in "set etiquette," which included avoiding the star's "eyeline," navigating around the Steadicam operator, and handling props. This set was designed to include several rooms, and in learning how to walk, I discovered that being an extra is not necessarily the simple, mindless labor that some believe. Being an extra on such a show requires physical as well as mental dexterity and endurance. Many of the shots we were needed for were called "walk and talks." For a walk-and-talk shot, which is generally captured by the heavy Steadicam strapped onto the camera operator, filming would start in one part of the set, with the principal actors walking and talking toward us in another part of the set, over a continuous period of up to three minutes (which is a long uninterrupted shot). The walk-and-talk shot requires tight choreography and synchronization on the part of everybody involved as the action has to appear seamless since the principals are walking (often briskly) through various rooms and turning corners, variously followed and fronted by the camera. The actor who enters the end of the shot to speak his or her lines carries the burden of executing perfect timing and line delivery so that the continuously filmed activity shot up to that point is not wasted. Since the camera is sweeping around a lot of area, extras—who are the scene's "crowd filler"—have to keep an eye on the traffic of other persons as well as the movements of the camera and the placement of various wires on the ground. It was a challenge to navigate around a fast-moving camera operator who wore a protruding 50-pound camera harness on his body that one could painfully and embarrassingly crash into. Initially, it was hard for me to know where the camera was at all times yet not look directly at it or for it, a faux pas that I committed on my first day. Through hasty instructions delivered to me by the second assistant directors that had been handed down to them from the first assistant director on set, I realized I'd have to improve my sense of rhythm for the walk-and-talk shots. Many of the extras had already developed what they referred to as a "sixth sense" for knowing where the camera was. The camera resembles that other powerful orb, the sun: actors and extras must refrain from staring directly at it, yet they want to be included in its glow.

To learn how to walk properly I was put under the tutelage of an extra I shall call Simon. Simon worked as background on this award-winning television drama for over five years. Off screen, however, Simon did far more than walk; he performed invisible labor that sustained the show. He occasionally worked as a stand-in (literally, standing in the place of the principal actor to whom he was assigned as the crew prepared lighting and camera angles so that the actor could go to the hair and make-up trailer or relax in his trailor). But first and second assistant directors also relied on him to instruct novice extras and visitors and relay information between various people, and between shots Simon sometimes helped to quickly move the chairs placed around the TV monitor for playback. He knew how to provide support to principal actors with an understanding nod or roll of the eyes after certain producers yelled at the cast. In many ways, an experienced extra such as Simon can be the glue that helps hold the set together and even function as an uncredited and unpaid second assistant director.

Simon was integral in teaching me set etiquette (which includes a quiet, nonreactive, and respectful manner, especially around high-profile key creative personnel). A savvy extra such as Simon on a show that has a large cast and group of extras knows how to find the script. Typically, not all the cast is given a full script (they are carefully monitored), and even regular extras find it a challenge to get their hands on one. But Simon knew to befriend the department head or department member who would let him find the "sides" (pages of the script being shot that day) to see the dialogue and the order of the actors speaking so he could have a general roadmap of the action. Simon also made it a habit to closely watch the TV monitor before and after he entered the frame of a walk-and-talk while the Steadicam was still rolling so he could map the Steadicam operator's choreography. Simon knew, after all those years, how to force a bubble around certain lead actors with whom he shared scenes. Perhaps more importantly, he also knew which actors to avoid.

On film and television sets, the camera organizes the space of techno-social activity of media production, imposing an ocular mode of discipline. While filming scenes for the television program, the assistant directors (there were usually four of them) were positioned at various locations throughout the set, controlling the traffic of the extras who walked in the background according to the directions given. The hierarchy of the assistant directors on this show was two first assistant directors (they would switch off to work on set for every other episode while the other one would work at the production office on the studio lot organizing logistics for the next episode); two second assistant directors; and one second second assistant director. On a show as large as this one was, extras would usually communicate with the second second assistant director and the second assistant directors as to the choreography of the shot and the placement of the camera, but less so with the first assistant director, who would work with guest actors, principal cast, department heads, and the director. The second and second second assistant directors were also responsible for retrieving actors from their trailers and communicating with above-the-line talent as to their transportation to the set. These assistant directors would crouch below, or hover out of, the camera frame during filming while watching their miniature, portable screens so that they would know when to cue off-screen actors to enter the frame. It was sometimes more interesting to observe these appendages of the director, hooked up to the main television monitor while simultaneously staring into their satellite screens and frantically receiving instructions and relaying communications through earpieces and walkie-talkies, than the scripted action.

The video-assist television monitors allows the director live, remote viewing on a monitor that displays the image that the audience will eventually see. Instead of hovering near the camera operator, as was the practice in the pre–video-assist monitor era, the director can opt to wear headphones that relay the recorded audio and be removed from the filmed activity. Not all directors opt for this. In Hollywood, many media workers refer to the cluster of personnel around this monitor as "video village"—an enclave of power, decision-making, and gossip, as the director dictates instructions to the script supervisor or confers with the Director of Photography. The distance from the actual shooting that the video assist system provides also allows the director to multitask and deal with off-set concerns, bringing the outside world into the space of the fictional world. Importantly, video village can be what one informant calls a "safe space" for the director—a refuge from other members of the production that the director may want to avoid. Sometimes actors also prefer that the director be cloistered within video village. Most of the people involved on the production floor (except the camera operator and the sound recorder and maybe a few second assistant directors who are crouching below frame in crowd scenes) also watch the filming from the television monitors placed at various locations on set.

When not walking in the background, I was frequently invited to sit near video village to watch what was being filmed. The director and production crew would be seated or standing around the monitor to view the framed shot. Sometimes I joined them, but my interest was primarily in observing the filming, unfiltered, outside the frame of the camera and standing or sitting right near it (unless the camera was a Steadicam, strapped onto the operator). Hovering in this liminal space, I would see that which was not intended for either the naked eye or the eventual audience. In doing so, I was able to note the facets of the performed emotions that are not enhanced or obscured by the transformative lens, and witness the gestures that appear so subtle with the naked eye but that are magnified by the camera. Observing from outside the lit and angled shot allowed me to witness the labor that occurs in the space surrounding the camera but outside its planned perimeters, such as the assistant directors who would crouch below the camera frame, and the operation of the snow machines in Hollywood and the pots of incense burning in Hong Kong. I was also able to discern the occasional leers and sneers of the crew and extras towards the actors that sometimes embarrassed them as they filmed scenes.

One day while on the set, I watched one of the lead actors film an emotional scene in which his character was required to gaze pensively into space. I had positioned myself near the camera to watch the filming of this shot in which the actor stared off camera at a spot near my head. After the director yelled "Cut!" and asked for a retake, one of the assistant directors warned me not to disturb what he and others called the actor's "eyeline"—in other words, to not stand in the actor's line of vision as he filmed his scene and thereby distract him, a common concern for actors. For some more than others it requires tremendous effort to ignore the distractions of work equipment, activity, and socializing of dozens of people around them as they summon up the scripted sentiment or construct their own fictional world. Gazing directly at the actor, and thus piercing the actor's eyeline, was occasionally, as I will discuss later, a form of challenge thrown down by below-the-line crew or extras on set to those working in front of the camera. This inter-penetration is one of the concerns in the production process between the actor and various media workers or guests on set, and reveals the tenuous partition between the spectacle being filmed and the spectacle of the off-screen production process.

"Who's the Chief?": Setwork and Authority

At one point during my research the cinematographer on this television drama turned to me and asked, "So, if you're an anthropologist, tell me: who's the chief here?" It was a good question, especially as the cinematographer (or director of photography) would break down the camera movements and lighting for each shot in preproduction and would often guide the different directors who would cycle in and out of the program so that the "look" of the show would remain fairly consistent, and coordinate between the director and the resident producers, executive producers, and writers of the show, especially the "show runner," or head writer. There are competing forms of authority and formal and informal status and power that a variety of media workers in such a packed space hold. The issue his question was getting at is particularly challenging for child actors on set, who also have to discern how their parent or guardian figures into this opaque and fluid hierarchy.

The set is a busy workplace with people carrying out different tasks. A set can be chaotic, despite controls, and offers little privacy. Issues of trust, conflict, and competition emerge. In both Hollywood and Hong Kong, television is primarily a producer's medium whereas film is a director's medium. On some Hollywood network shows, directors are cycled in and out through the Directors Guild and may carry little authority on the set. Other crew contracted for the season, in contrast, can hold tremendous sway over a principal actor, influencing him or her to make demands of the producer. A makeup artist I spent a lot of time observing told me,

> I've seen makeup artists basically create an insecurity for an actor, an insecurity which of course only that artist can fix. Then that artist can manipulate the actor, and start making demands for the actor to have more time, more accommodations in their contract. What's great is when the makeup artist makes themselves completely indispensable to the actor. If that actor is a celebrity, then executives better watch out.

As I observed in makeup trailers, actors are sometimes at their most vulnerable when in the makeup chair, preparing to face the camera and crew, and highly vulnerable to suggestions. The comments of the makeup artist can hold more weight for the actor than those of the director or producer, diffusing the distribution of formal power on a set. Yet at the same time, the makeup artist (or hairstylist or wardrobe assistant) may offer more sympathy and compassion for the actor than managerial personnel or executives.

Most of the production personnel I observed on set in Hollywood were white men, although the wardrobe, makeup, and hair departments were more diverse in terms of gender and, to a lesser degree, race. Gender and race bias and discrimination in hiring decisions was very evident there. In both Hollywood and Hong Kong, I observed sets that were very male-dominated with predominantly male management and executives, although there are prominent female directors and producers available to work in both industries (overall, though, women are more visible in production offices from support staff to executives and, particularly in Hollywood, in the preproduction spheres of writing and script development).

With the extreme dependence in both Hollywood and Hong Kong on the need to be seen as a "team player" on set and not disrupting the status quo in an already very masculinized space, there is little impetus or infrastructure in either site for women (whether a female celebrity actress or a female camera assistant) to complain about any harassment they may experience or witness. With the growth in flexible labor systems in both sites, subcontracted labor markets disempower female workers from organizing and fighting for improved conditions (Harvey 1991: 155). Panels on chauvinism in production have been organized within a few Hollywood unions, but transparency and accountability regarding discrimination and harassment remain incomplete and inadequate. Possibly, the 2015 investigation by the Equal Employment Opportunity Commission into the legality of extreme gender discrimination toward female directors in film and television in Hollywood hiring practices will result in some kind of change, although racial parity still remains largely unaddressed (see Chapter 3 for more on gender and race in Hollywood).

The Hong Kong entertainment industry's association with *lo pin moon*, combined with many media workers' and executives' own paternalistic views about female labor and bodies, has had negative consequences for some female media personnel there. For instance, some female actors in their thirties, forties, and even fifties had to contend with parental and familial disapproval about "making a spectacle" of their bodies on screen (or working off screen around others who presumably did), and concerns about working at night far from home with mostly men and supposedly consorting with dubious male entertainment and business figures. (Similar pressures for actresses in Hollywood were less explicit and were granted less import by the actresses as they saw themselves as more individuated.) Reasons why some Hong Kong female media workers were subject to close family scrutiny of their jobs included their financial inability to purchase their own residence, and strong familial expectations of living at home and fulfilling multiple familial roles. While professional Hong Kong women have made enormous inroads in upper management in the city-state's financial services sector, many of their media industry counterparts still bear a trace of local stigma.

Spectacle and the "Cinema of Attractions"

Visual spectacle is documented in early American and Chinese film and film historian and theorist Tom Gunning develops its import in his notion of "cinema of attractions." "Cinema of attractions" refers to early film's key feature of provoking emotional stimulus rather than disseminating an ordered storyline (Gunning 1990). Media scholars claim that contemporary disaster and science fiction genres as well as crime, medical and supernatural-themed television programs have retained elements of cinematic spectacle, and "attractions," which were certainly evident in the film/TV media that I observed such as explosions, fires, stunts, and gore (Gunning 1990; see also Caldwell 1995). I link film studies and media anthropology here to show that this early period of filmmaking—inspired by late 19th century mass entertainment such as live magic shows, vaudeville, and the circus—continues to permeate the character of commercial film/TV media production in Hollywood and Hong Kong. The set and the studio retain some quality of the fairground, and the attractions that amusement parks such as Universal Studios sell to visitors, such as staged shootings and floods, were described as one of the advantages of the daily work experience on set for these media workers, and indeed part of the lure for them. I use Gunning's discussion about attractions to illustrate my point that forms of interactivity are happening long before "the audience" sees the finished product.

In his work on early film, Gunning locates what he terms a "cinema of attractions" (Gunning 1990). "Cinema of attractions" refers to pre-1906 American (and French) film that lacked the linear, cohesive narrative structure that would proliferate in the later, classical cinema of Hollywood (Bordwell, Staiger, and Thompson 1985), as well as French and Chinese film. In the cinema of attractions, a curious and even visceral response was evoked in spectators through the display of a series of stunning and thrilling images such as magic tricks, train crashes, and stripteases, unlike the sequential narrative that would unfold from traditional theater and literature (Gunning 1998: 258). In this kind of cinema, Gunning points out that narrative was less important than the image, which was "itself an attraction and the point of the film" (Gunning 1990: 58). These attractions originated in the mass entertainment of the late 19th and early 20th centuries such as vaudeville, burlesque, magic shows, medicine tent shows, circuses and amusement parks. These films strove to show the viewer an illusion or an astonishing feat in order to provoke a sense of fear or awe, and show the "magical possibilities of the cinema," including the cameras themselves (Gunning 1986). Filmed magic shows were a common attraction, wherein a magician would gesture at audience members in this "act of *showing*" (versus *telling*, as with narrative film) (Gunning 1990: 56, italics mine). Gunning writes, "The cinema of attractions directly solicits spectator attention, inciting visual curiosity, and supplying pleasure through an exciting spectacle—a unique event, whether fictional or documentary, that is of interest in itself" (Gunning 1990: 58).[1]

Cinema of attractions inspired modernists such as the Futurists, Dadaists, and Surrealists, who saw the interactivity of exhibitionist film and its hailing of the spectator as a revolutionary art form because of its "accent on direct stimulation"; its *participatory* character was a legacy of live entertainment with the heckling, cheering, and singing along of audiences (Gunning 1990: 59). As I discuss later, the extras and production crew on some of the film and television sets also heckled and cheered key creative personnel on set (although to no revolutionary end). The cinema of attractions is not restricted to Western film: scholars of Chinese film Chris Berry and Mary Farquhar note the emergence of a "Chinese cinema of attractions" in early Chinese film in the first several decades of the 20th century (Berry and Farquhar 2005: 28). The Chinese cinema of attractions emerged from popular forms of Chinese entertainment such as peep shows, shadow-play, operas, and acrobatics (Berry and Farquhar 2005: 28). Some of them were enjoyed as "marvelous spectacles rather than as onscreen drama" that also actively addressed a spectator (Berry and Farquhar 2005: 30). These transnational flows of cinemas of attractions, intended to astonish and stimulate, offering "the thrill of display" (Gunning 1990: 101), would later be overtaken by the narrative turn in Hollywood in 1907 and China in the 1930s (although its form was never entirely lost in either cinema). The narrative turn entailed an ordered, self-contained world that draws viewers in to speculate about the development of the film characters and their psychology.

Considered in conjunction with anthropology, Gunning's history of film helps us think about how commercial film/TV media come to constitute the forms that they do. In examining the production of media, Dornfeld and Ganti see film and television producers as "evaluating" what they produce on film/TV sets (American documentary series and Bollywood films, respectively) for their intended audiences (Dornfeld 1998; Ganti 2002). Dornfeld has illustrated how in documentary filmmaking, producers are "surrogate audience members, putting themselves in the place of their potential audience as they react to the material they are shaping into programs" (Dornfeld 1998: 87). Yet what I observed was less the above-the-line producers serving as proxy audience members and instead a range of media workers, including extras, makeup artists, stunt workers, camera operators, and grips, constituting an uneven audience distinct from the conventional abstract, anonymous "audience." This immediate audience formed a spectatorship inflected by a professional fascination with tricks, stunts, and melodrama as well as the frustration of short-term contracts. Since much of what I observed being filmed and what interlocutors discussed was as much (if not more) image-driven as story-driven, elements of the legacy of the "cinema of attractions" that media scholars claim remains apparent in on-screen contemporary, commercial film/TV media *also* become evident in the production processes of such material.

Gunning asserts that, "Clearly in some sense recent spectacle cinema has reaffirmed its roots in stimulus and carnival rides, in what might be called the Spielberg-Lucas-Coppola cinema of effects" (Gunning 1990: 61). The tradition of eliciting shock and awe continues in the contemporary production of spectacle, and therefore media workers are enlisted in this dynamic engagement with visual and affective stimulus. Media workers themselves are frequently not immune to the spectacular images and themes they conjure and convey to audiences; their production processes provoke and thrill them—the immediate audience. Filming dangerous stunts and prolonged and graphic death or torture scenes was for some media workers exciting and pleasurable, for others harrowing—and for many of them an affective engagement with their craft and a transformative opportunity for them and their self-perceived worlds.

The Reel Audience: Mediating in the Immediate

Surprisingly, I found that despite the imperative of maximum profit accumulation in such commercial film/TV industries, the media workers themselves constitute in many ways the most essential audience. The imagined audience of film and television viewers is in fact an abstraction sometimes ignored by media personnel. As they mediate in the immediate space of the set, media personnel in both sites perform and perfect their crafts for each other—to impress and to bond together. They do this for their own aesthetic pleasure as well as their need to find future employment and sustain their industry. A sense of enjoyment would periodically emerge amid the routinization of the production process. "I love creating a look," a makeup artist told me as she stroked different layers of color onto an actor's face, after having complained about her consistently early call time before 6 am. She continued,

> I studied art history in school, and that's come in so handy in my line of work. You have to know about color. See how this taupe is blending with the pink? I'm just blending the colors here. It's all about layering. I feel like an artist, I'm actually able to be an artist.

On the set of a horror film filmed at a Hollywood studio, I noted the enthusiasm with which another makeup artist smeared fake blood and saliva on an actress who was made up with a prosthetic, gouged eyeball and torn cheek and throat. During the filming of this particular shot, he watched the monitor closely and rushed to the actress between takes to daub more blood on her face and throat. After about the fourth take, in his bespattered apron the makeup artist asked the director with a grin if he could "have more fun" and throw even more fake blood on the actress. The director acquiesced and then decided to "join in the fun" and throw some fake blood on the actress as well. The shot they were filming lasted only about 15 seconds, and it was the only shot in which the actress was required to look bloody and beaten, yet the glee with which they conducted their work was very evident.

In conceptualizing the staggered audiences of production (imagine a concentric circles chart), I discerned that, in addition to the final audience of consumers (the outermost circle), there is an intermediate audience of postproduction staff such as editors, visual effects artists, and color coders, as well as (in Hollywood and Hong Kong) upper management such as production and studio executives and marketing departments who wield decision-making power. Yet it is what I refer to as the *immediate* audience of media workers on the film and television sets—the core—with which I am most concerned. The actors, directors, camera operators, carpenters, wardrobe assistants, electricians, and so are an important audience through which the first wave of performance is filtered: an audience that evaluates, intervenes, and modifies performance and image for the *final* audience of consumers. Media workers would frequently scrutinize the video-assist playback television monitors to assess how their work looked on screen, whether it was an actor watching a playback screening of her performance, a member of the prop department checking to see if the props looked in order, or a member of the wardrobe department checking to see that the garments looked clean and draped correctly. Media workers frequently conferred over the images they were producing together. This is not to say that the final audience is irrelevant to media workers. On the set of a popular television program a principal actor called aside the head of the hairstyling department one day during filming. He told her that he had noticed while watching the last few episodes of the show on television that his hair was hanging in his eyes and that her crew needed to do a better job of keeping his hair out of his eyes since, as he told her, "I act with my eyes." Amid the activity of the equipment being set up for the next shot, he repeatedly emphasized to her the importance of his eyes being unobstructed so that he could reach his audience with his eyes, telling her repeatedly, "This is how I act, how I communicate to the audience." This actor's concern illustrates how, even with dialogue and sequential plot structure, he relied upon the visual draw of his eyes to display affect; recalling Gunning, this actor's eyes were the "attraction" and showing, not telling, was integral to his performance. (And later that night, upon perusing several fansites for this TV show, I found that fans indeed noted this actor's eyes as his primary way for communicating sentiment and story.) But as the next section illustrates, the immediate audience is an audience that exists for its own ends.

The Spectacle of Attractions: Explosions, Wizardry, and Tricks

The atmosphere in which media workers mediate images retains an aura of "attractions," providing an enjoyably visceral, even violent, experience for media workers. On a cold winter night in 2004, I watched as television media personnel blew up a building in what was acknowledged as a bid for bigger ratings. Orange blazes shot into the air, and the heat seared off the building, with clouds of smoking making some of us cough. Moments later, the first assistant director yelled "Cut!" Several members of the studio fire department rushed to quench the flames that were consuming the remains of the structure. The second assistant directors yelled excitedly to one another on their walkie-talkies with voices hoarse from the smoke to ascertain the safety of the principal actors, the crew, and the background artists in the vicinity, motioning us watching this spectacle to keep our distance from the fire. The camera operators, sound technicians, gaffers, grips, and teamsters were alert, poised to tackle any hazards.

We all experienced the very real effects of the acrid smoke, which made our eyes tear up and most of us cough. Producing such spectacular imagery can be fraught with potential hazards for screen workers, inviting chaos and risk. Yet many of the personnel with whom I talked expressed a sense of excitement at the spectacle of the explosion, and the possibilities that such stimulus can offer them. "How often do you get to work on something where you get to blow shit up?" an assistant director exclaimed to me. "I live for this shit!" another excited crew person told me. Keyed up by the blazing fire, many of the crew members kept breaking out in smiles, high-fiving one another and applauding the pyrotechnic team's efforts. Such spectacle enlivens a frequently dreary labor process, and, much like the rollercoaster sensation that early film provided to audiences, this production process arouses excitement for some media workers—the thrill that comes from not just viewing such stunts and effects but creating and enacting them. The illusions that variety theater's magic shows offered audiences in the late 19th century are orchestrated through different means and methods in contemporary film and television: the standard crime or medical television drama's shot of an actor's inner organs, such as the chest cavity, being exposed while lying on a hospital gurney is achieved by having the actor lie on a specially built mattress in which the section for the torso dips, allowing the actor's body to lie concave. The property department and makeup department then place a prosthetic of an open heart or chest cavity atop the torso, which oozes fake blood.

Amid the rationalized timetables and organization of industrial production, many media workers, especially in Hollywood, spoke of the "magic," "fantasy," and "glamor" that they created. "Imagineers" and "dreamers" are part of that self-congratulatory and aggrandizing language that Hollywood in particular promotes. Yet these references were not just in the context of boasting, or justifying the pressures, instabilities, and drudgery of the production process; for many, there was true excitement that lurked within the process. Within the controlled environment of the studio lot, the mythic power of media workers appears limitless. They make someone look dead, or dying, and then bring them to life again. Seasons are simulated with rain, wind, and snow machines; with the manipulation of lights and shadows, night becomes day and day becomes night. The perils of filming pyrotechnics and performing dangerous stunts empowered them to feel control over the ordinary coordinates of time and space.

Even some of the types of people attracted to work in contemporary production sites call to mind those who worked in early film as well as earlier forms of popular entertainment. Early in my fieldwork I visited Central Casting in Burbank to observe the people who sign up to become extras in Hollywood. Inside was a sign listing the special talents that hopefuls should note on their applications if they possessed. Evoking the "attractions" that early film shared with the circus, carnival, and vaudeville, skills such as fire swallowing, horse lassoing, unicycle riding, and trapeze artistry were among those listed as desirable. Apparently, the appeals for the extraordinary were not unfounded; while standing in the line for those who needed to supply information for employment, I started chatting with a young man who in a matter-of-fact manner informed me that he was a wizard. He was dressed in an ordinary manner with no visible accoutrements of sorcery, yet he was firm in his insistence on his supernatural powers and his hope of finding a profitable venue for performing them. He described his move to Los Angeles as "inevitable" since he saw only this popular entertainment center as an environment where he could peddle his wares. (He did admit that despite his supernatural powers, he, like all the other hopefuls at Central Casting, had to submit to the bureaucratic practices and gatekeeping of the industry.)

In noting the interactions that media workers have with the images they create, it is worth remembering that early cinema was experienced alongside other new contraptions at fairgrounds such as the rollercoaster—a new technology also intended to shock, stimulate, and astonish. Other live entertainment of the time also provided stimulus: "A night at the variety theatre was like a ride on a streetcar or an active day in a crowded city" (Gunning 1990: 60), an experience not unlike a film or television set today, with unusual and provocative sights such as gouged eyeballs or exotic animals. I saw the latter on a Hollywood studio lot when I had walked past the facades and recreation of city and suburb blocks that stand in as locations for New York City and "Anytown, U.S.A." As I turned a corner onto the generic "Main Street" that is ubiquitous to Anytown, U.S.A., I suddenly encountered an elephant standing not more than six feet away from me. The elephant was being allowed to wander around between filming scenes for a period-piece film being shot at the other end of this lot.

Clearly, commercial film production still calls upon the talents and labor historically associated with the attractions of vaudeville, the circus, and magic shows. This applies to Hong Kong as well, where children of opera performers, kung fu artists, and film technicians have in the past been expected to drop out of school and follow in their parents' footsteps. In Hollywood, while overseeing the set of a medical drama on a particularly busy day that included approximately 60 extras, 10 principal actors, and a crew of 50, the first assistant director stood on a chair and called out to me, "Look! It's like I'm at the circus, and I am the ringmaster!" His reference to the circus was particularly apt. Insider terms that recall the fairground linger in production, such as "honey wagons" (a term used for trailers with toilets and dressing rooms for non-featured actors and extras). Many late 19th-century and early 20th-century circus and vaudeville shows, as well as Chinese opera troupes, were traveling acts that required mobile equipment and stage pieces. The shifting between film sets and location sites and the continual transformation of space on studio lots today also recall the movements and renovations typical of traveling exhibits.

Some personnel, such as Hollywood stunt workers, actually worked in the circus prior to the film and television industries. Numerous stunt workers and stunt directors I observed and interviewed came from a background of clowning, aerial acrobatics, and gymnastics in circuses in England and the United States (see Martin 2012). Some of this training resembled that of Cantonese and Beijng opera that several Hong Kong informants underwent as children and young adults. Circus performers and opera performers had to learn and perfect dangerous feats such as jumps, trapeze, gymnastics, and work with rope, sticks, and knives. Having performed live in circuses and on stage, they are trained to perform stunts in fewer takes (as the more takes that are filmed, the higher one's chances are of injury). All of them understood the necessity of entertaining the masses via extraordinary skills that translated into enormous physical risk for themselves. This was countered not just by practice but by cultivating a positive attitude toward risk taking, similar to competitive sports with its focus on adrenaline, not fear. "We're thrill-seekers, not daredevils," stunt doubles and coordinators told me over and over—the distinction being the careful calculations and refined practice of the former as opposed to the perceived impetuosity of the latter.

The ways in which people perform their jobs are socially mediated, and on film and television sets there is also a very social *display* of skills for the sake of each other, as fellow entertainers, illusionists, and tricksters, as future employers, as competitors—not just the final audience of consumers. These film and television workers constitute something akin to a contemporary vaudeville audience, responding to the displays of skills and tasks on and off camera. Applause and sniffling were not uncommon reactions among cast and crew members while watching the execution of stunts such as jumping out of burning buildings or the enactment of tragic scenes. Vocal expressions of astonishment and appreciation were not unusual when a new set was dressed or costumes were assembled and displayed.

Animosities and alliances were also evident on Hollywood sets. Once, while sitting among some of the grips and gaffers on a set, I noticed that bets were quietly being placed when a certain actress was required to shoot a scene with lengthy dialogue. I soon discovered why: this actress apparently had difficulty remembering more than a few lines and would frequently make a mistake, leading to retakes. Not only would these crew members benefit from the extra time spent on the retakes by bringing them closer to overtime pay from the production company, but the lucky winners would also profit from the bets placed on how long the actress could make it into the scene without flubbing her lines. A few would even openly laugh at her mistakes while cheering at the overtime and wins she brought them while she appeared to enjoy repeating her performance. There would sometimes be back and forth banter between actors and the crew, bringing to mind the participatory nature of early live entertainment, in which audiences would heckle and talk back to the performers.

A thumbs-up from a below-the-line worker when a principal actor tried a new line-reading would encourage that actor to take more risks in his or her performance. "In beer gardens, minstrel shows, Chautauquas, amusement parks, Wild West shows, burlesque, vaudeville and melodrama, spectators were expected to laugh, to sing, to speak, to comment, even to argue" (Altman 2007: 279; see also Butsch 2000). Similarly, media workers (from above-the-line to below-the-line) occasionally ogled actors, especially female ones, in the middle of filming. In Hollywood in particular, some of the sensationalistic outfits and appearances chosen for actresses because of their presumed capacity to entice viewers would also elicit subtle (and not so subtle) reactions from media workers, who serve as the first wave of an audience and respond to the "attractions" of commercial spectacle (see also Mayer 2008).[2] While media workers in both Hollywood and Hong Kong are expected to conduct themselves professionally, responses to imagery and performance ranged from the indifferent to the enthralled, and provided immediate feedback to stunt workers, costumers, prop masters, actors, and special effects make up artists on the effectiveness of their work in the moment of production.

Some of the workers have a way of demonstrating the difficulty of their particular task for their colleagues. I encountered instances of, and heard about, gaffers and grips dropping a tool during filming, actors forgetting their lines, camera operators fiddling unnecessarily with their gear, and makeup artists exaggerating facial flaws all as tactics to call attention to their various jobs and to put their own particular stamp on their task. Stunt doubles, who often help the actor they are doubling for prepare for a scene with low-impact stunts, also have ways of asserting their power. In Hollywood, stunt doubles usually provide the actor with the appropriate amount of padding needed in the action shots that the actor films (as the stunt sequence is a joint effort between the actor and the stunt double). A stunt double named Clara told me that when the actress she doubled for was rude to her, she "disciplined" her, as Clara put it, by underpreparing her for a fall scene; she did not provide the actress with enough kneepads for the stunt. Other stunt workers who had seen how Clara was treated encouraged her to let the actress hurt herself first to "put her in her place" and allow Clara to assert herself.

Principal cast members could become frustrated with the very social workplace of the film set, which sometimes entailed noisy executives, a loud crew, rowdy extras, and a camera operator in their face. This was understandable as some actors had to concentrate deeply to imagine themselves into a different time and space, even with the aid of costumes and set design. One Friday night at 10:30 on the set of a television drama I saw a lead actress yell at the first assistant director for not maintaining control of the set and then scream at everyone to "Shut up!" After being on set for 12 hours she was trying to film a scene in which she had to subtly convey melancholia and anxiety. While some of the crew and extras were joking around and chatting with one another between shots, this actress was trying to retain the mood she was supposed to project on screen.

Tensions Between Extras and Actors

Extras in particular constitute an audience who mediate in the immediate environment of the set. Actors must deal with being scrutinized as they strive to remember the dialogue and choreography of the scene in front of an audience of extras who are evaluating their performance—and who may actually hold more experience and credentials than them. Once when an extra and I observed a director give direction to a principal actress, Cyndi (one of the extras who befriended me) commented of the female director, "She did it quietly, privately, to the side, so that the extras can't hear—that was nice." Cyndi then went on to say, "Many extras say, 'Oh, I can do it better than this star,' but that's not true. It's very hard. It's an emotionally and physically draining job." As a few assistant directors commented, from a management perspective the presence of the extras subtly disciplines the principal cast by serving as a reminder of the teeming hordes of "undiscovered" hopefuls who covet the principals' careers and from whom the principals must continuously strive to differentiate themselves. According to several assistant directors who were also personal friends with many of the principal actors on this show, the principal actors were aware of this tenuous hierarchy.

There existed an enormous disparity in pay and status between extras and the principal cast. Extras often scrutinized principal actors and critiqued their acting as a way to learn more about what many refer to as their "craft." The aspiring actors among the extras would frequently try to watch the filming, pointing out their "favorites"—principal cast members whom they admired, tried to chat with between filming, and even solicit acting tips from. These extras would compare various deliveries of a line from the script and debate which was the actor's best "take," evaluating the performance as a way to instruct one another on the emotive and technical labor involved in performing, even giving one another a thumbs-up and vigorous nod or high-five when the actor in question completed a shot in a manner they admired. Other extras were seasonal labor, such as educators seeking supplemental pay during summer months, and would marvel at or critique the activity on set. Some extras appeared entirely indifferent to the filming process—reading the newspaper, doing crossword puzzles, exchanging stories about their time in the industry, and even sleeping between takes. Some would whisper gossip to one another about the principal cast, crew, and executives on the program—a form of information sharing as well as critique. I also met people who chose to be extras because of the proximity to famous people. Members of the principal cast were aware of the diverse reactions from the immediate audience of extras and sometimes tried to avoid making eye contact with the multiple gazes directed at them.

Extras are generally "casual, part-time, short-term labor" (Scott 2005), subcontracted by a casting agency and therefore not hired directly by a production company. In Los Angeles, extras are drawn from a wide assortment of people—actors, gawkers, truckers, schoolteachers, and people who simply want to be paid for hanging about. To the rest of the production personnel, above and below the line, this disparate crowd represents fans, critics, and even ignorant strangers. When I worked as an extra on a television drama, I felt the occasionally hostile tone of the crowd of extras, the understandable resentment and envy of a labor sector who worked in such close proximity to the principal actors, brushing up against their person and literally rubbing shoulders with them in certain scenes, yet so distant in terms of income and status. On one particular show, numerous principal actors were earning approximately $3 million a year at the time of my fieldwork (one of them was making double that amount) while an extra was making between $50 and $130 for an eight-hour day, depending on whether he or she was in the Screen Actors Guild. In many cases, an extra and a principal actor who earns an annual salary of $9 million may hold identical credentials and forms of expertise, such as a Master of Performing Arts degree or tutelage under the same acting coach. As a result, some extras audibly disparaged the principal cast and even entertained other extras with imitations of those they mocked. Standing beside me while we watched a lead actress listen to direction from a director on the set of a television show, an extra with whom I was working in the same scene whispered loudly to me, "It's not fair, is it? She's not so great. A lot of people here feel they could do better, that it was just good luck that she's there and we're here"—"here" being the sidelines. On that set, several extras had worked on the show longer than some of the principal actors, leading to frustrations about seniority versus status.

For the principal actors, extraneous equipment and other people standing off camera are difficult to filter out of view while filming.

Avoiding the actor's eyeline is occasionally even a condition written into an actor's film contract. Besides maintaining the fictional world they have constructed for themselves, many principal actors are famous to varying degrees, and the informal rule on some but certainly not all sets is that status and privacy should be respected, and thus "extras" in particular should not initiate or invite such intimate visual contact. Because many principal actors do not want to actually articulate their desire to keep their eyeline clear, retreating to their trailers between scenes for privacy is preferable, especially on sets with large numbers of extras who may stray from their "holding pen." Small props, items of clothing, and photographs compiled for continuity occasionally go missing, and extras were often the ones to whom guilt was attributed. On-line leaks about the show or film is also sometimes attributed to extras. Some of the crew viewed extras with suspicion as they are not part of the production "team" but rather day players whose allegiance to the project is not assumed.

A few extras made a point of throwing off an actor in the middle of their performance or immediately after the director yelled "Cut!" with a direct look, breaking their eyeline. Taking this bold step of staring straight into the eyes of the principal actor can momentarily subvert the prescribed hierarchy of on-set relations, since the actor is under pressure (particularly in an intense, emotional scene) to perform under time constraints and (as actors told me) may feel exposed or vulnerable. This direct gaze of the extra, alongside the scrutiny of the camera, illustrates how media workers with low status and low pay seize the visual advantage. Their gaze is a subtle yet firm way of piercing the actor's aura as well as the industrial hierarchy, achieved with the convenient excuse of needing to be nearby for filming. This interaction can in turn heighten pressure and tension for the actor and thus impact the rest of his or her performance. A deliberately loud whisper, a guffaw, or a snort to another extra can affect the principal actor's performance in the next take.

Sisyphean Efforts of the Subcontractor

Returning to the extra mentioned earlier, despite the enormous help Simon provided the production team, he was a subcontractor, infinitely replaceable, working on a week-to-week basis, with no guarantee for the following week. This resembles the situation of subcontracted labor the world over. Recalling Camus' essay about the repetitive efforts of Sisyphus who toiled in his "futile labor," Simon awaited confirmation at the end of each week from the casting agency as to whether his background or stand-in skills would be needed by the production company for the following week. Occasionally he was not rehired. Rarely was he given a line of dialogue on the show. He had been on the show for so long that he was trusted by some of the principals more than the new principals added to the show. However, that didn't guarantee him stable, long-term employment on the show. Simon told me that he didn't try to audition for speaking roles on other shows. "This set is like family," he told me. He said that he loved the writing, he loved the show. There was prestige in being associated with it.

As with Sisyphus, we can sense something absurd: the absurdity of repetition with no hope of security. While so many production personnel are flexible and mobile, learning new skills and languages, finding new markets, transforming their bodies and appearance, Simon resisted that kind of flexible innovation. He worked the same show, the same job, at the whim of employers who granted him no guarantees. He worked on post-Fordist terms with something of the Fordist spirit. Camus claims that Sisyphus found greatness in striving even as he was aware of the futility of his labor. Simon's access to respected actors to chat about their shared craft of acting and to compare notes about films recently seen appeared to enrich his time on the show. Unlike most other extras, he was able to address the first assistant directors directly; he was treated with a certain amount of respect by pretty much everyone on set. I was so impressed with Simon's efficiency and earnestness when he first mentored me on set, and I found Simon's devotion to the set—the team—poignant. Camus insisted, "The struggle itself toward the heights is enough to fill a man's heart. We must imagine Sisyphus happy." I cannot imagine Simon happy with the precarious conditions of his labor, but it seemed that there were aspects of the job that were fulfilling to him. And so the subcontracted labor of entertainment industries—its exploitations and its enchantments—grinds on, an integral part of the spectacle.

PART II

Local Sets, Global Forces

CHAPTER 3

Gambling, Striking, and Assemblage

Hollywood on (Its) Location

Dollar Day

"It's Dollar Day!" exclaimed Pete, a member of the lighting department on a Hollywood network television drama. We were on set, and he reached for his wallet to put a $20 bill into the jar being passed around. On the set of this television show (and on other Hollywood sets), I observed a betting game called "Dollar Day"—an unofficial and unsanctioned game through which money is placed and redistributed within the on-set production team. Dollar Day was on Fridays, and almost everyone, from the extras to principal cast to directors, participated. Players put a dollar bill into the "pot" (in this case a glass jar) with their name written on it, which was folded over. Some of the principal cast submitted higher bill denominations, such as a $20 or a $50. Assistant directors told of how on other sets, well-known actors would drop in a $100 bill. At the end of the shooting day, someone was chosen to cover his or her eyes and pull a bill out of the pot; whoever the bill belonged to won the whole pot of money. This amount could be in the hundreds, even thousands, depending on the amount of people on set that day, and the number of individuals who chose to contribute a large denomination. A camera operator described this ritual as a "boredom buster" on set, intended to boost morale with the hope that a production assistant or a similarly low-paid individual would win (even though it was expected that the winner would buy a treat for everyone; one wasn't supposed to keep it all). It was considered bad form for famous actors to put their name on the bill, as the pot's winnings were geared toward those below-the-line. It became fun even for me to imagine, as the money was being collected and the bills were filling up the jar, who the lucky winner would be. On that set, the winner would typically pay for drinks that night at a bar after filming.

Dollar Day came at the end of a week that would typically run into overtime, with filming on Fridays on this show often not starting until late in the morning given the union-mandated turnaround needed after filming until late the previous night, sometimes around midnight. People were exhausted by Friday, and this competitive ritual fostered a sense of cohesion. When I was on set, everyone was welcome to put something in the pot, even day players and extras; a "team spirit" was encouraged (I declined). But in addition to pitting individuals against each other, it also pitted departments against one another ("lights got it last week, cameras better get it this one!"), thereby building departmental loyalty. For some, especially below-the-line workers, it was also exciting to imagine winning earnings from a highly paid celebrity actor—to upset even temporarily the order of things on a set and the enormous differences in salary between a celebrity and a production assistant, which could be in the millions of dollars.

Dollar Day provided a sense of release from long workdays and nights; the celebrations (and complaints) when the winner was selected allowed for loud exclamations, foot-stomping, hand-clapping, and cross-department ribbing in a worksite whose members must be silent, whisper, or speak scripted lines when engaged in its core task: filming. Many people I spoke to said that they just enjoyed the thrill of betting, of taking a gamble. They happened to be doing so within the workspace of an already high-stakes profession; even a popular television show can suffer low ratings if a popular cast member leaves or is cut from the show, or a new program overtakes its lead. The network can cancel the series. Thus the risks and uncertainties of media production are emblematized through this ritual. Participation in it encapsulated the "dream" that many below-the-line (and even above-the-line) workers share of "making it" in show business, of success.

When I returned to this set in 2006, I discovered that Dollar Day had been discontinued: one of the assistant directors told me that studio executives claimed that gambling in the workplace was illegal. Not everyone on set was happy with that decree, as it had been considered a morale-booster. What is of interest is that this gambling practice, on the studio soundstage, had occurred *within* the corporate and rationalistic structures of Hollywood studios, owned by a media conglomerate. The very gamble of television production was replicated in this ritual on set for the years that it lasted. On the set, people had found a way around the bureaucracy of budgets and subcontracting and union rates to (re)distribute value, to make sacrifices, to surmount official status, and to reveal (and revel in) the unpredictability of success. Studio heads in the 1930s opened their own race track, betting on horses becoming a popular past-time for them. Appealing to chance and "the breaks," as Hortense Powdermaker described the gamble of film production in Hollywood over half a century ago, this ritual on a television set underscored the current of "irrationality" that runs through the industry (Powdermaker 1951).

Dollar Day, in fact, represented what Comaroff and Comaroff refer to as capitalism's increased capacity for mysterious ways of making money, and the rise in pyramid schemes and financial scams that indicate people's desire to get rich (Comaroff and Comaroff 1999: 281). Working 12 to 18 hours on set a day is extremely tiring, and while long-time members of the guilds can make six figures on a project, most personnel did not make the millions a year that a few principal actors and producers did; surely, the incredible income disparity with which many media workers came into intimate contact every day ignites a desire to optimize one's financial fortunes. This is particularly the case for extras and featured actors who made the gamble to move to Los Angeles and pursue their dream. This Friday ritual on sets represented a graduated series of gambles: Dollar Day operated within the gamble of the show's success, which operates within the gamble of Hollywood industrial uncertainty, which operated within the gamble of global capitalism. Perhaps it's not so surprising that the seemingly harmless Dollar Day thrived within an industry that has a long history (and rumored present) of illicit financing, and corporate and conglomerate ethical dubiety as well, that the world of network television programming shares with its sister site across the Pacific the *lo pin moon* of Hong Kong media production. The set, in this case, doubled as an extra-legal space, and made manifest the ethos of risk that drives commercial media production.

Keeping in mind this ethos of risk that surfaces in rituals such as Dollar Day, in this chapter I look at production processes on both television and film sets in Hollywood, and trace how the presence of China (and its Special Administrative Region of Hong Kong) wound throughout them during my fieldwork—demonstrating the permeability of these production centers. I start by examining one of the key features of production—flexibility—and how individual workers and departments experience the disjointed process of filming a one-hour network television show at a Hollywood studio. I then look at flexibility on a wider scale: its mode of production and accumulation that requires offshoring and outsourcing, and the ways in which this became articulated during Hollywood's 2007 Writers Guild of America strike. The broader threat to the mooring of local production in Hollywood is the same threat that haunts production in other industries under the conditions of global capitalism. The Hollywood sets on which I observed were among the decreasing number of locally filmed scripted productions. I discuss my impressions of the Writers Guild strike to demonstrate the awareness of the structural issue of offshoring and outsourcing to film and television sets. Combining attention to Hollywood's displacement with the transnational elements of media assemblage, I then turn to the experiences of Hong Kong media personnel who came to work on the set of a Hollywood studio film in Los Angeles. I provide an example of how Hong Kong and Hollywood film personnel worked together on a Hollywood set of an American adaptation of an Asian horror film, which suggest how issues of globalization (outsourcing, gendered and transnational labor, racism, xenophobia) can seep into the insulated film (and television) sets of Hollywood amid fears of a loss of historic place-based industrial production. In this particular film's "ensemble of heterogeneous elements" (Ong and Collier 2005: 4–5), the Hong Kong filmmaker's particular cinematic expertise—performed as a subcontractor—is combined with global capital (a U.S.-based studio owned by a multinational conglomerate). The concept of media assemblage is not intended to confer a benign gloss to the diversity of participants; instead, attitudes on set toward the Hong Kong director at times recalled those toward a foreign laborer rather than an international "expert" (see Ong 2005). The simultaneous globally encompassing and locally encroached experience is a key part of the Hollywood production experience.

Standard Instability

The filming of a script in most Hollywood entertainment is a disjointed process in which actors struggle to maintain affective continuity, especially for dramatic scene work. As opposed to a staged play, films and television programs disassemble the scenes, which are then filmed out of order due to various contingencies. These include scheduling and availability of actors, technical constraints, financial expediencies, access to outdoor locations, and weather conditions. Production personnel had to adjust to the varying constraints such as strictly regulated work shifts for child actors and animals, and working with technology that required lengthy setup (such as pyrotechnics or cranes), or in outdoor locations that require hasty filming. Due to these concerns, filming does not entail an orderly, sequential creation of a text, but rather a chaotic ensemble of visual imagery and affective registers. I found that in many ways this was most challenging for actors, as they had to be able to quickly slip into the scripted role amid the disjointed and disorganized production process.

For instance, sometimes the conclusion of an episodic television drama or film is filmed at the beginning of the shooting schedule, and so some actors complain that they are not able to develop the emotional momentum necessary for the emotional climax. Sometimes two different episodes for the same show are shot at the same time, a challenge for the actors who strive to keep the chronology of the plotlines straight. I observed on a television set the frustration of an actor who filmed an intensely emotional scene in which he had to perform rage and sadness. The filming for the scene was broken up throughout two days, so he struggled to maintain his affective register throughout such a fragmented process. "I don't like these broken-up days. I prefer to shoot in one long day; it's much easier to stay in character and concentrate," he complained to the director as we stood around the set waiting for the crew to set up for the shot. For all the painstaking planning that goes into filming this format, various exigencies emerge and throw the production schedule into disarray (in this case, the child actor became ill). This actor and others feel the additional frustration of becoming stuck in an emotional loop and not being able to "let go" of the mood they are portraying throughout the day, while at the same time losing their hold over the affective pitch they want to convey in their performance. On the second day in which the production was trying to complete this scene, the actor was summoned from his trailer multiple times, only to be told to return to it while they filmed something else. At other times throughout the day he was taken aside for a meeting with the show's writers, whisked away by the wardrobe department for fittings, contacted by his agent during his one-hour lunch break, and introduced to VIP visitors to the set that day—all activities that made it difficult for him to retain the emotional continuity and focus needed for the scene. By the time he was finally summoned for the last two shots to complete the scene, he complained of feeling drained. Finally, during one of the takes he became frustrated by the loss of his grip on his character's affective state and slammed his fist against the wall of the set. As the actor took a few moments to refocus, an assistant director and I discussed the actor's outburst. Despite her having breezily relayed the delays to this actor, she expressed sympathy:

> It's very hard to remember how your character relates to another one without the continuity. He's had so many interruptions today. And after being told to "take five" and "let's do it after lunch" and all that, it's very

frustrating to hear the director sitting there in the chair say, "Do it again, but this time with more intensity."

Media workers in other departments on set must also contend with the fractured performance and production process. Maintaining the physical and material settings is the responsibility of the rest of the production personnel. Wardrobe, property, design, and hair/makeup departments captured a particular look by taking Polaroids and digital photos for reference. Yet these media workers rarely experience the affective disjointedness that actors do, although some are impacted by the tenor of the material and performances, which I discuss later.

Television in both Hollywood and Hong Kong is considered primarily a producer's medium and film a director's medium, since in television creative and financial control rests primarily with the production company and its resident producers (who may also direct episodes) and writers (the key person being the "show runner"), whereas in film, much of the creative control lies with the director, although all answer to network and studio executives. When I was observing in Hollywood, directors who are members of the Directors Guild of America were frequently rotated in as guest directors throughout the filming season, with the television show's internal producers also stepping into the director's chair for a certain allotment of episodes. These "hyphenates" (producer-director) are considered by principal actors on the set to have a more thorough knowledge of, and allegiance to, the program than the guest directors and thus represent a more trusted source of direction. On the other hand, a guest director can offer a new sensibility to the show than a resident producer, who may also bring a history of prior financial and logistical tussles to a process that actors may envision as purely creative. In Hong Kong, the directors' guild does not have the same kind of stipulations with production companies or studios. Television producers may double as the show's director, like in Hollywood. The individuals who are hired to direct television episodes are seen as needing to possess more technical, rather than creative, skills. On the set of a Hong Kong television show that I observed, for instance, the director was largely responsible for physically choreographing the scene, whereas the show's producer helped the actors to understand the timeline and history of the characters.

Further complicating flexibility of performance in the Hollywood context, there is a particular relationship of ownership between actors and their roles that occurs more explicitly in television than film. The process of constructing a scripted character is a decentralized process involving multiple departments, sectors, and individuals. In Hollywood's project- and episode-based structure directors are rotated in, writers come and go, and even craftspeople such as costume designers or makeup artists who may contribute to the signature look of a particular character also move from project to project. Yet numerous Hollywood television actors I've interviewed see themselves as possessing the essence of their scripted character. As an assistant director on an episodic television show pointed out to me, because of this sense of ownership, principal actors can be hostile to guest directors:

> Actors will tell the director who's rotated in through the Guild to fuck off if the director tries to tell them how to play "their" character. They can be possessive. Some of these actors have been here longer than even some of the producers and writers.

Actors who play the same role for multiple seasons can even feel "possessed", as one described it, by the persona of their role, their character. "Sometimes it's a little unclear to me where I end and my character begins!" an actor rue- fully told me.

Transnational Flows, Gender, and Race

As the Dollar Day ritual epitomizes, there are many uncertainties and risks inherent to industrial production. The fragmentation of production manifests on broader levels as well: a film developed and financed out of an American-based studio may opt to film overseas not for artistic reasons but for economic ones. The same goes for television shows. Often, though, these films and television shows are conceptualized primarily for American audiences and tastes (although that has been changing), and es- pecially for television, it's the American-based ratings that determine a show's success (in film, it's commonly accepted now that foreign box office is crucial for big-budget, tentpole films). This decentralized process for a television project—developed in the United States, financed by an American network, filmed out of the country with some of the actors and crew hailing from different countries, aired in the United States—is an- other example of media assemblage, combining as it does various local, regional, and international elements. These heterogeneous forms bring op- portunities for some (limited though they may be, as production person- nel in virtually any offshore site lack the status and income levels of Hollywood executives and elites) and obstacles for others.

During fieldwork, I heard rumbles of a looming risk in production offices and union meetings, an issue that has come to define global capitalism: offshore production. Offshoring took the form of out-of-state and overseas production, or, as the industry calls it, "runaway production." The issue was with productions that filmed overseas or out of state less for creative reasons and more for economic ones—to lower production costs. On set I noticed technical workers (especially members of the light and camera crews) wearing T-shirts emblazoned with slogans about keeping Hollywood local. In people's downtime I heard concerns and complaints about jobs leaving town for extended periods of time, and reluctance to relocate.

In the day-to-day activities of my own fieldsites in Hollywood, the media workers described themselves as (and sometimes acted as if) insulated from concerns outside of the United States. In talking with and observing actors, camera operators, directors, development executives, assistant directors, technicians, producers, and writers, problems within Hollywood were largely attributed to Californian and internal American policies and attitudes. However, they did acknowledge the financial incentives to film not just in other states but overseas which unsettled the Los Angeles–based production site as it meant that fewer Los Angeles-based, and U.S. based, media workers were needed, even though these films and television shows were created for a primarily American audience and sensibility (with the assumption that even "global" blockbusters should offer an American sensibility). These incentives, in the form of foreign subsidies offered by other countries and particularly Canada, and film tax credits in other states such as Louisiana to bring in state revenue (Mayer and Goldman 2010), were increasingly described as "runaway production"—a phrase that captures the perception that an activity has fled its home base. Production workers and scholars have become critical of out of state and overseas production. While Louisiana became what media scholars Vicki Mayer and Tanya Goldman call "Hollywood's premiere remote back-lot," its "system of tax credits is like every other bloated financial system in the U.S., moving capital between elites while workers live with exaggerated job insecurity, declining market value, and uncertain futures that make up the rest of the workforce" (Mayer and Goldman 2010, "Hollywood Handouts: Tax Credits in the Age of Economic Crisis").

Yet during my Hollywood fieldwork (at the production company and on various sets), "foreign markets" such as China or Latin America represented sites where their own products were sold and marketed (and China posed a vague threat), but many interlocutors described, and seemed to operate within, a cartography in which the United States determined the rise and fall of commercial film/TV everywhere. Certainly the people and community I knew felt very embedded in the Los Angeles locality, as the production sites were filled with people who had lived in Los Angeles for years, especially technical and crafts workers. Yet Hollywood is networked into businesses, industries, and infrastructures around the country and the world, and its products pervade the globe in both legal and pirated formats. The business of it emerges as far more transnational than is assumed by some of the technical workers and teamsters on set, with communications, contracts, production and postproduction, and exhibition spanning far beyond the United States. For instance, the Chinese conglomerate Wanda Group has acquired AMC entertainment, which is North America's second-largest theater owner, as well as Hollywood studio Legendary Entertainment; the South Korean conglomerate CJ Entertainment has a stake in SKG's DreamWorks; Sony continues to back Chinese filmmakers; Disney has struck a co-production deal with Shanghai Media Group; the Chinese company DMG invested in the Hollywood film *Ironman 3*; and Huayi Brothers has announced it will invest $120 million to $150 million in former Warner Bros.' Jeff Robinov's new Media 8 company. Certainly, if one looks at Hollywood blockbuster and tentpole films, the transnationality of the financing and star talent hired indicates the "global" marketing of film projects to international audiences (such as *Transformers: Age of Extinction*'s Li Bingbing, *Pirates of the Caribbean: At World End*'s Chow Yun Fat, *The Mummy III*'s Jet Li, *Karate Kid*'s Jackie Chan, and *Blackhat*'s Wang Lee Hom). Yet regarding Hong Kong or China, few Los Angeles–based production personnel had little to say. Many non-local media workers based in Hong Kong (Chinese and expatriate Westerners), however, frequently articulated how their personal trajectories and experiences were linked to what was happening within Hong Kong, with China, the East Asian region, and production in Anglo-American sites.

As an example, one of my interlocutors from Hong Kong, an actress called Linda, traveled between Los Angeles and Hong Kong every year to visit family in both cities. In Hong Kong, she took me to the set of a TVB drama, where I met everyone involved in filming. A year later, when she was in Los Angeles, I took her to the set of a television network drama there. It was a fast-moving, busy day, but the cast and crew were very happy to quickly meet her, and she was given a chair to sit in and was invited by the director to listen to the audio on headphones as they watched the filming on the video assist monitor. A principal actor on the show quickly offered Linda advice on joining the Screen Actors Guild in the United States before he had to shoot a scene. Linda was very pleased with the warm welcome she received, as was I. However, these introductions did not lead to anything more substantial to help her navigate the vast machinery of Hollywood, as both she and I hoped it might. I also noticed the perfunctory interest and attention expressed by the Hollywood personnel toward Hong Kong and its television industry. While they were certainly busy filming to meet their deadline, it was also apparent that the focus was on *here*, on Hollywood—the ostensible center of the entertainment universe.

Gender and racial disparities were starkly apparent on set yet rarely commented upon. The visible evidence was a challenge to the "liberal" narrative that Hollywood members often tell about their industry. At the time of writing, the Equal Employment Opportunity Commission is investigating the issue of gender disparity for female directors in Hollywood, an investigation prompted by the American Civil Liberties Union. Women, people of color, and the LGBT community have for years been underrepresented on screen and behind the camera in proportion to their national demographics. In a USC study of the 100 top-grossing films over a seven-year period which includes 2007, only 28 women worked as directors. The study also confirms the lack of racial diversity in commercial film: "Across 700 films, 5.8 percent of directors were black or African-American and 2.4 percent were Asian. There were no Asian directors in 2014. In the seven-year span, only three directors were African-American females and just one was an Asian female" (Smith, Choueiti, and Pieper 2015).

To get a sense of most sets on which I observed in Hollywood, the breakdown on this production call sheet for a network television show on which I observed in 2005 is fairly representative (excluding the female camera assistant). It lists the camera department as led by a male Director of Photography, with a male operator and one male and one female camera assistant (all white). There was a five member all-male grip (camera rigging) department and a 6 member all-male electrical department, most of whom were white. The wardrobe department lists five women and two men, and the make-up department two women and two men, also mostly white. All the departments except wardrobe were headed by a man. In a study examining film labor in 2008, a year after my fieldwork, Martha M. Lauzen found that women accounted for only 1 percent of key grips and 1 percent of gaffers for the 250 top-grossing domestic films of 2008; they made up 25 percent of production managers, 44 percent of production supervisors, and 20 percent of production designers (Lauzen 2009). By 2014, women accounted for only 20 percent of the personnel working in key production jobs on the top 700 theatrically released films (Lauzen 2015). Lauzen also found that the gender of the director is significant, as the director decides who is hired for many key positions: "films with women directors employed substantially higher percentages of women in other key behind the scenes roles than films with exclusively male directors" (Lauzen 2015b: 1). In the 700 films considered, women formed just 13 percent of the directors and only 9 percent of the cinematographers; 92 percent of the films had no female cinematographers (Lauzen 2015). These numbers challenge Hollywood's "progressive" descriptor, revealing a complete lack of gender parity, and bias and discrimination in hiring patterns. Paternalistic concerns about whether women are tough enough to call the shots for action films or are to be trusted with large budgets emanate from studio executives and investors, most of whom are male and white (similar concerns are held by men in the Hong Kong industry). Women tend to fare better as producers (who are often in offices, not on set). In 2014–2015 primetime television, women accounted for "27% of creators, directors, writers, producers, executive producers, editors, and directors of photography working on broadcast programs" (Lauzen 2015a: 1).

"Strike!"

During the Writers Guild strike in November 2007 I heard complaints linked to economics and politics. The primary issue of the strike was the writers' efforts to acquire a share of DVD and Internet reuse revenue, or residuals; the Internet residuals were considered the most urgent matter. Without writers for scripted television shows, thousands of production personnel were laid off, and with the increase in reality television programming, many did not immediately return to employment when the strike ended in early 2008. With not only California's governor but also presidential candidates weighing in on the strike, Cynthia Littleton of *Variety* wrote on December 19, 2007, that the chief economist of the Los Angeles County Economic Development Corp. estimated that the strike had cost L.A. County more than $342.7 million. Many production personnel I knew were upset about the lack of work in Los Angeles, but writers insisted that the share they were asking for was very little in comparison to the profits the media corporations would accrue.

When I visited the picket lines outside the studios (Photos 3.1 and 3.2), more than a few writers, directors, and actors I spoke with commented that the move against unions and local production was connected to the ailing U.S. economy and "political stuff." The picket line had become a place for mostly white, self-described liberals to vent about politics and

PHOTO **3.1** The Writers Guild of America Strike Outside the Studios in 2007 *(Credit: Author).*

PHOTO **3.2** The Writers Guild of America Strike Outside the Studios in 2007 *(Credit: Author).*

what someone described as "the ills of globalization." A few striking writers told me that "even we artists" were not immune from the threat of off-shoring that had already destabilized the below-the-line technical and craft labor for film as well as television. The organization FilmL.A. documented that, leading up to the strike, principal photography in California for feature films had declined from 11 of the top-grossing films in 2003 to six in 2006 (FilmL.A. Research 2014: 3).

China was repeatedly the most named threat in my conversations on the picket line without my ever bringing it up, a nativist sentiment echoed by informants in Hong Kong for somewhat different reasons. As a female writer said to me, "This strike is about protecting our work. What we make, China can't make." This sentiment pervaded Hollywood: that a white, American national identity, education, and cultural sensibility was the creative Hollywood default (especially for comedy writing), although "American" was not specified by them as white. Someone else on the picket line said, "The conglomerates can't outsource what we do to China," explaining that the Hollywood sensibility for the written comedic word in particular could not be assembled in China. Their insistence betrayed their doubt. These comments also recalled TVB producers in Hong Kong telling me that the Hong Kong writing and filming style, so revered in China, cannot be replicated there. As Arjun Appadurai writes, "It is not difficult to see that the speed and intensity with which both material and ideological elements now circulate across national boundaries have created a new order of uncertainty in social life" (Appadurai 1996: 228). While his statement was made in the context of the rise of ethnic violence amid globalization, we can see this uncertainty emerging as members of the Hollywood industry fear displacement. China would continue to figure as both a rising, innovative competitor and a racialized symbol of oppressive factory labor in these picket line conversations. The salience of this sentiment for Hong Kong, a Special Administrative Region of China, is discussed in more detail in Chapter 4; here, I note that most of my interlocutors in Hong Kong scoffed at the news of the strike in Hollywood, claiming that everyone in an industry suffers when one sector refuses to work. To them, residuals were a luxury, as they are not the norm in Hong Kong. The guilds in Hong Kong are not powerful labor organizations that represent creative labor such as the Writers Guild of America, West and the Screen Actors Guild with the American Federation of Television and Radio Artists in the United States, which were founded in the 1930s (SAG-AFTRA) and 1950s (WGA-West). Many Hong Kong media workers I spoke with in fact hoped that the labor dispute would open up opportunities for them to find work and develop projects in the United States.

Hong Kong in Hollywood: Media Assemblage

Around this same time, Hollywood had been busily adapting East Asian horror films. In 2007, I observed on the set of such a remake, in this case a film directed by a Hong Kong director on a major Hollywood studio lot. This production represents another facet of the media assemblage, with a combination of foreign talent, local workforce, and global capital (the studio backlot used for filming was owned by a multinational conglomerate). On this film set I had the opportunity to witness a few of the subtle ways in which uneven relations play out. The director, Chow, and his director of photography, Leung, were not permanently relocating to Hollywood; rather, they were brought to Los Angeles on work visas authorized by production executives to work specifically on this film—Chow for six months to direct and later supervise editing, and Leung for two months to film principal photography. Also hired for this project as a director's assistant was a Hong Kong woman. A director's assistant is different than the first assistant director, who breaks down the script into a film schedule and acts as second in command on set to the director, overseeing all the departments involved in on-set activity as they execute the commands handed down to them; the first assistant director is also frequently male. The director's assistant, Grace, was supposed to be the translator between the director, Chow, and the rest of the crew, even though Chow spoke very good English (but said that he was not very comfortable speaking it, especially while working). Besides the director, director of photography, and director's assistant hailing from Hong Kong, the production team that I observed on the set of this U.S.-based remake consisted mostly of white, American men, with more women in the wardrobe, hair, and makeup departments. Prior to visiting the set, I discussed the film with a Hong Kong colleague of Chow's. This friend referred to the Hollywood production company's choice of hiring Chow for an American remake of a Asian horror film with the sarcastic comment, "Yeah, we Asians are spooky." This colleague was referring to what many Hong Kong media workers see as Hollywood's essentializing strategy: corporate and studio sectors lumping all East Asians into one ethnic bloc, especially for horror-thriller genres. At other times, however, various sectors of Hollywood strategically differentiate between East Asians for marketing purposes, as became apparent during filming. Yet Chow was also a noted director in Hong Kong and overseas, and his expertise in "Asian" and horror film was seen as an asset by a few of the studio executives.

It had been decided that the project would be filmed with the Panavision Genesis HD system, a relatively recent video camera system at that time that boasted visual precision and a 35mm depth of field, and both Chow and Leung were excited about using it; it was one of the attractions of the project for them. As an example of transnational flows of local production practices, Chow and Leung had performed the *baai sahn* ritual for protection at the beginning of production. According to one of the producers, the American crew enjoyed it.

During the evening, Chow, Leung, and I watched the dolly track for the camera being rigged by the male crew members who were laying down the tracks and hammering away. The dolly track resembles a train track. Chow and Leung commented that watching the mostly white male crew work on the dolly track reminded them of the images of the Chinese brought out to build the railroads in California a century earlier. Chow and Leung half-joked to me that they enjoyed watching this, a reversal of a historical pattern of transnational labor. Their enjoyment was short-lived, though, as the crew worked at a steady, not speedy, pace. As the time passed, Chow and Leung started to complain that a Hong Kong crew would have completed the task much quicker. "*Fai di la!*" (Quicker!) they quietly repeated to each other as they watched the crew. Our conversation then turned to a critique of Hollywood unionized labor as responsible for slowing down the pace of production in general. As if to illustrate Chow's point, during our conversation one of the grips stopped to light up a cigar while he was rigging the dolly track. Although it is very common for media workers in production sites all over the world to smoke a cigarette while they work (including Hong Kong), a cigar conveys a tone of luxury more appropriate to a salon than a set. Chow nodded at the cigar-smoking grip and complained quietly to Leung and me, "It's like they are standing around at a party, so social." Chow also complained that whereas on his Hong Kong film sets the department heads make decisions, on this American film everyone came to him asking him questions all the time. "Here, no one wants to make a decision," he said, implying that no one on the Hollywood set wanted to be accountable, although being in control of all aspects of creating a "vision" is considered the hallmark of cinematic auteurism. Chow and Leung recounted that on Hong Kong films there is more room for improvisation, and changes can be made to the script on the spot. Yet they also emphasized that they appreciated the resources available to them on a Hollywood studio production and at the set of this large, historic studio lot. As Leung, a veteran cinematographer, said, "It's my honor to be able to light

PHOTO **3.3** A Typically Spacious Hollywood Backlot That Is Used for Filming Exterior Shots at a Studio *(Copyright: © RanaPics / Alamy Stock Photo).*

such a big space. We don't have studio spaces like these in Hong Kong anymore. We film in the city. Only in China do you have such big sets. Space like this is becoming a thing of the past." Both the camera technology and the spatial dimensions of the studio (the latter exemplified in Photo 3.3) were seen by Chow and Leung as technological and aesthetic opportunities that a transnational collaboration could provide.

When filming finally started at around 11 p.m., I joined Chow inside the set piece of a house where the director's playback monitor was set up for him and the producers so that they could watch the scene that was being filmed outside the house from their "video village." As another director had told me, the emergence of the video-assist technology for filming can reduce the director to somewhat of a voyeur as opposed to the formerly more visible and active authority and technical participant when sitting or standing next to the camera operator during filming. At this shoot, viewing what was being filmed on the monitor from video village inside the house protected the director and producers from the cold night air. Chow, who had spoken a combination of Cantonese and English before filming and while the crew were readying the set, switched to only Cantonese during filming, both when yelling from inside the building to Grace and Leung outdoors as well as talking into his mouthpiece on the walkie-talkie.

PHOTO **3.4** A Hollywood Director and Crew Huddle Around the Video Village Monitor to Observe Filming *(Credit: Logan Boettcher).*

During this nighttime shoot, I shifted between sitting with Chow and the producers by the monitor inside the house and venturing outside to observe the filming, which was a running sequence. This scene called for smoke, but Chow became annoyed with the operator of the smoke machine about the lack of coordinated timing between the smoke and the movement of the actors, which to some degree was beyond the control of the smoke operator and his assistant. Managing the direction and speed in which smoke blows can require a lot of time when filming outdoors in a cold wind, but time, as Chow kept muttering into his mouthpiece to Grace, was in short supply.

Smoke was not the only issue for Chow and the crew. Grace had the challenge of quite literally mediating between Chow's directives in Cantonese and the rest of the American crew. At one point during the night, while the crew were setting up a shot, one of the producers sitting at the playback monitor said to me, "This film is so international: an Asian film, directed by a Hong Konger, in the U.S., and some scenes in the movie that take place in Europe." He then motioned at Grace and marveled, "She's so Westernized, she gets every nuance because she went to school in the U.K., yet she's from Hong Kong." Grace had to navigate being Chow's female mouthpiece, yet not thwarting the authority of the first assistant director, who on Hollywood productions usually assumes that role. This set, despite being so "international" and bilingual, remained English-centric. At one point Chow became frustrated by a miscommunication with one of the camera operators over how many frames per second they were running. The subsequent three-way Cantonese conversation between Chow, Leung, and Grace (with Grace yelling messages back and forth from her halfway point between Chow seated inside the house by the monitor and Leung outside in the middle of the filming activity) was observed by the rest of the crew with some puzzlement, especially after Grace gave only terse instructions to the first assistant director in English after Chow had shouted a lengthy commentary to her in Cantonese about the production coordination.

During a break for setup between shots, an executive came to sit with the director and two producers by the playback monitor. He sat behind Chow, next to the two producers, and did not address Chow. He observed the next couple of shots being filmed and, during the next setup, said quietly to one of the producers, "So, what's the logic here of having a Hong Kong director for this remake?" While this was an interesting question, the timing and place of it were not optimal. Looking at Chow, who was adjusting his earpiece while watching the playback of a previous shot, one of the producers quietly responded, "Ah, based on our market research, we think this is a good match . . . you know, the China market." The executive nodded and responded, "Well, at least this director hasn't made any decisions I don't like yet." All of these comments were made directly within earshot of Chow, whom the executive ignored, perhaps assuming that Chow was absorbed in watching the monitor and/or could not understand English (which he did). To the executive, the choice to hire Chow represented a potential mismatch that could threaten the authenticity of the film's Asian yet non-Hong Kong identity, even though the remake was reworked into an English-language American and European setting with mostly white actors. In his exchange with the executive, the producer glossed Chow as generically Chinese, eliding his Hong Kong identity and dismissing the need for a specific cultural sensibility in the pursuit of profit accumulation from the monolithic "China market" that compresses the diversity of East Asia.

These various interactions on the set of this film show how convergences even on the micro level of a film set rest upon and also generate certain tensions. Chow satisfied multiple needs for the Hollywood production team and executives: lacking name-brand recognition for a mass American market, he would be more malleable to executive pressures (in their eyes, at least). At the same time, Chow brought with him the cachet of film festival accolades for American and European fans who keep abreast of Hong Kong cinema. He also arrived with previous success from an acclaimed Hong Kong horror film geared toward East Asian audiences. Thus, Chow served as a flexible, all-purpose Asian filmmaker whom Hollywood marketing and distribution could capitalize upon, given the growing spate of Asian horror and ghost films appearing on the global market. In Hollywood, Chow was seen as Asian, and in some cases a part of China and therefore assumed by white Hollywood executives as more likely to garner mainland Chinese appeal. At the same time, Chow was also identified as a Hong Kong filmmaker, accredited with a commercial horror film sensibility and savvy that mainland Chinese filmmakers ostensibly lack given the PRC's ban on such genres. The specificity of Asian countries and territories thus receded at certain junctures in this project and came into focus at others. Chow's own experiences were also mixed. On the one hand he was frustrated: the constraints imposed by the project (short filming schedule, union labor, and studio infrastructure) could hamper his ability to accomplish a Hollywood debut that would propel his own career trajectory. At the same time, he was very appreciative of the range of financial and material resources made available to him on this project. As Chow told me, he would be able to market the fact that he had directed a film shot on the Panavision Genesis HD technology, a camera system at that time not commonly used outside of Hollywood. Further, the cachet of directing a Hollywood film would provide him with more leverage for future film projects, especially those based in East Asia. Thus, the relations of mutual dependability illustrate the contingencies and heterogeneity of such media assemblages. This encounter also demonstrates that film sets are not separate from structural issues such as globalization. A transnational ensemble can be a discomforting lived experience, and not just a feel-good celebration of multiculturalism. Recalling what the Hollywood writer said to me on the picket line about China not being able to make what Hollywood makes, we must ask what counts for "authenticity" in a production process that research shows is made up of predominantly white, Euro-American men. In an American adaptation of an Asian horror film, what counts as "American" and what counts as "Asian," especially given location filming, the diversity within East Asia, flexible citizenship strategies and the U.S.'s extended work visas for Chinese professionals? Hollywood's localism isn't just found on screen: it also haunts the production process, particularly amid the perceived risks and rewards of the China market, which at times is embodied by individual Hong Kong media personnel.

....

CHAPTER 4

The Death Narratives of Revitalization

Colonial Governance, China, and the Reconfiguration of the Hong Kong Film Industry

The Death Narratives

> "You know how long your study will take you? One day? No, one hour! We are nothing anymore."
>
> —HONG KONG film star, interview, August 2005

On a winter afternoon in 2006, I was invited to observe a film production crew film a stunt scene on Hong Kong Island. Members of the production took up their designated positions for filming the stunt scene. Behind the protective bar that separated observers from the production team, we watched as one of the young stunt workers, dressed in a black tracksuit, ran down the street as an oncoming car, squealing around the corner, collided with his body. His body slammed against the hood of the car, his torso thrust against the windshield, as the car screeched to a halt (Photo 4.1). The stunt man then rolled off the hood of the car and collapsed on the ground, and the director yelled, "Cut!" The stunt man jumped up, shook himself off, and, as the crew applauded, the driver emerged from the car to enthusiastically shake the hand of the young stunt man.

As we applauded, one of the production coordinators told me that this stunt had been performed by a father–son stunt team: the father drove the car that hit his son. The father is in fact one of Hong Kong's premier stunt choreographers.

PHOTO **4.1** The Young Stunt Worker's Body Is Filmed Being Hit by the Oncoming Car, Driven by His Father *(Credit: Author).*

After filming was completed, I was introduced to the father, Fred, who had driven the car.

AUTHOR: So how did it feel to hit your own son with the car?
F: Oh, it felt great! [pumps fist in the air]
AUTHOR: Really? Why?
F: Well, he's well trained. He knows how to do it, I taught him, he wouldn't do it otherwise, I wouldn't let him.

As I continued to express awe at the father–son stunt work, Fred paused, stopped smiling, and said, "It's important to me—this is a family tradition, this is what we do. I teach my son. But our film industry is dying out. Who will my son teach?"

Fred's query illustrates how even the most physically robust members of the Hong Kong film industry—the world-renowned Hong Kong stunt men—have become highly vulnerable to its deterioration. Hong Kong stunt men have for several decades been famous among fans of martial arts and action films around the world for performing death-defying stunts (Desser 2000; Teo 2000). Some of these stunt men were trained in the martial art of kung fu in kin-based labor systems whereby their fathers and grandfathers, who performed such acrobatics on the Cantonese Opera stage, trained their sons and grandsons alongside them.[1] Others were trained in the Peking Opera tradition. Some of these performers transitioned to working in film and television adaptations of Cantonese operas throughout the past century in Hong Kong. Yet as the Hong Kong film industry goes into decline, and there are fewer films in which to feature such crafts, these Hong Kong stunt men fear that their craft will become obsolete.

Almost all of the Hong Kong media personnel described their film industry as not merely suffering a lapse but as a vanishing entity—"dying" or "dead." "We are dying, and you are here to record it," an actress in the Hong Kong film industry repeatedly told me. Tapping on my notebook, a producer instructed me, "Write this down, what I am telling you, so people know who we were." "Let's toast the last of the Hong Kong film industry," another producer-director suggested over tea, proffering his teacup. During these times, which anticipated some of the sentiments that drove Hong Kong's 2014 Occupy protests and Umbrella Uprising, I felt as if I were being given data for a eulogy instead of an ethnography. Informants described their cinematic art form as rapidly becoming an artifact to be excavated, and their distinctively "Hong Kong" commercial filmmaking practices (known for their stylistic action and fast-paced shooting schedules) as becoming extinct. These "death narratives," as I labeled them in my fieldnotes, reflected the salient downturn with which the Hong Kong film industry has been struggling to overcome for nearly two decades after the decline started in the early 1990s, and the scholarship that explores it.[2] The turning point was the 1997 return to mainland China as a Special Administrative Region under what is called a "one country, two systems" form of governance; this has bred tensions, most evident in the Umbrella Uprising in 2014. Yet in critically reading these death narratives I illustrate that despite the demonization of China as depleting Hong Kong of its resources, it is also the policies of colonial administration played out in a global city formation that have led to the current demise. In other words, the very government rhetoric and policies about "openness" and "laissez-faire" that are attributed to the growth of businesses and industries in Hong Kong such as film were in fact what led to its decline. I also suggest that the demise of the Hong Kong film industry has generated a new configuration of film production bolstered by China.

The moniker "Hollywood of the East," as the Hong Kong film industry came to be known by the film community and film scholars, invites us to consider the basis of the comparison between film industries in Hong Kong and the United States. The basis lies in the mass production of films located in a particular site. While the Hollywood comparison should not be belabored nor the term "Hollywood of the East" reified, it is nevertheless useful to note that film industrialization in Hong Kong has been largely unprotected by its government, unlike the American film industry. Thus, the laissez-faire capitalism of the film industry and Hong Kong itself that has been so deeply valorized by businesses, government officials, scholars, and film personnel has in fact contributed to its vulnerability.

"King Kong in Hong Kong": The Specter of Return

To film workers during my fieldwork, the specter behind the narratives of demise appeared to be China. Explicitly and implicitly, industry discourse and imagery attributed the desiccation of Hong Kong's film industry to competition from China's growing media industries, which were entering the global marketplace and supported by a vast (albeit lumbering) governmental infrastructure undergoing market reform. Hong Kong's cinema, and even Hong Kong itself, was understood by many film workers as being subsumed by China. In the 2002 Hong Kong film *Runaway Pistol*, one of the storylines revolves around a young Hong Kong boy who is kidnapped by a pair of mainland Chinese immigrants. After Hong Kong's return to China and the subsequent increase in cross-border traffic, anxieties regarding the penetration of the city-state by immigrants (legal and illegal) have arisen—an anxiety that films such as *Runaway Pistol* play upon. In the film, the boy is forced into a child slavery ring with other Hong Kong children who have similarly been abducted deep into China.

This film's imagery of vulnerable Hong Kong bodies snatched up by corrupt mainland Chinese was one of a growing collection of on-screen representations that depicted fears among many Hong Kong people (and film industry workers in particular) of China as an entity that is inducing the demise of the Hong Kong population and depleting Hong Kong of its resources (Davis and Yeh 2001). Even though Hong Kong existed under Chinese sovereignty until its capture by the British in a series of Opium Wars, and many Hong Kong Chinese have parents who grew up in China, most of the Hong Kong film personnel I encountered expressed a strong sense of a Hong Kong cultural identity that was formed largely under a laissez-faire capitalist system introduced by British colonial rule. I will posit later that the fears of the absorption of Hong Kong bodies and the depletion of Hong Kong resources should also be attributed to the U.S. media conglomerates as a result of Special Administrative Region (SAR) government policies that uphold colonial practices and manifest in the global city of Hong Kong.

In my interactions with film workers in Hong Kong, I was frequently confronted with commentary about "primitive" and plundering main-landers, who, in a less dramatic manner than the Chinese couple depicted in the film, participate in the depletion of Hong Kong bodies, labor, and knowledge. Strains of this discourse were echoed in some of the print and popular media that I encountered, and is captured in Rey Chow's essay "King Kong in Hong Kong: Watching the 'Handover' from the US" (Chow 1998). Rey Chow likens the specter of China in Anglo-American political, legal, and media discourse to the spectacular beast King Kong—an image that resonated with how many Hong Kong film workers and some mem-bers of Hong Kong society spoke to me of mainland Chinese. Lawless and looming over a population that many informants described as "civilized" by colonization, China served as the monolithic Other against which many Hong Kong film workers defined themselves. In January 2006, William, a Hong Kong producer and director, discussed filming co-productions between Hong Kong and China in China and expounded on his attempts to raise money from mainland investors:

> People in China need a long time to be educated, to be polite, to be civi-lized. Most people are farmers and most now have money. They suddenly get rich, but they skipped certain stages of development. They really are primitives. They didn't have to think, they just got the money [from the government]. But they need a long time to come up to speed. Like in Hong Kong: we are also Chinese, but we learned how to think from the British.
>
> When I was last in China to make a film, I noticed that the changes within China are going too fast, they haven't developed a business acumen. The investors there, they are not sophisticated like Hong Kong investors, the way the British taught us. They don't really know how to invest. Thank God for the British! Thank God they taught me how to invest money.

William's comments were not unique; many of the directors, producers, and actors that I interviewed articulated similar sentiments, although some expressed more tolerant views of mainland Chinese people's per-ceived rush to integrate capitalist practices. His comments should also be seen in the context of fear of becoming disposable; when we met a year later, he was morosely contemplating leaving Hong Kong for good. While many Hong Kong entrepreneurs and filmmakers hoped to capitalize through mainland China "opening up" their market for financial gains, with Hong Kong serving as a bridge to China's market, many personnel I interviewed also expressed concerns about China's propensity to plunder Hong Kong's industries and to dislodge Hong Kong as a key global Chinese hub in the East Asian region. They expressed a fear that "unsophisticated" mainland Chinese film workers would leech off principal Hong Kong creative personnel (such as writers, cinematographers, stars, and directors) their knowledge and skills as Hong Kong film workers crossed the border to work on mainland Chinese productions or co-productions and Chinese film workers crossed into Hong Kong to work.

Such cross-border work was made possible by the Closer Economic Partnership Arrangement (CEPA). In fact, what the Hong Kong Trade Development Council (2004, 2005) refers to as the "revitalization" of the Hong Kong film and television industries has been supplied in many ways by the mainland Chinese government. The CEPA between mainland China and Hong Kong, put into effect in 2003, is a free-trade agreement that facilitates the integration of mainland China's recently liberalized industries with the capitalist ones of Hong Kong. CEPA also attempts to repair the Hong Kong film industry's downturn by allowing Hong Kong filmmakers access to mainland Chinese investment and distribution markets. The Hong Kong government touts the revitalization of Hong Kong's economy and its film industry in particular through joint film productions. CEPA has been implemented in various phases: during my fieldwork CEPA moved from Phase II to III. The benefit of CEPA for Hong Kong audiovisual industries is that as long as Hong Kong film and television scripts receive approval from mainland censors, Hong Kong films and television shows are not subject to import quotas and are distributed as domestic products in mainland China. Under CEPA Phase III, Hong Kong production companies may own more than 50 percent of the copyright of films co-produced, and Hong Kong residents may represent more than 50 percent of the total principal personnel in the motion pictures concerned. The ostensible benefit to mainland Chinese production personnel is the opportunity to work on these media and acquire filmmaking skills from crews and principal personnel who possess extensive experience in commercial filmmaking. The purpose of CEPA is not just to assist Chinese industries as they liberalize, but also to help Hong Kong's ailing industry. Yet what triggered a decline such that Hong Kong's film industry required revitalization?

Industrial Decline

The Hong Kong film industry has over the years been referred to by scholars and practitioners as the "Hollywood of the East" for its mass production of films that for decades were consumed by both local and transnational audiences. A Cantonese-language industry, with the rise of the PRC after World

War II and subsequent upheaval in Southeast Asia, Hong Kong's film industry became dominated by mainland Chinese and Singaporean filmmakers
who relocated to Hong Kong (e.g., Shaw Brothers and the Cathay) (Fu 2000:
72, 78). Consequently, local Cantonese cinema "became a nonentity" within
Hong Kong up through the 1970s as Mandarin-language cinema dominated
locally and with overseas audiences (Teo 2000: 91), although, as Laikwan
Pang asserts, a Hong Kong sensibility remained in these films (Pang 2007:
10). By the late 1970s, local filmmakers reclaimed the industry, sparking
the New Wave (Teo 2000: 102) and ushering in the highly commercial era
of the 1980s and 1990s. After some fluctuation in the 1990s, however, the
"Hollywood of the East" started to experience a significant downturn in
the early 2000s (Table 4.1).

In 1984, Hong Kong's return to China was negotiated by the British
government in the Joint Sino-British Talks, in which Hong Kong people
had little say about their city's autonomy. The hovering date of return to
China in 1997 sparked nervousness among Hong Kong's top talent, resulting in a rash of film workers moving or seeking more work overseas
as people were uncertain how a "one country, two systems" form of

TABLE 4.1 Decline of Hong Kong Film Productions

YEAR	NUMBER OF HONG KONG FILM PRODUCTIONS
1992	138
1993	242
1994	190
1995	154
1996	116
1997	94
1998	92
1999	146
2000	151
2001	126
2002	92
2003	79
2004	64
2005	55
2006	51
2007	50

Source: Chan, Fung and Ng 2010: 13.

governance would impact Hong Kong's liberalized economy, its "democratic" colonial government, and its political and cultural autonomy.[3] As I was conducting research in Hong Kong a decade after 1997, a sense of expiration—a looming countdown to an ending with a planned 2047 convergence of Hong Kong and China—pervaded the Hong Kong film community. As a veteran film producer and distributor said to me in February 2007,

> What's going to happen to Hong Kong people? In ten years China will have a healthy [film] distribution system, but right now they need Hong Kong people and others to do it for them. In 80 years, in two generations, they can do it themselves. And in two generations Hong Kong film people won't be around. They [the mainland Chinese] won't need us anymore. They need to catch up. And when they do, that's the end of Hong Kong film.

A cinematographer, Henry, also predicted that within the next 10 or 20 years, his skills as a cinematographer would no longer be needed in China as camera technicians there would absorb the knowledge he currently passes onto them when he works there through CEPA. Henry interwove his comments about the redundancy that Hong Kong film workers face across the border with complaints about the threat from mainland Chinese people within Hong Kong, including the film industry. Increasing numbers of Chinese come to Hong Kong to shop, work, and make money, and in a preview of the 2014 protest commentary, Henry warned of Hong Kong's standards of "good taste" being eroded by mainland sensibilities. "The market in Hong Kong is toned down to cater to mainland tourists. Have you noticed that the styles and models of things like clothing and cameras have gone down?" he said. The siphoning off of knowledge and taste was a recurrent theme alongside the decline of films produced and consumed.

1997 was also a critical year for the film industry due to the Asian financial crisis, which, triggered by the collapse of the Thai currency, spread throughout the Southeast Asian economies and caused film investors to retract their financing from what many considered to be risk-prone ventures. Combined with investors' skittishness about China's impending governance of Hong Kong, local and regional financing diminished. The decreased investment, combined with smaller audiences for an abundance of local films, damaged the film industry. Aggressive marketing and distribution of Hollywood films throughout the 1990s resulted in a reduction of consumption of Hong Kong films, further slowing financial investment in them. The increased capability to produce pirated films also hurt the film industry. Yet the death narratives I encountered were also, I argue, a response to political-economic factors that rendered the Hong Kong film industry vulnerable; these causes emanated from Hong Kong's colonial mode of governance.

Structural Causes of Decline

Colonial policies extending into the postcolonial phase and its iteration in the global city model reveal that the "open," "free" economic environment of Hong Kong that many film workers championed to me is actually one of the prime causes of its vulnerability. These policies mean that such an industry cannot withstand challenges to it that its American counterpart, Hollywood, has been able to withstand with its federal and state financial and legislative support as well as research and development from high-tech and education sectors and the U.S. military-industrial complex (see Miller, Govil, McMurria, Maxwell, and Wang 2005).

While government officials and economists such as Donald Tsang Yam-kuen and Milton Friedman have declared Hong Kong to be a haven of free-market practices with minimal government interference, scholars have also pointed out that Hong Kong's colonial government played a decisive role in the economy, in a policy that came to be known as "positive non-interventionism" (Castells 2000; Ngo 1999b; So 2004). which I argue had implications for the film industry. Positive non-interventionism, a policy pursued by Hong Kong's Financial Secretary John Cowperthwaite in the 1960s, was the colonial policy of maintaining an open and "free" economy with little government intervention—a policy that was already in development since Hong Kong's early days as an entrepôt. Yet, citing Manuel Castells in his discussion of Hong Kong's rise as a global city, Wai Kit Choi points out that the British colonial government *did* intervene in Hong Kong's economy, through the realm of collective consumption (Castells 2000: 270–276; Choi 2007: 396). In response to widespread poverty, the colonial government offered public housing, universal health care, free education, and subsidized public transport, food, and social services. Thus, by intervening in the realm of collective consumption rather than production, the colonial government allowed manufacturers to maintain workers at low wages (Castells 2000). Choi also notes that governmental policy did not allow Hong Kong's low-cost, low-end industries to move into the high-technology sector (Choi 2007: 396–397). Many of Hong Kong's industries that had initially thrived in the entrepreneurial environment for which Hong Kong is famed entailed small and medium-sized labor-intensive companies that manufactured textiles, clothing, electronics, watches, plastics, and food (most of which were family owned and run). Hong Kong's success in its export-led industrialization thus emanated from a form of state intervention that chose not to grow domestic businesses and industries. Unlike other developmental states in East Asia, which received government support for research and development as well as capital to upgrade, Hong Kong's colonial government refrained for the most part from investing in the development of industries. So, for instance, as Choi explicates, in 1994 the total spending on research and development as a percentage of gross domestic product was 2.29 percent for South Korea, 1.80 percent for Taiwan, 1.18 percent for Singapore, but only 0.10 percent for Hong Kong (Berger and Lester 1997: 77; Choi 2007: 397).

As Stephen Chiu, K. C. Ho, and Tai-Lok Lu (1997) assert, without state support for scientific and technological development, most Hong Kong industries were not equipped to transition from their low-technology and low–value-added status into the more specialized knowledge-intensive production niche that South Korea, Taiwan, and Singapore formed. Thus, in order to compete with manufacturers in other East Asian developmental states in the early 1980s, most Hong Kong factories, instead of upgrading, moved to China, where labor was cheaper (Choi 2007: 397). Challenges to Hong Kong industrial production that MIT researchers Suzanne Berger and Richard Lester summarize (and which I posit encompassed the film industry) include

> gaps in human resource development systems; low investment in new technology development; the limitations of family ownership of business enterprises [such as limited transparency which is necessary to secure bank loans]; the low rate of formation of new technology-based enterprises; the scarcity of specialized technical knowledge in government; and high labor and land costs. (Berger and Lester 1997: 59)

Many Hong Kong production companies were run as flexible family labor systems, or were formed to make only one movie, and so did not sustain an organization structure that was invested in long-term technological or creative growth (see also Fu 2000: 77). The family-run (and sometimes triad-connected) film businesses rarely featured human resource development systems. As a lawyer at a Hong Kong studio recounted to me in 2005, legal departments and contract lawyers are a relatively new phenomenon for Hong Kong film companies, which (similar to Bollywood's film industry) existed in a system of oral as well as written contracts, arcane payment methods, informal management, and secretive records (see Ganti 2002). Technical drawbacks also became apparent when films were screened in newly built cineplexes in the 1970s; the improved audio system installed in the theater only served to amplify the poor quality of audio recording, revealing the outdated recording equipment used in production and post-production at that time. Subpar lighting in the studio also detracted from production values "by creating unnecessary shadows" (Fu 2000: 77). The film industry would technologically upgrade over time, but without state support, and as Joseph M. Chan, Anthony Y. H. Fung, and Chun Hung Ng point out, filmmakers continue to complain of "a lack of technical back-up infrastructure, for example post-production facilities and studios" (Chan, Fung, and Ng 2010: 21).

While in the process of deindustrializing in the 1980s, Hong Kong's colonial government transformed Hong Kong into a "global city" that facilitates the transnational flow of finance capital (Sassen 2000, 2001). The global city model of development entails the establishment of regional headquarters of multinational corporations, investment banks, law firms, accounting firms, and other transnational service providers, such as Citibank, Goldman Sachs, Bank of America, Deloitte, and Royal Bank of Scotland (Choi 2007: 398). By the 1990s, Hong Kong became the financial center of Asia and the third largest financial hub in the world, after New York and London (So 2004). As Choi argues regarding Hong Kong's loss of sovereign autonomy, many domestic businesses within Hong Kong participated in this global city model only by offering the requisite physical infrastructure to maintain this complex of financial services, such as office and apartment space, a telecommunications network, and a power source; thus, "[g]iven Hong Kong's dependence on the presence of a multinational specialized service complex, it cannot have a new institutional structure other than the one it has always had since the colonial days" (Choi 2007: 399). Civil servants in Hong Kong's colonial government remained in place after Hong Kong's return to China (Choy 2005: 9), hence maintaining continuity in policy and personnel between colonial and postcolonial SAR governance. Therefore, as Choi posits, Hong Kong's SAR government (with China's consent and participation) retained its colonial mode of governance in the first 10 years after the handover.

Consequences of Decline

This lack of sovereign autonomy and government intervention has had significant consequences for Hong Kong's film workers, such as its stunt community. Joe, an active member of the Hong Kong Stunt Man

Association, comes from a family of three generations of stunt workers. He remarked to me that while he has been able to survive jumping off buildings eight stories high, he cannot endure the steep decline of the Hong Kong film industry. In the early 2000s he petitioned the Hong Kong government for funding for the film industry but has met with very little support. The current SAR government of Hong Kong has continued the former British colonial policy of "positive non-interventionism" in many aspects of Hong Kong society—in this case meaning minimal involvement in the realm of local cultural production (see also Chan et al. 2010: 19, 82).

Yet it is not solely Hong Kong's stunt community that has experienced the Hong Kong government's active indifference spanning both its colonial and postcolonial phases; other film workers such as directors, producers, and actors complain of neglect and preferential treatment for overseas (and particularly American) productions. In November 2007, the Hollywood production of *The Dark Knight* chose to film in Hong Kong for eight days. The director was quoted in Hong Kong news media as wanting to feature the spectacle of Hong Kong's famed skyline and world's longest escalator for certain action sequences in his *Batman* film. During the eight-day film shoot, the production required the use of local film crews who could work around-the-clock shifts. The production also received permission from the Hong Kong government media authorities to close down local businesses surrounding the escalator in the busy financial and tourist center of Hong Kong Island for filming. The production was additionally granted law enforcement personnel for managing crowd control in order to accommodate outdoor filming. The government even asked business owners to comply with the production's request to keep the skyline lit throughout the night for an entire week, an enormous drain on the territory's resources of electrical power at a time when the Hong Kong government had started to heed environmentalist calls to promote energy-saving practices among its residents (Crawford and Chan 2007).

Although the stars and principal creative personnel of *The Dark Knight* derived from the Hollywood establishment, this Hollywood production relied upon the lax labor laws and loose environmental and safety regulations of Hong Kong. This process is what Miller et al. (2005: 111–140) refer to as the "new international division of cultural labor" in which the Hollywood-based production disperses its filmmaking process to various parts of the world where labor is cheaper and contingent. During the *Dark Knight* film shoot, Hong Kong filmmakers as well as environmentalists objected to what they saw as the appropriation of Hong Kong's resources. Renowned Hong Kong filmmaker Johnnie To publicly accused the Hong

Kong SAR government of "discrimination" by continually facilitating the needs of U.S. and overseas productions while repeatedly ignoring the requests of local Hong Kong filmmakers for similar forms of government assistance (Ho 2007).

To's accusation echoed what I had heard throughout 15 months of fieldwork in Hong Kong from a range of film workers who had continually complained about the lack of assistance from the government's media authorities, such as the Hong Kong Film Services Office. A leader of the Hong Kong Stunt Man Association had complained bitterly of how for several decades the government authorities had not safeguarded crews filming outdoors when threatened with theft and extortion by local gangs in Kowloon and Hong Kong Island. Several producers had complained that instead of protecting local film crews, the Hong Kong police patrolling the area being filmed had harassed them while demanding to see permits. Of the double standards, a film producer told me:

> I would tell the police that my films were promoting Hong Kong, making it look good, but they didn't care. We'd get into huge shouting matches in the street and they'd waste my time. But when foreigners film a Coke commercial here, that's a different matter. Everything is available to them.

Production crews recounted how filming outdoors had been difficult without the support of the government bureaucracy and the free or low-cost protection of law enforcement for crowd control. Several producers complained that they had to pay police officers to work as private security in their off-duty hours, without the aegis of their police uniforms to keep gangsters away. This was in sharp contrast to the access to various locations and forms of assistance that overseas filmmakers generally receive through the Hong Kong Film Services Office, a division of the Hong Kong government's Trade Development Council.

Hong Kong's government seeks to attract and associate with transnational capital without simultaneously developing its own cultural industry, since Hong Kong positions itself as offering Anglo-American–style financial services in a liberalized economy. Informants complained that film and television programs at most Hong Kong universities have until recently been underfunded and underdeveloped (see also Chan et al. 2010: 55). Paradoxically, by offering up the city's scenic landscapes, labor, and energy resources to Hollywood conglomerates such as Warner Bros. as part of a strategy to internationally promote Hong Kong's image, the Hong Kong government contributes to the deterioration of its own, place-based "Hollywood of the East" legacy.

As a result of the multiple causes of decline, the stunt performers and other Hong Kong film personnel have become highly mobile workers. A famous stunt coordinator has been able to find work in Hollywood and China. Joe and other stunt workers I observed have also worked as consultants on Hollywood productions, and, as a result of CEPA, trained mainland Chinese film workers in stunt work. In doing so, these film workers have recently also had to become flexible in ways that their martial arts training did not prepare them for, in some cases learning new languages later in life (such as Mandarin and English), renewing family ties in China, and training in new skills, such as computer literacy and film budget software. Since Hong Kong film workers do not have strong unions and the government has provided little in the way of infrastructural resources or support, these increasingly entrepreneurial film workers fear that the craft that initially put Hong Kong cinema on the global stage will soon become a lost art within its own region and among its own community, regenerating only within the American and mainland Chinese film industries.

Conclusion

The global city model of development has had implications for Hong Kong's film industry, such as unimpeded access for foreign-based media conglomerates (including Colombia and Sony, Warner Bros., and Walt Disney Co.). While several family-run Hong Kong film production companies such as Golden Harvest and Shaw Brothers went public, the 1980s filmmaking boom was financed by many independent production companies whose investors were also involved in real estate and jewelry businesses, and which disbanded after one or several productions. It has not helped that the SAR government, as with the colonial government, has not held the film industry in high cultural regard, instead for years seeing it as what many interlocutors described as *lo pin moon* (involvement in dubious business), girded by marginal entrepreneurial forces (see also Curtin 2007: 75). Many of the films of the late 1970s and 1980s and early 1990s were made with entrepreneurial capital. Even though some Hong Kong filmmakers were only indirectly linked to illegal networks, the perception shaded the tone of the industry. Yet the prevalence of illicit activity within the film industry is due in part to the marginality in which governmental forces have encased it. In fact, the Hong Kong film industry has for decades been a shadowy capitalist enterprise. A major exporter of Hong Kong icons such as Bruce Lee, Jackie Chan, John Woo, and Chow Yun Fat, the Hong Kong film industry constituted a virtually spectral presence in the annals of British commerce. A glance at the official British almanac of businesses and industries in 1982, a year in which Hong Kong's film industry was particularly profitable and visible throughout international film markets, revealed that while so many other local industries were accounted for, such as textiles, jewelry, and wig making, there was no mention of the film industry.

It was intriguing that so many Hong Kong film workers frequently pointed to the developmental state of South Korea and its strong government support for cultural production as an example of a successful East Asian film industry with its quota system (see also Chan et al. 2010). The "death narratives" both emerged from and articulated contradictory desires. On the one hand, Hong Kong film workers claimed that they are members of what numerous informants referred to as "a people" who are not predisposed to political organization, and they wanted to uphold the practice of minimal government interference. On the other hand, some of these same film workers held up the South Korean film industry as an admirable model of national government support in maintaining a place-based industry. It is noteworthy that the Hong Kong film industry grew in popularity in the 1950s amidst the backdrop of the Cold War, with films made by "anti-Communist companies such as Cathay and Shaw Bros." at a time when Hong Kong came to "see itself as an outpost of the 'Free World'" (Jarvie 1977: 33). When I asked about past and future attempts to form more viable unions, many informants brushed off unionization as too closely related to communism. One producer told me,

> The Brits wouldn't allow unions—they represent communism. A while ago, Hong Kong Performing Artistes tried to form a union. But also, we Chinese, we are very different. It's in our genes to not align with other people to fight for a cause unless it's something very personal.

Although this producer's comment was historically inaccurate (unions did actually emerge under British colonialism), his sentiment reflects a popular anti-union stance on the part of many in the managerial class. It is also worth pointing out that the business of making films—whether for capital accumulation or aesthetic pleasure or family tradition or other reasons—has indeed become "very personal" for many film workers. The disavowal of the kind of protection that unions or collective bargaining ostensibly offers (the latter not being allowed in Hong Kong), juxtaposed with many informants' envy of South Korean government support of its film industry, revealed the complexity of attitudes and ambivalence as the film industry undergoes dramatic shifts. One of the main issues underlying such tensions is the fact that Hong Kong is not a nation-state such as South Korea, and its film industry is not a *national* industry such as South Korea's. Hong Kong is a city-state, and historically it has been a territory of China, then Great Britain, and now China again as an SAR.

In the 10 years since the handover, the Hong Kong government has started to recognize that its film industry can be a profitable way to promote its international image and interact with transnational capital. Moves of support from the SAR government include the opening of the Avenue of Stars promenade at the Victoria Harbour in 2004, which is a monument to the stars of Hong Kong cinema (featuring their handprints in cement) and serves as a popular tourist destination; the 2001 opening of the Hong Kong Film Archives (which offers exhibits, screenings, and

PHOTO **4.2** Hong Kong Movie Stars Tony Leung Chiu-Wai and Carina Lau at the 2011 Asian Film Awards *(Credit: Author).*

scholarly resources of Hong Kong cinema); and the Hong Kong-Asia Film Financing Forum, which links Asian filmmakers with film financiers, producers, bankers, distributors, and buyers. Hong Kong has also hosted FILMART since 1997, the year of the territory's handover to China, an event which positions the SAR as a regional hub for entertainment distribution and co-production deal making, and in 2007 the Film Development Council was established by the Chief Executive to provide funds and training. The Hong Kong Entertainment Expo organizes FILMART as well as the Asian Film Awards, which draw Hong Kong's remaining stars (Photo 4.2). However, these sources of support were overdue and didn't adequately address the industry's need for support, which has also been hampered by an overall "deficit of information technology and skills and qualified labor" in Hong Kong society (Pun and Wu 2004: 127). Recently, there is a sense that there will be a rebirth of local film production (see Szeto and Chen 2013), especially after the 2014 Umbrella Uprising. Yet the rootedness of the Hong Kong film industry within the territory, and the style and sensibility of its films for which it became renowned, seemed, to many media personnel, to be vanishing.

The kind of support that the Hong Kong film workers attributed to the South Korean government is similar to the support that the mainland Chinese government is providing provided for its film industry. And it is mainland China's government support, through CEPA, that has arguably rejuvenated Hong Kong's film industry. For instance, Hong Kong produced 51 films in 2006. Six out of the top 10 films were made as co-productions with China. These co-productions brought mainland revenue to Hong Kong filmmakers. Since the handover, and as a result of co-productions with China, nonlocal industry personnel and audiences have resumed their prevalence in what Mirana M. Szeto and Yun-Chung Chen refer to as the Hong Kong film industry's "mainlandization" (Szeto and Chen 2013, Mainlandization or co-production section). As Szeto and Chen emphasize, "since 2006, almost half of the 50 'Hong Kong' films made every year have been co-produced" (Szeto and Chen 2013). And so we see that it is China, through CEPA, that is indeed positioned to "revitalize" Hong Kong's film industry. But while the "death narratives" that I encountered expressed fears about "parasitic" mainland Chinese making Hong Kong film workers redundant and depleting their vitality, it cannot be overlooked that the imperatives of global capital in the form of Hollywood productions (including the recent *Transformers 4: Age of Extinction*) that seek cheaper production sites such as Hong Kong's also deplete the territory's labor, energy, and resources. Quite a few film workers expressed admiration for the legacy of the British experiment in laissez-faire capitalism; a film producer told me, "The Brits did a great job with Hong Kong, and I wouldn't be like this, the way I am, without them and Hong Kong wouldn't be a great-planned city, a world-class city, without them." Yet the consequence of the management of this "world-class" global city is that this realm of cultural production requires bolstering by the governmental infrastructure of China.

PART III

Performance and Possession

CHAPTER 5

Of Ghosts and Gangsters

Capitalist Cultural Production and the Hong Kong Film Industry

The Underworlds Emerge

While watching a stunt crew prepare to film a scene in Hong Kong, members of the production gathered together in front of a table heaped with food. They held sticks of burning incense above their heads and bowed in various directions several times (Photo 5.1).

It was 2006, and stunt workers were performing *baai sahn* ("worship gods"), a Buddhist and Daoist ritual derived from Chinese popular religion in which sticks of incense and sometimes paper money (or "ghost" money) are burned not only to worship gods but, importantly, also to appease ghosts who, through such propitiation, can be persuaded to protect their propitiates instead of plaguing and possessing them. Hong Kong cosmology acknowledges the entanglement of the world of the living with that of the unliving (Constable 1994). Some film personnel, especially stunt workers, have been trained in Cantonese opera or come from opera troupe families, who are known to attribute accidents to ghosts. Opera troupes historically acknowledged ghosts as spectral audience members who enjoy the entertainment of opera (Chan 1993), and this belief has been loosely transferred to film sets, where ghosts may be drawn to the action. Therefore, appeasing mercurial ghosts is for many film personnel a casual yet indispensable part of the production process, even if they practice Christianity or Catholicism. To be sure, many personnel do not believe in ghosts, and some participate in such rituals only to appease their

PHOTO **5.1** Members of a Hong Kong Production Team, Including Stunt Workers, Burn Incense *(Credit: Author).*

boss, who in turn may only want to be seen respecting the custom. The hazards of performing violent stunts on a fast-paced schedule, however, sometimes without long-term insurance, renders ghost appeasement a shrewd tactic. As discussed in the Introduction, since some film personnel follow the convention that they may risk spirit possession when playing dying or dead characters, producers or directors usually budget a nominal fee to be dispensed to personnel as *lai see* ("lucky money") as payment for their performance and a token of respect for such provocative labor.

Yet Hong Kong film personnel are at times obligated to appease members of another unpredictable and powerful Hong Kong underworld: gangsters. Rooted in 17th-century China's imperial Qing dynasty as male secret societies, members of Hong Kong's organized crime (known as *hak seh wui* ["black societies", or triads]) have for several decades been financially and creatively involved in Hong Kong film production (see also Curtin 2007 and Stokes and Hoover 1999). Besides offering ready cash for film ventures as a ploy to launder illicit money, gangsters have a history of physically coercing actors and directors to work on gangster-financed film projects. Illicit practices are easy to perform and hard to track in an industry whose production companies ran largely on verbal agreements and secretive accounting until the late 1990s. It should be noted that graft is not unique to the Hong Kong film industry: organized crime and black market profiteers have at various points over the past century played a role in other mass-production film industries including the Hollywood, Bombay, and Cairo commercial film industries (see Ganti 2004; Horne 2001; Vitalis 2000). Yet gangster violence became so extreme in the Hong Kong industry that, in 1992, dozens of actors led by Jackie Chan marched in the financial center of Hong Kong to protest against the blackmail and firebombs, rape, and even murder of film personnel and to demand police protection. Gangster activity operates at multiple scales in Hong Kong film production, including extortion on location filming. Members of the film community spoke of triad members who have approached the film crew to demand "protection money" while filming on gangster turf in Kowloon or in the villages of the New Territories. These interruptions cost the production money and time and reinforce the shady reputation of the film industry.

The commercial film industry of Hong Kong is world renowned for its ghost and gangster films that feature spectacular on-screen images of possession and coercion. Yet I discovered that ghosts and gangsters must be taken seriously as a powerful presence *off* the screen among film personnel. In this chapter, I argue that members of these cosmological and criminal underworlds emerge as legitimate participants in the production process, influencing financial, creative, and logistical resources and decisions to play an uneven yet undeniable role in film production, alternately hampering and helping film personnel. The Hong Kong film industry has over the decades had to seek protection and render payments and propitiation to these underworlds. Thus, I posit that the diverse local practices of Hong Kong are threaded into not just representations of Hong Kong cinema but the very conditions in which filmmaking occurs; specifically, the supernatural and the criminal are woven into the operation of these late capitalist companies. This is particularly evident given that location filming, which constitutes much of the footage in Hong Kong films, sometimes occurs in actual graveyards or on gangster turf, demonstrating that scripted media are created in evocative and unruly "social spaces" (Spitulnik 2002: 338), not just rationally managed studios. Such production practices also reveal that while ghost and gangster films have become carefully censored for the mainland Chinese market across the border (due in part to their "feudalistic" content), these distinct Hong Kong experiences and worlds remain embedded in the filmmaking *process*, evidence of the resilience of Hong Kong culture in the face of Hong Kong's 1997 "handover" to China as a Special Administrative Region.

My intention here is to demonstrate that by situating media production processes in their broader cultural context, we see how sociocultural forces that are generally considered beyond the scope of Western media institutional and organizational studies play several salient roles in the production process. There is less gangster involvement in very recent years, but it has left its mark on the industry. These underworlds constitute material forces that have over the years created conditions and contingencies in the filmmaking process. Traditional Chinese organizations such as male secret societies that used violence extend to contemporary commercial film production. Accounts of "culture/al industries" such as film and television typically analyze how "collaborations" are formed and "constraints" arise and are addressed (Hesmondhalgh 2007: 37; Levine 2001:68). Here, I examine how in the Hong Kong film industry members from the two underworlds also collaborate with and constrain film personnel in the production process. In contrast to a process that has been largely addressed in conventional political economic and industry terms, cosmological and criminal underworlds demand alternative forms of payment occurring during film production. These include ritual payments to ghosts such as the *baai sahn* (incense and ghost money) and the *lai see* to vulnerable actors and stunt workers, as well as protection money to gangsters who harass film crews on location. These seemingly marginal entities, in fact, exert control that at times resembles managerial power, demanding terms of labor even from star actors. Since the majority of the gangsters involved in film production and the managerial class of film personnel are male, female film workers are a particularly vulnerable segment of the labor force. Male gangsters may constrain female film personnel in particular whether they work in front of or behind the camera, contributing to the film industry's dubious social status within Hong Kong. The film industry has historically been considered by many in Hong Kong society to be *lo pin moon* (involvement in a "slanted door" business, as opposed to a 'straight door' business such as law or medicine) (see also Curtin 2007: 75). Further, my analysis reveals the paradox that while Hong Kong is frequently characterized as a hub of market rationality (Ong 2006), these cosmological and criminal elements that appear to be "outside" the rationale of law, science, and reason are in fact part of a modern, capitalist industry.

I contend that the presence of cosmology and crime in filmmaking illustrates that media industries are not "disenchanted"; filmmaking does not necessarily occur in a "postsacred, postfeudal" modernity (Singer 2001) as many studies of media industries and organizations have assumed. Nor are the enchantments of industrial production confined to "other" locales such as Hong Kong. As Hortense Powdermaker noted and

I observed during research in Hollywood, the production processes of the Los Angeles-based film industry are also not free of religious practices and illicit economic activity when addressing risk and accountability. Studio sound stages, numbered, would skip "unlucky" thirteen. Media personnel on Hollywood sets gave tarot card readings between shots on film and television sets, especially among extras and in actors' trailers, made visits to psychics, and collected icons of St. Clare of Assisi that were brought onto the set and into trailers. Indeed, a range of cultural expressions are apparent in media industries, especially those located in liberalized environments where we see the growth of "hyperrationalization with the exuberant spread of innovative occult practices and money magic" (Comaroff and Comaroff 2000: 292).

This chapter demonstrates that authority and labor control can operate beyond conventional managerial forces or corporate structures. I illustrate how the two underworlds are linked through a shared logic of propitiation as well as violent claims on the bodies of film workers, both even evoking the specter of death. Apparently it is not only the product but also the process that features violence. By making these shadowy underworlds visible in the process of filmmaking, the visceral, possessive nature of production becomes more apparent. Ghosts are understood to be drawn to displays of violence, capable of interfering with the filmmaking process by breaking camera equipment or possessing an actor. Performing violence on a film set is provocative as it renders film personnel vulnerable to spirit possession. Gangsters also make claims on the bodies and labor power of film personnel, such as physically and financially coercing film workers into working on films and dictating the financial terms of their labor. They are known to invest as a form of money laundering as well as resorting to coercive control tactics, and some film personnel commented that gangster associations are among the reasons why the colonial government did not support the film industry. The participation of ghosts and gangsters in film production has become evident to the public in relation to star actors, as news reports have covered the harassment of star actors (for whom the gangsters are valuable commodities in trying to secure funding) and the spirit possession of star actors, even though less visible film personnel are also at risk from these forces. Yet while ghosts and gangsters provoke risk-filled conditions for film personnel, they also provide favorable filming conditions such as accident-free film shoots or the financing necessary for a film project.

As Sylvia Yanagisako argues in her ethnography of Italian family firms, capitalist work and culture are not separate domains but mutually constituted through everyday practices with workers shaped by culturally and historically specific contexts (Yanagisako 2002: 5–6). The unlikely combination of ghost and gangster collaborators in the production process testifies to how cultural logics, even seemingly irrational ones, are not separable from rationalistic production processes. We must be attuned to the culturally specific ways people understand labor uncertainty and exploitation. Ethnographic study of such cultural activity also unveils the perils of production at the heart of capitalism that results in phenomena such as zombie labor and spirit possession found in South Africa and Malaysia (Comaroff and Comaroff 1999; Ong 1987). Performing violence and death in the context of mass production invokes shady elements and specters of death. Nighttime work, remote locations, gangsterism, and a lack of codified regulations for physical and financial protection amid the stark wealth and social inequality of Hong Kong can lead to expressions of locally nuanced anxiety and exhaustion. Jean Comaroff and John Comaroff's writings on "occult economies" are relevant here, since in their examination of capitalism they use this notion to characterize the ways in which wealth is achieved through the involvement of the supernatural and the criminal as market reform is an uneven and uncertain experience. The instability of the labor systems that postcolonial, postsocialist, and postrevolutionary societies generate, combined with neoliberalism's invocation to privatization and entrepreneurship, lead Comaroff and Comaroff to conclude that occult economies operate beyond *"the conventional, the rational, the moral"* (Comaroff and Comaroff 2000: 316, italics added). Corruption that has occurred in both the colonial and postcolonial Hong Kong film industry becomes apparent through gangster tactics such as physical and financial coercion, and, combined with spirit possession on film sets, reveals another iteration of the vampiric nature of capitalist production (Comaroff and Comaroff 1999: 289).

These payments and appeasements of ghosts and gangsters may not appear to be conventional film production processes; nevertheless, they encompass Hong Kong's commercial film industry. Yet in contrast to accounts of spirit possession and shamanism as ambivalent reactions in emerging market economies (see Buyandelgeriyn 2007; Kendall 1996; Ong 1987; Taussig 1980; Weller 1994a), ghost appeasement among Hong Kong film personnel is not a new response to the introduction of capitalism. Indeed, industrial capitalist relations have predominated in Hong Kong for many decades, with Hong Kong's post-World War II laissez-faire policy as evidence that "colonial Hong Kong has long been operating on a logic similar to neoliberalism" (Szeto and Chen 2013: 241). Ghost appeasement in the film industry represents a casual yet common business tactic in confronting the various risks of production (it is also a protocol among many small business owners). In fact, the specter of ghosts and the practice of *baai sahn* in Hong Kong have remained even as the capitalist colony transitioned to nominally communist leadership under China as a Special Administrative Region in 1997. The juxtaposition of cosmological and criminal entities emerges in a fashion other than expected in a territory that is commonly presented as a hub of market rationality and capitalist calculation (Ong 2006). What becomes apparent, then, is that payments and appeasements to the underworlds—which signal the risks of film production—are expressions of the diverse economic and cultural practices that make up capitalist production.

Performance, Payment, Possession

The Hong Kong film industry consists of a variety of film production companies. Some are divisions of multinational firms based in Southeast Asia and China; some are small independent companies based in Hong Kong that are formed only for the production phase and then disband; some are vertically integrated firms with distribution and exhibition divisions. The industry lacked government subsidies and import quotas. The prevalence of studios such as Shaw Bros., which discouraged unions (Rodriguez 1999), and some of the gangster-related production companies helped create the conditions in which marginal social forces, particularly gangsters, could come to act as material forces in the production process. Fast-paced filming and quick turnaround by both major studios and independent production companies meant that film personnel worked long hours on film projects without consistent union protections, as was particularly the case during peak production in the 1980s to the mid-1990s (Stokes and Hoover 1999).

Colonial and local indifference and minimal regulations in both the colonial and postcolonial periods have allowed gangsters to exert force within the industry and dampen union efforts. The lack of colonial and postcolonial government support and involvement in the Hong Kong film industry is one of the main reasons its productivity has declined (see also Chan, Fung, and Ng 2010). The absence of a film commission and minimally enforced or consistent police protection for location filming and personnel were other challenges to industry sustainability. Aggressive pre-sells and money laundering, as well as predation and extortion on film sites, granted gangsters something akin to managerial power. Reports of spirit possession and interference occurred while working on around-the-clock productions funded by triads, revealing the intersection of the two underworlds.

It is therefore not surprising that ghosts and gangsters constitute integral and interrelated features of the discursive frameworks from which film personnel create media, since both ghosts and gangsters figure as common referents in the actual sociocultural landscape of Hong Kong. Popular religious practices combining Buddhism, Daoism, and Confucianism among Hong Kong people include ghost appeasement (Constable 1994; Feuchtwang 1974; Wolf 1974). This practice, *baai sahn*, is used when making offerings to supernatural entities. Gods are also propitiated, and in film production offices and studios I observed altars dedicated to the God General Guan. However, I focus on ghosts in this account as it is they who threaten to interfere with filming by breaking cameras, can ruin a shot by appearing in it, and possess personnel.[1] Like gangsters, ghosts are morally ambiguous forces, whereas gods stand apart as revered, virtuous figures. Gangsters, infamous for combating corrupt officials with their fraternal force and loyalty (see Ong 1999), hold near-iconic status in the popular culture of Hong Kong. There is frequent media attention devoted to the exploits and capture of gangs; moreover, they operate and own many of the clubs, bars, massage parlors, and brothels that ordinary Hong Kong people frequent (Chu 2000).

Ghosts and gangsters feature in the production rituals, processes, and reflexivity of film personnel. Film projects frequently start with ritual offerings to ghosts, as well as gods, on astrologically auspicious days, and protection money is paid to gangsters. Even in extratextual discourse such as "behind-the-scenes" footage on DVDs, as well as film production company websites and Chinese—and English-language print media, film productions are seen attending *baai sahn* or *hoih geng laih* ("open lens ceremony"). *Hoih geng laih* is the ceremony conducted by the cast and crew for the first day of filming; it includes eating barbequed pig, lighting incense, and asking for good fortune from a range of spiritual forces, including ghosts. This event is usually covered by Hong Kong newspapers and magazines.

The gangsters have also left their mark on the film industry and the Hong Kong public's perception of it. A few films parody the Hong Kong film industry and even show the financial and physical involvement of gangsters within the film industry.[2] These are among the ways in which the film industry represents itself to the public.

Ghosts •

Ghostly involvement in entertainment is in part a legacy of Chinese opera, which attributed accidents to ghosts and also acknowledged them as audience members who are drawn to the entertainment of opera (Chan 1993). Some film personnel—especially stunt workers—were trained in Cantonese opera or come from opera troupe families. According to popular Chinese religion, ghosts are the unsettled spirits of generally disreputable individuals— rogues and thieves—who met unsavory deaths or are people who died far from home (see Constable 1994; Feuchtwang 1974; Weller 1994a and b, 2000; Wolf 1974). The landscape is believed to be haunted by restless ghosts who are "hungry" for food and entertainment and for individuals to possess. Since ghosts are believed to be roaming through the world of the living, seeking amusement, theater troupes schedule publicly staged operas for the ghosts' entertainment (Constable 1994: 111), even leaving some seats empty for these spectral spectators. Various festivals throughout the Chinese lunar year, such as *Yu Laan Jit* (Hungry Ghost Festival), are devoted to feeding and entertaining these roaming ghosts. Ghosts are usually believed to lack descendants to propitiate them, and many Hong Kong Chinese are willing to placate possibly troublesome ghosts to show respect. People make substantial offerings to them, which include lighting incense and burning paper money and even paper effigies of material goods for which they think the ghosts yearn in their afterlife, such as cellphones, Manolo Blahnik shoes, and cigarettes. Ghosts are also perceived as lingering near businesses where socially ambiguous behaviors are enacted, such as bars, massage parlors, and performance sites. Many industries and independently owned businesses in Hong Kong feature altars where employees burn incense and paper money and make offerings to gods for success and ghosts for appeasement.[3]

Filming on location can be particularly perilous for film personnel. Outdoor filming in urban centers is neither a simple nor an inexpensive matter: it entails permit licenses and fees that must be budgeted for, as well as hiring security or law enforcement to subdue traffic and passersby. Outdoor filming is generally quieter and cheaper late at night. Yet late-night filming in dark, quiet places can also attract "hungry" ghosts who are emboldened to appear after dark, thus rendering nighttime shoots a spiritually hazardous time for film personnel. Performances on film sets, especially in dark, abandoned, open-air locations where they may already be prowling, provide amusement for ghosts and perhaps the opportunity to temporarily possess vulnerable personnel such as tired camera operators or injured stunt workers. According to many film personnel, filming content of a violent nature renders one particularly susceptible to spirit possession. Film personnel shared stories of spirit sightings or possession on film sets, or spectral interference in the form of equipment suddenly breaking and unexpected changes in weather.

Stunt coordinator Wong, who has worked in the Hong Kong film industry for over 35 years as a martial arts and stunt performer, comes from a long family line of Cantonese opera performers and martial artists. While recounting his experiences as a young teen performing opera with his grandfather, he explained that the spectators who enjoyed such performances were not solely human: included among them were ghosts. Wong explained,

> Operas are performed to entertain ghosts. When I was on the stage I did *baai sahn*. If we don't worship, then there'll be an accident. Or a possession. People sometimes ask the possessed, "Why are you in the body?" There may be a voice, "I just want to watch a performance!" Sometimes, a person is possessed by the ghost of a dead performer.

Yet ghosts were integral to the behind-the-scenes activity as well. Acrobatics and stunts were performed on the stage without wires or extensive safety regulations, and, given such risks, performers prayed for successful performances, since accidents or misfortune would be commonly attributed to angry or mischievous ghosts. In fact, it was not uncommon for sticks of burning incense to be placed at the edge of the stage to appease the spirits and deities that performers believed would protect them from falling off the stage (see also Chan 1993: 176).

And as with opera, ghosts are also drawn to film production sites because they can enjoy the performances for the camera, and possibly possess a vulnerable individual. As Wong indicates, the relationship between cosmology and performance existed even before films were made. Barbara Ward points out that opera troupes have been hired by local communities to perform at temple festivals in honor of local deities, even performing exorcisms for members of the community in the manner of priests and mediums (Ward 1979: 32; see also Chan 1993: 176). Some actors also worshipped Wah Kwong (the god of fire), while crew members worshipped Lu Ban (the god of construction). Ward calls particular attention to the liminality of actors in many societies; "in some strangely uncanny way they appeared to incarnate or act as mediums for spirits, whether of gods, mythical beings, or heroes, or—at the very least—men and women other than themselves" (Ward 1979: 33). Given the historical religious role of actors, the rationalistic and secular assumptions in organizational and industry-based media studies need to be reconsidered.

Gangsters

While filmgoing offers escapism for audiences, filmmaking offers gangsters the lure of rapid enrichment through the alchemy of laundering and theft, methods increasingly used in other liberalized economies (Comaroff and Comaroff 1999: 293). While on the set of a producer whom she admires for his "clean" tactics, an actress who chooses her film projects carefully told me, "Hong Kong is trying to look like the West, but it's still the 'Wild West.' Permits aren't needed, and it's run by gangsters." The gangsters, or triads, control many of the bars and discos and much of the drug dealing and prostitution in Hong Kong through "protection" services (Chu 2000: 43). Gangsters usually invest in many industries for a quick profit and are a palpable socioeconomic force in Hong Kong. The gangsters have been mythologized in popular culture as male secret societies formed by Shaolin Temple monks during the Qing dynasty that fought to restore the native Chinese Ming dynasty. However, as the archives of the Qing dynasty have become accessible, scholars have discovered that the *Tiandihui* (Heaven and Earth Society) was established in 1761 or 1762 as a "mutual protection society," which evolved as a response to social conflicts among ethnic groups in southern provinces of China (Chu 2000: 12; Murray and Qin 1994: 1). In the 1760s, the *Tiandihui* and associated clusters formed a decentralized unit that linked unknown men into various brotherhoods and offered protection to people migrating through southern China to Hong Kong (Chu 2000: 12). From its earliest days, "members were involved in different types of organized crime, especially the selling of private protection to those who needed to travel frequently for a living" (Chu 2000: 12). By the late 1780s, the *Tiandihui* and associated clusters were deemed illegal by the Qing government and "were forced to go underground" or change their name (Chu 2000: 12–13). The *Tiandihui*'s activities included "mutual aid, collective violence, and rebellion" (Murray and Qin 1994: 22). Starting in the 19th century, local labor markets in Hong Kong such as street hawking were overtaken by various triad societies, increasing gangster visibility and control. A few years after occupying Hong Kong, the British outlawed triads, some of which were involved in criminal activities such as opium smuggling, piracy, and theft, as well as Republican activities across the border (Sinn 1989:13); for instance, Sun Yat-sen used secret societies to overthrow the Qing dynasty in 1911. In the 20th century, gangs spread across East Asia and into various Western countries as transnational networks. In contemporary Hong Kong, gangs are understood to be organized as "small pyramids led by area bosses at district level and connected by a form of cartel" (Chu 2000: 135).

The lore of gangsters as resisting state or foreign powers has surfaced in Hong Kong culture, especially cinema. The gangster genre is one of the most popular in Hong Kong film, and even in films that are not labeled a crime or heist genre, there are frequent depictions of mostly male gangsters. Contemporary gangsters have been canonized in Hong Kong films for upholding the values of fraternal loyalty and heroics and fighting against the corruption of (mainly British) state officers and control (Ong 1999: 161–165). According to recent scholarship on triads, they enter certain businesses in order to monopolize a market or recoup stolen property or debts. As Yiu Kong Chu argues in his study of triads, gang members of varying ages "offer" what he refers to as "protection services" to male and female entrepreneurs in uncertain economic climates (Chu 2000). Many businesses are forced to accept (or in some cases, solicit) protection from a particular gang so as to stave off attacks from rival gangs. Thus, displays of violence are understood by some gangsters and businesspeople as necessary for substantiating gangsters' reputation as protectors.

The Spectral in the Spectacle: Constraints and Collaborations

As mentioned in the Introduction, some Hong Kong people consider photographing or filming the deceased as disrespectful. This perspective is expressed in the film community; numerous informants remarked that filming the deceased is a dubious action that can invite misfortune for the living from offended ghosts, a consideration in an industry where death is frequently simulated and filming occurs in cemeteries. The threat of offending spirits necessitates respect for the risk undertaken in these spectacles of death through the offer of *lai see*, which can be as little as 100HKD (US$13) to avoid possession. The payment serves as a form of protection to the performer as well as the rest of the production team to appease any *gwei* ("spirits") who may be drawn to the performance and imagery of death and violence. Spirits may already be lurking among the living

Ghosts constrain film personnel in multiple ways, and avoidance and appeasement tactics are incorporated into film production processes as rituals including burning incense and paper money. Many film personnel attributed the breakneck speed of production, the long hours of filming in uncomfortable conditions, especially at night, and in some cases filming in locations with bad *feng shui* (such as dark, cold, abandoned places) to spectral forces. As a result, time and money may be spent on ceremonies to protect film personnel from ghosts. Production companies may bring in a *sifu* ("master") who can exorcise ghosts if there has been exposure to them—a hazard of filming in provocative public spaces such as cemeteries. Kelly, a costume designer, attended location scouting for a ghost film.[4] Days later, production members alerted Kelly that something "ghostly" had been captured in still photos taken at the cemetery they scouted. Everyone involved was asked to attend a ceremony in which a *sifu* hired by the production would assess each person to check for any lurking ghosts, and exorcise them. Kelly did not believe there were any ghosts in the photos or around her and was one of the few who did not attend the ceremony, a decision respected by her co-workers. Yet she was not surprised that something was detected in the photos and that a ceremony was planned, reflecting how commonplace such a confrontation with the supernatural in the pursuit of cinematic spectacle can be.

A female producer, Jessie, commented on the attitude of respect toward ghosts as a production tactic:

> There's a Confucian saying about ghosts: "Respect them but keep a distance." You never know til your dying day if they exist—so show respect. It's ok to burn incense on location. Movie-making is not like math; it's a bet, a gamble—who will make money? I think movies are a business that needs positive energy. Positive energy is more important than anything else. So you burn incense for every location and show respect to them.

When I asked Jessie if she would make a ghost movie, she laughed and cringed: "I'm too scared to make a ghost movie! To write a ghost film, you really have to really engage with ghosts. This can be a problem. And we only have creative meetings at night—9:30 pm to 3:00 am. And ghosts are there."

Local folk beliefs about social spaces such as cemeteries intersect with the risks of a production process that frequently continues around the clock. One summer night in 2006 I attended a late-night film shoot in Kennedy Town. This film was directed by Jack, a veteran director of many ghost and action movies. The crew hurriedly yet deftly moved camera equipment about in hushed tones while the director rehearsed a scene between two actors playing gangsters who fight in a car, demonstrating for one of the actors how to angle and fire his prop gun at the other. Even at 1 a.m., it was hot and sticky, and the smoke from the actors' cigarettes hung in the humid air, as did the smoke from the sticks of incense burning in a small incense pot on the ground. The *cha seui* ("tea-water lady") came around to offer the cast and crew cool, moist towels and cups of tea. The atmosphere on set was tense, as they were under pressure to complete a series of action shots that night. I asked one of the crew about the burning incense. "It's to keep the ghosts away, and the mosquitos," she answered. On this frantic production schedule, there was no time for ghostly interference in the form of accidents or rain.

A few days later, Jack told me that in his effort to run a "smooth set," conducting *baai sahn* is very important. He commented that although ghost films are financially practical to make (darkly lit film sites are less costly because they require less electricity), they pose spiritual risks. Filming during the night, especially in remote or abandoned sites, can invite ghosts who may interfere in the filming process by possessing a member of the film. He recounted a ghostly episode from the making of a popular Hong Kong film that he had directed about people coming back from the dead:

> A scene was shot in an unused part of town in the middle of the night. The lead actress was supposed to react to the evidence of ghosts, created through special effects. At the end of each take, the production assistant would replace the props and set the shot up again. The crew was very alert. But a few production personnel saw that far away there was a guy who didn't respond to their calls to leave the area while we were filming. They would call out to him, but they saw that this person had no reaction. So instead of scaring the rest of the crew, they just made a traditional sign used to ward off a spirit possession, in this case putting two chopsticks on either side of the middle finger. It worked, and the guy reacted. He then seemed shocked to find himself so. It turned out that he was one of our crew guys. This crew person was temporarily possessed, due to it being a dark, abandoned place.

Another director shared his experiences with avoidance and appeasement tactics. On a late summer afternoon, I met Andy outside a Daoist temple in Sheung Wan, which he had visited for a previous film project with several producers to perform rituals to propitiate the ghosts and gods. Andy explained that it is important to perform *baai sahn* when dealing with lurking ghosts who may be attracted to the performance as well as the technical equipment used on film sets. While sitting in a cafe, he shared pictures of himself with his producer and lead actress lighting incense on the set of his last film, and then recounted how, while filming a scene for this movie in a cemetery, the camera suddenly stopped working:

> It's funny, because the camera had been working that day in all the sites we shot in, but once we got to the cemetery, in the middle of the night, it

just stopped. You know, the cemetery was being exhumed . . . that may have had something to do with it.

The release of supernatural energies during the exhumation posed a risk for the film production, as well as the usual logistical constraints of filming at any location. Yet the curious episode did not stop there:

> After filming in the cemetery all night, we saw on the playback [monitor] a white blob rush past the camera. But there was no one there, and then I realized it's a crew guy being lit from behind. But the D.P. [cinematographer] says he only lit in one place and didn't put the light where it would need to be to have lit that crew person. You know, I watched that footage over and over, and I know I saw something there. It wasn't the crew guy, but what was it? So of course the next day we lit more incense!

As with many other productions of ghost and horror films, it was cheaper and easier for the production to film in an actual cemetery than to take the time and effort to recreate one in a studio. The filmmaker also felt that the setting lent the film shoot the sense of realism that is so fetishized among many filmmakers. Creating spectacle in these dark, abandoned, socially ambiguous places can evoke the spectral forces that are already implicit in the production process.

Stunt coordinator Wong, who has performed death-defying stunts himself, recalled witnessing a possession while working on a film that required the cast and crew to work nearly around the clock for many days:

> It's an old place, very early in the morning, when ghosts are around. I had worked many hours; for one week, I never went home once. I drove my car to the set, and as we had a break, I took a nap in my car. I asked my assistant to wake me up when my crew arrives. So he slept somewhere, and I found out later that all the other guys had also napped there in the same place. They said to me, "Wong, do you feel something wrong?" I didn't. Everybody who slept there got possessed, but I'm the exception. When you're possessed, you don't move, you feel a certain way. Another guy took a nap there where we were, and suddenly he awoke and he couldn't move. A little boy comes over and complains to him, "Why do you sleep on my bed?" But there is no little boy on set there that day. No boy should be there on set that day. The guy couldn't yell, he couldn't get up, he couldn't do anything. You can feel it when you are filming in old, abandoned places.

Wong recalled the days when he first performed film stunts in the 1970s, and how the threat of physical injuries was intensified by having to perform under very tight deadlines. These deadlines were imposed by the demand for mass-produced films, shot on the quick and cheap, underscoring how dangerous work conditions are shaped largely by the market and managerial forces:

> You need airbags and pads for high falls, it's a must for stunts. But if you fall from so high, it's no use. I've done falls from seven stories high. For the falls, they use crates, they put all of them together, and put mattresses on them, that's it! When I was a stuntman, I was injured a lot, everywhere. There was no protection. And always, there is the pressure of time and money. You have to work so fast. It is hard to be so safe when you have to work so fast.

Given the physical dangers and uncertainties of film production and the fact that many of Hong Kong's first films were adaptations of Cantonese opera, it is not surprising that theater superstitions and ghost appeasement resurface in film productions, connecting contemporary cast and crew members to the film industry's historical roots in traditional Cantonese opera theater. Even today Hong Kong stunt workers rely upon the goodwill of their fellow stunt workers if they are injured, since many film productions lack adequate long-term accident insurance or worker's compensation.

Accountability is another feature of cultural production with which film personnel must contend. While ghosts carry the potential to harm film personnel, they can also help others, particularly the managerial class. Ghost appeasement serves as a way to manage the unpredictable, and producers and directors have told me that in many cases they prefer to attribute accountability for problems that might arise to nonhuman forces instead of themselves, a shrewd tactic in an industry rife with speculation and risk. "Why should I be responsible when failure can be blamed on an angry ghost?" one producer in Hong Kong asked me. This sentiment was echoed by many producers and directors. "It is better to fail because of the ghosts than to fail on your own account," several other directors told me.

Producers and directors also encourage their crews to appease ghosts on film sets as a team-building activity that they claim provides a sense of unity. Many of the cast and crew refuse to work without *baai sahn*. In fact, film workers often casually refer to it as "insurance," since not all Hong Kong film productions have in the past been able to buy accident insurance for their cast and crew members, and in the absence of strong unionized labor, there are very few organizations that represent the interests of film personnel.[5] One director who would frequently express skepticism about *baai sahn* complained that sometimes it is instrumentalized as a cheap solution to considerable technical and safety issues. Yet this same director said of *baai sahn*, "When I've done it, the shoot is great; when I haven't, it's catastrophic. That's the thing—it always somehow works," he laughed. Wong said,

> On every film I'm always asked by the boss [film producer] to do *baai sahn*. Whenever there is any kind of accident, there is always the quick response of "Burn incense!" You know, have you heard that expression, "There's no such thing as accidents"? During filming, there's no "accidents."

After I observed a new film company gather together to light incense for a successful venture, one of the production company members told me that a spirit possession is sometimes glossed as a "safety valve" for workplace tensions. Working long hours late into the night together in frequently physically uncomfortable conditions can lead to flared tempers. Even tabloids occasionally attribute discord between co-workers to spirit possession.[6]

Holding ghosts accountable may add to the mystique of why a film succeeds from its inception to reception; it also reinforces the extra-rational dangers of the conditions of the commercial filmmaking process.

Gangsterism: Constraints and Collaborations

Film productions have learned to budget for protection payments on location filming. One of the biggest quandaries for film personnel in these situations is authenticity: which is the real gang the production should pay? Filming on the streets of Hong Kong (versus filming inside a studio) has become a site for "turf wars" between rival gangs. The production risks losing more money than was budgeted to the competing gangs. Below are shared experiences of film personnel in dealing with gangsters on location. One of them, Jessie, describes how she used her gender, which was seen as a handicap in advancing within the film industry and dealing with gangs, as leverage to resist gangster intimidation in public space.

When Jessie started out in the film industry, she worked as a production assistant. Typical of that time, Jessie's family was not enthusiastic about her choice of career, given that the film industry was not considered entirely respectable for young women to join, due in part to its long hours in remote locations, nighttime filming schedules, exposure to a largely male workforce, and association with criminal elements. Jessie promised her family that she would not pick up smoking and swearing from her male film colleagues. Popular films were kung fu and stunt action, and the off-screen dynamics of creativity and production were "chauvinistic" according to Jessie: "It was better to be a guy. Men think women work in the industry as a production manager, not a writer or director. Be a coordinator or secretary. There were no women producers or directors." Nevertheless, Jessie was excited to pursue her dream of making films. She was soon promoted to production manager:

> As a female production manager I was good and hardworking. Those days were chauvinistic, but women are more hardworking than men, we have more stamina. We are more tolerant than men, "face" is not so important to us. My personality helped me rise. I was a hard worker and persistent. When I scouted apartments for location, I was not afraid to look at dozens of apartments and hear "no." I was optimistic. But it was hard.

Jessie soon learned that part of her job was dealing with the contingencies of location filming, which can constitute as much as two thirds of the film shoot schedule. Thus the immediate public space in which filming occurs—and its inseparability from the social landscape of the territory—to a large degree determines the terms of filming. This can include not only weather and crowd control but the interference of gangsters, who may control certain districts of the city and demand "protection money" from restaurants and other businesses on their "turf." A gangster, generally a large man, would position himself in front of the camera and in some cases threaten to break it or steal it if not paid. Gangsters may also exert control in the rural areas of Hong Kong where a lot of filming occurs, such as the New Territories. The remoteness of rural areas allows gangsters to aggressively demand payment from the production crew, whether it be in the form of protection money or "donations" to village temples.

The potential for gang interruption could impede a female film worker's involvement in the industry because for location work, female personnel are seen as more vulnerable to triad intimidation. Numerous women I interviewed attested to this. Jessie explained that the common perception within the industry was, "Guys are better with the triad, with the protection money guy. Especially in the New Territories." Jessie described,

> In the New Territories, sometimes the person approaching us would ask: "Do you know who this area belongs to? Do you know the rules?" They will stand in front of the camera. It's annoying, it wastes your time and time is money. You must negotiate with them. You have to make sure *this* is the right person to bribe, because you can pay the wrong

person, someone pretending to be in charge, and then you have to pay again, the real person. And then you can exceed your budget. So you have to have your assistant go to the location first and ask around first to see who to deal with, who can protect us. I always had a man do this.

Of the urban districts Jessie said,

In Wan Chai, Tsim Sha Tsui, Western, it's hard. We need some connections so you don't pay twice. For one day of filming with a triad asking for protection money, I would call police. But for more days of filming, I need to make a deal with them. Because I will be there longer. And it's always a risk. You never know who'll approach you.

Jessie explained, however, that she played upon the gender dynamics when dealing with male gangsters. In urban film locations, Jessie assumed that bystanders would protect her from triad brutality in the open. Laughingly she recounted, "In the city I was bold, I made a good deal [with them]. They wouldn't attack me in the street in front of people, I assumed. A woman."

In scenarios resembling a plotline from Hong Kong films, various film productions that participants worked on over the years would be harassed and held up by gang members while filming on location. Wong explained that when he worked in the film industry, the Hong Kong government maintained its distance from the predatory tactics of gangsters toward the film community:

In different districts, all over Hong Kong, different triad come up during location shooting and threaten to disrupt it. They ask for who is in charge of money and threaten to make noise while we were recording audio, or they throw rubbish at the camera. It happened all the time. This was a real problem for us. This is why we need the police to stay. It's cheaper for us to pay a cop to protect us than to pay off triad. But in Hong Kong we can't hire cops to clear the street. The police tell Hong Kong productions that they lack the manpower. They [the cops] do it afterwards, after hours, as an extra job, with no police uniform. They are then a security guard. It's good for the cop because he gets double pay. But it's not good for us, because without a cop in uniform, he doesn't scare the triad away.

Gangsters have become dramatis personae off screen. When first contacting film production companies and studios in Hong Kong, a few informants advised me against asking pointed questions about illicit activity or connections in interviews. As a director remarked, "In Hong Kong, our movies are influenced by triad culture, because production already has those kind of people. The triads run everything, just like in the movies." Starting in the 1990s, members of organized crime who saw the opportunity to launder their "black" money from illegal activities by proffering it as available cash for filmmaking began to play a bigger role in film production (Curtin 1999: 37–38). With local films backed by illicit money, production schedules had to move very quickly so that the "black" money was washed within a short period of time, thereby avoiding the scrutiny of legal and administrative sectors. While many gangsters left the film industry after it started its descent in the late 1990s, some remain involved in the industry, particularly distribution and piracy. Their reputation for intimidation, for coercion in the labor process such as who performs in which films, their pay, and their terms of involvement, led most informants to respond to my queries about the lack of unionization within the film industry with replies about gangster control. Some film personnel have left Hong Kong due to the strong-arm policies of triad. Ties to gangsters have even affected some film personnel's ability to obtain entry to and citizenship of various countries.

There are various ways in which gangsters manage the labor of film personnel, such as physical and financial coercion (see also Stokes and Hoover 1999: 30–33). One of a producer's main tasks is called "pre-selling," in which they assemble "bankable" stars for lucrative film projects so that they can sell the rights to (usually overseas) distribution companies. The pre-sell is crucial since it provides the capital and cash necessary to make the film, which, once distributed and ostensibly popular due to its star power, will reap a profit. Yet the distributors' money from the pre-sell is not always enough to sustain the length of the production, and producers are usually desperate for a cash infusion toward the end of filming. This is the point at which gangsters enter: they save the film by injecting amounts of cash at a phase in production when producers are vulnerable, making them susceptible to extortion. The gangsters also formed their own production companies, or stables, wherein they themselves would assemble star actors, which they would then pre-sell as a package to distributors. Gangster producers have used their particular brand of force (such as blackmail and physical and sexual forms of brutality) to pressure film personnel to appear in or work on film projects of the gangster's choosing; on occasions when actors, their managers, or producers or directors have been reluctant, there have been harmful physical consequences. Gangster employers are also notorious for not paying the cast and crew their full salaries.

Actors are among the film workers most coerced by gangsters since they are highly commodified: it is their star power that can frequently secure funding from overseas investors. Hence, there is a somewhat paradoxical division in labor control among film workers: while below-the-line camera operators, makeup artists, and sound technicians may be able to self-manage their careers, the high-profile and higher-paid actors (and, in some cases, directors) sometimes lack control over theirs. The exploitation of star power has led to several high-profile Hong Kong actors choosing to work outside of Hong Kong. Some actors I observed and interviewed were forthcoming about the role of the illegal sector in the film community. An actress introduced me to an actor who has worked on both Hong Kong and Hollywood productions. She told me, "He doesn't work with triad. And so he doesn't work much." The actor and I discussed the difference between Hollywood and Hong Kong film productions—the hours, the organization of labor, and the ways in which actors were treated. When I asked him about the lack of unions in the Hong Kong film industry he said, "We don't have unions. We have the Triad. They are 'the union.' While they remain involved we will never have real unions. This is just something you have to deal with in Hong Kong."

Although technically there are unions and guilds, this remark was echoed by many members of the Hong Kong film. The industry's shift from a Fordist mode of production to post-Fordist capital accumulation did not extinguish the persistence of mafia-like labor systems, some of which are family run and frequently patriarchal in character (Harvey 1991: 152). Unions—which are intended to safeguard workers' rights and protect salaries and the rights of film workers – do not really resemble gangster-controlled production as some Hong Kong film personnel claimed. Film personnel are largely the instrument of coercive forces that exploit their labor, whereas unions are ostensibly an organization for film workers' empowerment and protection, facilitated by collective bargaining (which was not allowed under colonial rule or now, under postcolonial rule). Nevertheless, many Hong Kong film personnel expressed their view that that there is some resemblance between the centralized power of a union and the gangsters.

Numerous female film workers spoke longingly of instituting standardized business practices and professionalization; they saw those as a way to confer more respectability on their work and protect them from harassment. For actresses in particular, modesty in on-screen behavior and off-screen morality were common themes. Several informants confided that their families disapproved of their on- and off-screen obligations, which included sexualized portrayals on camera and sexualized demands made of them off screen. An actress, at the beginning of her acting career, was expected to entertain dubious producers and their cronies at late-night parties and karaoke bars as a supplement to her paltry income. The prevalence of male gangsterism in the industry has reinforced the patriarchal characteristics of capitalism—characteristics that, recalling Jessie's family members' concerns, likely contribute to why there are fewer female directors and few female cinematographers.

At the same time, Jessie acknowledged that gangsters played multiple roles in film production, and as collaborators, they facilitated film production as they could provide the finances necessary to get the project launched. They could also provide creative inspiration for filmmakers. "When I first started, one producer brought in a mafia guy—oh, he was very interesting, she laughed." Numerous filmmakers have over the years spoofed gangster figures in a few films. Importantly, some filmmakers benefit from the heft and scale of contacts for film production and distribution that gangsters can provide, particularly for distribution in China. "Their relationships in China can be very helpful," Jessie stated, underscoring the need for a robust and resourceful social network within a vast and diverse media landscape. "They can be very generous. And sometimes very knowledgeable about film," she said.

Reciprocity and (Self) Censorship of Ghosts and Gangsters

Intriguingly, there is an intimate relationship between off-screen ghosts and gangsters that illuminates the risks of filmmaking and reveals their participation as both collaborators and constraints. In a reciprocal manner, gangsters propitiate ghosts and ghosts protect gangsters, and this interconnectivity comes to be expressed within the workings of the film industry. While many people propitiate ghosts, gangsters in particular appease them since they can expect to receive the protection of ghosts who, unlike Chinese gods, grant requests without regard to their morality because they are so desperate for worship. Ghosts are attracted to businesses of an ambiguous nature, including the film industry. These *lo pin moon* businesses have historically been controlled by Hong Kong's gangs. Gangsters are popularly regarded as among the most superstitious sector of Cantonese society since the "slanted door" businesses they own are considered most in need of spiritual protection. Since many of the ghosts were themselves involved in illicit dealings in their earthly lifetimes, they are considered particularly receptive to the pleas of those who similarly engage in *lo pin moon*. And gangsters, like ghosts, enjoy popular entertainment. According to research participants, gangster membership also requires participation in religious rituals that revolve around ghost appeasement. Thus, gangsters are in essence worshiping kindred spirits—similarly dubious individuals. These opportunistic relationships link the two underworlds in business ventures such as massage parlors, discos, and film production companies (Chu 2000).

Ghosts and gangsters remind us that production is full of pitfalls and the laboring body can be possessed in unexpected ways. Payments that appease ghosts and gangsters are not always officially noted in production budgets, but they constitute expenditures and they indicate the involvement of other worlds in the realm of filmed entertainment. There is a cost to film personnel such as star actors or directors who have been coerced by gangsters to work on films that they produce or finance. There is also the payment made to gangsters who demand hundreds or thousands of Hong Kong dollars for permission to film. If any equipment is broken by gangs, the costs of the equipment add up. Additionally, time and expenses are accrued for the *hoih geng laih* ceremony or even incense burnt at the start of every filming day.

Censorship is another area in which entities from supernatural and illegal activity intersect with film production. Since Hong Kong returned to mainland China in 1997, censorship has increasingly encroached on the terms of representation of both ghost and gangster films. Ghost films have come under scrutiny because ghosts supposedly incite "feudal superstitions" that the Chinese Communist Party has outlawed, and gangster films are censored since they expose neophyte capitalists to graft. How ghost and gangster plotlines are developed and how filmmakers negotiate censorship with officials of the People's Republic of China—which can continue during the filming phase—thus constitutes part of the production process for film workers. Censorship is managed in part by the Closer Economic Partnership Arrangement (CEPA). In some cases, as a result of the censorship that is applied to the Hong Kong film community within the larger "one country, two systems" geopolitical situation, Hong Kong filmmakers who make ghost or gangster films must correspondingly create what informants referred to as "one movie, two endings"—a film that offers the original ending for Hong Kong audiences and another, sanitized ending for the mainland Chinese audiences.[7] Another tactic may be used for films dealing with the supernatural: contemporary ghost and vampire movies are frequently adapted as mythological historical films in order to win government approval. Situating the supernatural in the past keeps the present supposedly free of mystical beliefs.[8]

Censorship has become controversial with the reunification with mainland China. Many Hong Kong film personnel I interviewed claim that this censorship, inconsistently applied by Beijing, hinders the supposed revitalization of the Hong Kong film industry, which started to decline in the 1990s. While discussing the difficulties of receiving script approval from mainland Chinese censor officials, a Hong Kong director told me,

> China, oh, they are too much with the censorship. CEPA says that China doesn't want mainlanders seeing films about triad. CEPA will kill the Hong Kong [film] industry! Movies are just movies. There is all this censorship against ghosts and gangsters, but these are the two main, most popular themes of Hong Kong films. And these are the most popular themes in Hollywood. There are good stories in the triad, power plays. You know, millions of people saw *The Godfather*, but they didn't go join the mafia. It's so ridiculous, the censorship. And the artificial endings which are engineered, such as the triad or ghost turns out to be a bad dream, or they become reformed at the end, silly endings attached, these are crazy. Please. CEPA will cut off both my arms—ghosts and gangsters!

I had been invited to observe this director as he worked with his editor to edit his latest film, the filming of which I had also observed on set. I was instructed to go to the film editing facility at 1 a.m., when they would start the graveyard shift edit session. Late-night film activity is not unusual, and amid these nocturnal activities hover the ambiguous presence of ghosts and gangsters.

The editing facility was located in an industrial section of Chai Wan on Hong Kong Island. The taxi driver dropped me off outside a dilapidated building. Once inside, the director led me to the edit bay, and we drank coffee as both of us stifled yawns due to the late hour. As we sat in a darkly lit room the faint lights from the buildings outside glinted through the windows.

After his outburst about censorship, I asked the director about any upcoming plans he had to make a ghost story. He smiled sheepishly and said,

> You know, I'd love to make a horror film, but I'm too afraid to make one. People who work on horror films say they see something; I know too many people who have been possessed or seen possessions to make one

myself. You should hear some of my producer's ghosts stories, they scare me. I have enormous respect for ghosts. I try to avoid them.

Censorship—whether externally imposed by the state or internally imposed by his personal fears—rendered ghosts a subject matter that this director was compelled to avoid in cinematic representation. Indeed, the specter of ghosts was so potent for him that even in his avoidance of them, they remained a powerful force.

Since gangster involvement is a sensitive topic among film personnel, I cautiously asked him how he felt about another controversial force on and off the screen: gangsters. He thought for a minute and then, not meeting my eyes, responded,

> This industry is full of negative power. Dark, negative things emanate from it, the industry, and even film sets have bad *feng shui*. The film industry is *lo pin moon*. I will leave it at that.

My visit ended a couple of hours later, and the director insisted on escorting me outside while I waited for the taxi that he had called for me. It was just after 3 a.m., dark and eerily quiet, and the hour at which, he reminded me, both ghosts and gangsters are most active. My taxi arrived and I climbed in. I turned to thank the director, but he had already vanished.

Intriguingly, while mainland China censors Hong Kong ghost and gangster films, these underworlds remain involved in the Hong Kong production process. Hong Kong film personnel I interviewed did not witness ghost propitiation or gangster interference on location filming in China. These ghost and gangster practices are thus distinctly local, a part of Hong Kong culture as the city starts to with China.

The Violence in Production: Possessive Power and Payments

As anthropologist Hortense Powdermaker pronounced nearly half a century ago, the industrial production of film, while emblematic of modernity, is not entirely free of the arcane, as evident in Hollywood studios' and executives' use of astrology, avoidance of the number 13, and religious symbols used by individuals on set. In demonstrating how ghosts and gangsters are multivalent participants in Hong Kong film production, alternately harmful and helpful, I have tried to extend our understanding of the production process beyond the rational, secular binary of above-the-line and below-the-line labor hierarchies. In an industry in which people work long hours yet see little prospect of job security or long-term reward, and must contend with the unpredictabilities of market rationality and capitalist calculation, ghost and gangster appeasement signal the myriad risks of capitalist film production. In the industrial process of creating imagery, film personnel labor across worlds—the worlds of the living and the dead, the legal and illegal.

Anthropology impels us to probe the possessive power of ghosts and gangsters in film and their broader significance. "It is to interrogate the *production*, in imaginative and material practice, of those compound political, economic, and cultural forms . . . by means of which space and time are made and remade, and the boundaries of the local and the global are actualized." (Comaroff and Comaroff 1999: 295, italics original). The process behind the film product geared for a global market reveals, as Comaroff and Comaroff note, the local imprimatur. Film, after all, is a process that manipulates the coordinates of time and space, and ghosts and gangsters have endured through the colonial and postcolonial eras; indeed, they both emerge from an earlier past—ghosts haunt us from a prior time and gangs are remnants of a pre–nation-state era. They haunt contemporary capitalist production. Thus we witness another iteration of capitalism— enchantments at work to procure profit and propitiation.

Finally, it cannot be overlooked that off-screen ghosts and gangsters are social forces that share two features: both are desperate to be appeased and both are also related in some way to death. Ghosts, after all, are the spirits of people who have died, and gangsters are sensationalized as frequently committing violence and involved in killing. Violence is also evident in the production process, whether it is dangerous stunts or the strong-arm tactics of triad involvement. Eros and Thanatos—enduring themes in cultural production—are visible in the sensationalistic images on the screen and are also discernible off screen among workers in the sometimes violent labor process that capitalist industrial production entails. During a time when almost every film worker I met complained about the demise of the Hong Kong film industry and fears of their industry being subsumed by the mainland Chinese film industry, it is intriguing to consider these on- and off-screen connections between money, death, and the perceived decay of an industry. Commercial film production can be a violent business that entangles the living and the dead, the legal and the illegal.

CHAPTER 6

....

Affective Labor

An Intersection of Performance and Possession

Introduction

> When performing, I get taken over by the character.
> I think it's just because you start a journey with a character,
> and you complete the journey with the character. But the
> journey is so intense that it's then very difficult to put that
> character to bed. And I've been in relationships with people
> where I observe that as well, and very often the person isn't
> aware of how much their character is affecting them. . . . A
> lot of actors get so involved in the spirit of the character,
> they're not in touch with their reality. And so people can get
> very badly hurt, when they actually come to earth again.
>
> —Tammy, Hollywood actress

What a nasty piece! Almost the whole film was on Steadicam so it was a great technical experience for me. But it was
depressing because of the subject matter [of female strip-
pers] and the way the writer and director were dealing with
women. During that film I wanted to quit the business.
The storyline in the script absolutely affects you even if you
are a technician, even though your skills are being used and
being improved upon. There are things about working on a

151

film that shape your outlook. That film wasn't worth it; I
became more particular about what I worked on after that.

—LENNY, Hollywood Steadicam operator
on a film about female strippers

I think the thing is, when you are an actor and you are
working in an intense situation, you make yourself really
vulnerable, you expose yourself so much that I believe that
there are all sorts of energies you draw into yourself without realizing you are.

—SUSAN, Hollywood actress

As the actors and camera operator above attest, performance and attendant labor such as camera operation to capture it is a provocative activity
that can haunt media personnel, a point which episodes of spirit possession on film sets in Hong Kong reinforces. Performance entails traversing
between perceived worlds of fiction and nonfiction, and such movement
on the production clock can eventually render performers and production
personnel confused, vulnerable, and exhausted. From the above quotes,
we learn that the vagaries of performance challenge common perceptions
of a mechanized production process. Many of the actors and actresses emphasized that they do not consciously employ Stanislavski's system (or
Strasberg's Method of emotional recall) in which the actor must "disap-
pear" into his or her role, particularly actors in Hong Kong. Yet, even if
they do, these various forms of being overtaken merit analysis since they
contribute to our understanding of media labor.[1] In this chapter, I demonstrate that it is not only actors who are transported or moved by performance, but also other production personnel who help mediate the
performances on the soundstages and studios, such as camera operators,
stunt choreographers, makeup artists, and producers.

Media workers cannot forget—are not allowed to forget—that the
labor they perform on the seemingly enclosed "production floor" of studio
soundstages or highly managed exterior sites is shaped in part by the demands of global logics of accumulation. From technicians to teamsters,
enormous numbers of media workers on Hollywood and Hong Kong sets
are engaged in manufacturing physical spectacle and thematic variations
on love, death, or conflict in order to create a product that is to be ex-
changed in global media markets. As discussed in Chapter 2, spectacle is
a visual form whose intended effect has been to stun and even incite viewers (see Gunning 1990). Given the dynamic processes of filming such

spectacle (and therefore the intimate relationship that media workers often form to the images they participate in), it is not surprising that media workers are themselves moved by what they produce. Yet media workers must create these spectacular images amid "rationalized" timetables, impersonal assembly-line techniques, and financial regulations governed by studios, multinational corporations, banks, and private investors, as well as shifts in the global political economy.

Anthropology has contributed to the study of the complicated relationships between an industry's producers and their products, demonstrating how production sites are replete with "meaning-making" (Ganti 2000:16; see also Freeman 2000; Kondo 1990, 1997; Ong 1987; Zaloom 2006). In examining the enactment and embodiment of film and television work, I consider how creating characters and worlds in industrial production sites requires quick immersion into and out of affective states—transitions that are not neatly conducted and are the result of socio-professional processes, not just a private, individual experience (Neff, Wissinger, and Zukin 2005; Schechner 2002). I examine multiple forms and meanings of "possession" that media workers experience as the worlds of fiction and nonfiction merge in their production of spectacle.

Affective Labor

I discovered that in commercial media production, media professionals balance a variety of skills and resources, dealing as they do with the technical requirements of equipment such as cameras, props, and prosthetics, the physical demands of action or action-oriented filming, and the emotional work of actors and those who work closely with them. The concept of affective labor helps to describes this complex process. As anthropologists Purnima Mankekar and Akhil Gupta explain in their article "Intimate Encounters: Affective Labor in Call Centers" which is based on their ethnographic research of call centers in Bangalore, India, affective labor captures the combination of cognitive, corporeal, and emotional work that is fostered in highly social production sites. Here, I aim to complement organizational and institutional studies of media (informed by the fields of geography, labor studies, and sociology) with ethnographic observations and narratives of experiential accounts of scripted television and narrative film. In their book *Empire* and elsewhere, Michael Hardt and Antonio Negri refer to affective labor as an aspect of immaterial labor which is "labor that produces an immaterial good, such as a service, a cultural product, knowledge, or communication" in a post-industrial, late-capitalist context (Hardt and Negri 2000: 290).[2] Affective labor characterizes socially interactive labor, especially the feminized work of care givers. However, Hardt and Negri also use affective labor to describe the work of people in the entertainment industry who produce information and sentiment, and who evoke what they refer to as "passion" in their recipients (Hardt and Negri 2000: 292; Hardt 1999:89). They specify "the entertainment industry" as a site of affective labor because of its "focus on the manipulation of affect" (Hardt and Negri 2000: 292; Hardt 1999: 96). My ethnographic research of film and television personnel helps ground and develop their conceptualization.

Affective labor also owes much to sociologist Arlie Hochschild's earlier theorization of "emotional labor" which describes how service workers (such as flight attendants and bill collectors) "induce or suppress" emotions in order to perform their work, such as providing "service with a smile" or stifling annoyance with testy customers (Hochschild 1983:7). Hochschild pointed out the exploitation and detachment that comes with emotional labor and public performances sold for a wage in the capitalist market. Similarly, the affect that media workers sell to audiences also calls upon a plumbing, and manipulation, of their own sentiments. However, commercial film and television personnel evoke sentiment and spectacle not only for the eventual and abstract audience "out there" but also for the more immediate audience of their colleagues on set, with whom they interact in quite intimate ways.

Signaling deep, embodied feelings and even irrationality (Mazzarella 2009; Yanagisako 2002), affect yields a new perspective on media's intersection of performance, risk, and enchantment. It taps into anthropology's challenge to modernity in what Michael Hardt conceptualizes as "the corporeal and intellectual aspects of the new forms of production, recognizing that *such labor engages at once with rational intelligence and with passions or feeling*" (Hardt 2007: xi, italics added). Hardt specifies that labor involving such contradictory elements includes the production of images and ideas – as with film and television. Over the past decade, anthropologists have engaged with the concept of affective labor such as when writing about the labor of overseas workers (Bautista 2015: 1). The concept is valuable for thinking through intimacy in capitalist work relations, particularly intimate production spaces in which one's work process is visible to most if not all co-workers and one's vulnerabilities can be witnessed by others. Purnima Mankekar and Akhil Gupta's contribution extends the concept of affective labor very effectively through their ethnography in which they complicate the notion of alienation by looking at very socially interactive labor. They theorize affect as the "intensities that passes between bodies and objects; between and across bodies; as existing alongside, barely beneath, and in excess of cognition; as transgressing binaries of mind versus body, and private feeling versus collective sentiment" (Mankekar and Gupta 2016: 9). This provides a useful way to think about setwork and its assemblage of art, science, and business, and its implications for rationalized industry.

Of their participant observation in the call centers, Mankekar and Gupta describe being struck by the "raw energy that crackled and swirled around us" (Mankekar and Gupta 2016: 3; 11), an experience which could easily resemble film and television sets especially when setting up shots. They noted intense interactions, and the taut body posture that reflected the call center agents efforts' to persuade and cajole their customers, their exclamations of joy and panic, and even their own fatigue from their ethnographic observations. Mankekar and Gupta write, "We have never been able to get accustomed to the affective intensities, the electric charge, of the floor in any of the call centers where we conduct our research: we are physically exhausted and emotionally spent by the time we leave" (10-11). They note the strains of night shifts on the agents, but also the enjoyable sociality of the call center work, even as the agents' labor was predicated on interactions that were highly structured by the demands of capital (Mankekar and Gupta 2016: 17).

As Mankekar and Gupta demonstrate, affect is a more socially distributed and interactive phenomenon than emotions, which Mankekar and Gupta see as an individual experience, reflecting interiority (see also Clough 2007; Massumi 2002). Mankekar and Gupta also deviate from Hochschild's emotional labor in that they are less concerned with questioning the level of authenticity in the observed emotions (see Manekar and Gupta 2016: 9-10), and more concerned with understanding the collective endeavor of such work and the intimacies formed which, as they claim, "enables us to conceive of the work of call center agents not solely in terms of their interpellation by ideological or disciplinary apparatuses of labor but also in terms of their capacity to navigate space and time, and to experience and inhabit their bodies in specific ways." In thinking through the physicality of call center work, Mankekar and Gupta point out the managerial instruction for agents to smile when speaking on the phone, as customers "would be able to 'hear' the agents' smiles in their voices" (13). This need to simultaneously employ cognition, the body, and emotion resembles the work of many media professionals, actors in particular, and helps us understand the individual and collective endeavor of media performance.

Laboring Between Worlds

Spectacle for the screen entails the simulation of what are in reality intense, tumultuous events, from explosions to disaster scenarios, and even sexual intercourse. Life is breathed into inanimate objects, such as rubber baby dolls designed by prop departments who remotely control their breathing. Rites of passage such as births, marriages, and death must be enacted. Media workers handle weapons such as guns with fake bullets and knives with blunted edges. Media labor provokes an unsettling of classifications, and as Mary Douglas noted in her seminal writing on classifications, the ambiguity that the blurring of categories and classifications entails for members of a community can produce confusion for them, yet also hold appeal (Douglas 1966). Media workers in key sites such as Hollywood and Hong Kong are laboring between what are conventionally conceived of as different worlds—the world of industry and rationalization, and the world of sentiment and passions; the world of secular concerns and the world of cosmological beliefs.

Many commercial film and television plots are structured around romantic storylines as well as violent scenes of death and dying that do not leave media workers untouched, threatening to dissolve the fragile boundary between what they perceive between their real and "reel" selves. Speaking of this permeability, an actress in Hollywood told me:

> [T]he character was something I created, I would put this mantle on, do my work, then take this mantle off and go home. But, as I've been working I feel that actually more of me has seeped into the character, or more of the character has seeped into me. So it just becomes a blend.

A Hollywood actress, Lynn, expanded on the confrontation between performance and commercial imperatives:

> One of the hardest experiences working on this show was when I worked with an actress whose character on the show was killed, and we try to save her. I found that filming really hard to do partly because the actress was leaving and her character had been written off the show, and so I felt for her. But also she had joined the show having just watched her family member die in real life. And so for the actress not many years later, to have to die herself, as her character, I just thought this was a very hard task the writers were asking her to do. And she had a very hard time with it, because of that. And so I felt extremely sensitive to her and what she was dealing with emotionally but also on top of that, my character

on the show was trying to save a co-worker's life. It was very difficult to hold myself together, very hard to control myself.

In her comment above, Lynn describes a situation in which demise occurred on multiple levels. First, the off-screen, managerial decision to not renew the other actress' contract and thus kill off her television character; second, the off-screen death of the actress' actual family member, which, according to Lynn and other members of the production, pervaded the filming of the death scene; third, the scripted, on-screen, and very graphic depiction of the stabbing to the actress' upper body to be followed by her death. This Grand Guignol-esque spectacle of suffering had been timed to occur during the Nielsen "sweeps" ratings, a time in which television networks promote sensational plotlines and visuals to attract larger audiences than usual.

To film her death scene, the actress was required to lie on a gurney, dressed with a prosthetic of an open chest cavity that exposed a prop heart and oozed blood and bodily fluids. Lynn had to rehearse with the the the medical consultant on the program, a doctor, on how to repeatedly plunge her hands and the surgical equipment into the prop chest cavity in a credible manner. Working with equipment and props while employing the reasoning necessary to take technical direction and also summon up the appropriate emotions exemplifies affective labor with its mix of corporeal, cognitive, and emotional work.

As we see from the scene that Lynn describes, actors may have to revisit and relive painful memories as well as embody them. This can be upsetting, although it can also be cathartic for an actor, exhilarating even. In this case, the producers expected the actress playing the stabbing victim to be professional and "rational"—to hit her marks, to be able to offer a realistic portrayal of suffering as a stabbing victim (the type of scene that may require an actor to plumb the depths of her emotions), and yet to be detached enough to take technical direction and film multiple takes of a brutal scene from various angles under the gaze of a camera crew with (mostly male) members telling her how to position her body, all the while without needing to take extra time to prepare or recover from such a scene that could hold up the day's schedule. Lynn explained to me that part of her struggle with the scene was due to her compassion for and friendship with the actress. The shallow and transient intimacies assumed of post-Fordist conditions of production with its short-term, part-time labor and subcontractor relations are offset by the burst of intensive emotions and socialities that the making of such spectacle entails. These observations also demonstrate the spontaneity and meaningful associations of the production process.

The commercial production of performance and specifically setwork draws upon a combination of precise technical skills, intense emotionality and empathy as well as physicality to create evocative images. Affective labor helps us understand how the creation of sentiment and performance, commodified for transnational publics, poses ontological risks (and possibilities) for media personnel (see Hardt 1999: 99). As we see in the Hollywood and Hong Kong examples, conventional understandings of rationality and irrationality coexist in production processes (also observed by Rosten and Powdermaker in Hollywood over half a century earlier). Further, Hardt recognizes affective labor's potential for illuminating "new forms of exploitation" in media production and the entertainment industries in his call to link the production of affects with the creation of images and ideas (Hardt 2007: xii).

A Hollywood actor whose film character mourned his deceased wife complained of being emotionally drained by performing the emotion of grief day after day, and his sense of "losing" himself, of feeling "possessed" by the subject matter. This actor spoke of having to continually submerge himself in that state, and how, even if he broke the mood when not filming by listening to upbeat music or playing sports, the long hours of having to perform mourning and dealing with death under the close scrutiny of the camera every day plunged him into what he described as an actual deep "depression." The filming schedule for this project lasted several months, and he was greatly relieved when it was over, although he admitted that he could not cast aside his shroud of sadness immediately. Similar experiences are often recounted by actors in print media interviews as well; as Kenneth Branagh told *The Guardian* earlier this year, playing an "angst-ridden" detective had left him anxious off camera, and his portrayal of a Nazi for another production caused him depression (Martinson June 24, 2015). People may scoff at accounts of media workers becoming superstitious while filming a supernatural-themed film as unprofessional, but such immersion in other genres are regarded as a commendable level of artistic commitment. For instance, when the respected American filmmaker, Steven Spielberg, told an interviewer recently that he felt "sad" after filming the "traumatic" Holocaust-themed film *Schindler's List*, there was no commentary criticizing or ridiculing him for feeling the story's effects (Masters, *THR*). Prior to my fieldwork in Hong Kong, an actor there faced some legal troubles; media workers I interviewed who had previously worked with the actor speculated that the actor had been unable to pull himself out of the dark mood into which he had immersed himself for playing a dark and bleak character in a film. Other Hong Kong personnel told me of an actress who became withdrawn since her last film and reportedly continued to suffer from lingering depression that resulted from her playing a tragic character—a hold from which she apparently could not "free" herself for a few years. In this type of labor where affect is elicited for, and within, industrial contexts and constraints, the seemingly bounded categories of "fiction" and "nonfiction" become porous and hence unsettling for media workers. The filming of torture and sexual assault scenes—the staple of so many thriller and action superhero films in any commercial industry—can also trigger actual fears, especially if the actress has to wear props such as handcuffs or chains. (Even an escapist, "popcorn" Hollywood comedy such as *Back to the Future* features a scene of a woman struggling against attempted rape from an overpowering bully.) So many scenes that feature women being sexually assaulted or taunted are filmed by a mostly male crew including a male director, cinematographer, and camera operator, which can heighten the sense of gendered scrutiny and vulnerability for the actress in a workplace that is already often marked by gender bias in hiring.

Technicians, craft workers, and other members of the production team are also touched by the themes of the images and stories they work on, as Lenny, the Steadicam operator, explained in the quote at the beginning of the chapter. An award-winning Hollywood makeup artist whose work in the makeup trailer I would observe told me how she became disturbed by the illness and disfigurements that she was often called to create on the actors' faces. Similar to the actor who portrayed a widower, her work sometimes depressed her: "What I apply on their faces is temporary, but for some people it's not. It's kind of eerie to make people look dead, when you think about it." Her extensive knowledge of blood, muscle tissue, epidermal layers, and bone structure came from hours of studying medical textbooks of physiology and illness, and morgue photos of decomposed corpses, as well as observing how weapons penetrate bone and tissue. When people close to her became ill, the task of designing faces ravaged by disease for commercial entertainment purposes became distasteful to her.

A Hong Kong director relayed to me how a producer colleague of his, while filming a television drama about gangsters, would act similarly to the gangsters whose lives he was depicting in the program. On location filming that took place all over Hong Kong Island and Kowloon peninsula, the Hong Kong police would interrupt filming to demand evidence of permits and permission from other media authorities. In response,

This producer would start acting like a gangster himself with the police, the show just rubbed off on him. He'd be yelling all the time, picking fights with the cops, swearing, throwing stuff around, acting just like these guys. He'd start acting like the gangsters. It just gets to you, it's unavoidable. And other people around you notice it. It's not good for you. And he'd have to deal with them [gangsters] as investors as well. Eventually he went to seek help about it.

Scholars have posited how an emerging feature of postmodern life is the decentering of the self (Gergen 1992; Kondo 1990; Turkle 1984). Dorinne Kondo argues that a person's self is relational and "permeable"— and, thus, "flexible"—arising out of varying social and familial contexts and power relations (Kondo 1990: 26). These episodes, however, point not only to the phenomenon of fragmentary selfhood but also to the interactive labor that the combination of media technology, performance, and the commercial market entails.

The affective labor required to produce profound emotions is not conducive to working within strict time constraints. On a one-hour Hollywood network television programs I observed, they generally filmed three and a half pages a day of a roughly thirty-page script in order to keep the production on budget. A dramatic one-hour episode generally took close to 10 days to film. In the account of the actress Susan getting upset while filming a scene about her deceased husband in the Introduction, the first assistant director and the unit production manager had to make a quick decision about how to proceed after Susan started crying. Organized by the production department the week prior to filming, her allotted time on set did not in this case allow for much flexibility with rescheduling; she was expected to keep filming. Since an actual baby was called for in a scene to be shot later that day (as opposed to a mechanical baby that was sometimes used), the first assistant director had to contend with conflicting schedules. He had to consult with the "baby wrangler"—Hollywood industry jargon for a member of the production who is responsible for managing the time shifts and care of babies on set, which must be coordinated between union-mandated sleeping and feeding times and remain within the boundaries of legal work hours for minors. The emotional breakdown of the actress could not be allowed to stagger the schedule for the rest of the day. Due to various logistical issues that day, the one-hour lunch break designated by the various labor unions (e.g., Screen Actors Guild [SAG], International Alliance of Theatrical Stage Employees [IATSE], Local 766) could not be moved up; if this had been possible, the first assistant director could have sent everyone to lunch while the actress recovered in her trailer and not wasted the production's time and money.

While the camera is understood by many interlocutors as the most important object on the set—the "window to the audience," and the apparatus that "captures our souls"—it is the budget, that mysterious, ever-evolving, often-invoked object, circulating among the upper management of production companies, studios, and networks, that, rarely seen, challenges it as the supreme authority. It is the budget, as much as the camera, that captures their souls. In the service of the budget, the production process cannot be derailed by the pitfalls of performance, such as human frailty. The production "machine" (as an actor described the process when speaking of the emotional upset and confusion that death scenes prompt) cannot come to a halt when the drama bleeds into the lives of the media workers. These pressures also put into greater context the use of religion in the production process, especially in Hollywood. Wearing religious icons under one's costume (such as a St. Christopher medal) may, to that worker, offer spiritual protection. Retreating to the privacy of a trailer to pray or read Bible verses, as numerous workers did, also allows for contemplation, and another method for reconciling the conflicting pressures and problems of work. These personal and private attempts at finding succor should be seen as a consequence of affective labor on the production floor.

Recent media production studies, concerned with issues of exploitation and alienation and committed to advocacy for union labor, social justice, and "good work" are highly valuable, and necessary (Hesmondhalgh and Baker 2008: 229). Yet in looking at media workers' complicated relationships to the images and themes they film, we find other concerns and meanings expressed alongside them. While media personnel may experience alienation in the Marxian sense—a dislocation from the self (Marx 1992: 74)—affective labor can also bring a sense of pleasure and even empowerment. For some actors, although the movement between different worlds may be difficult, the set of circumstances or character may represent an exciting possibility—an escape or an aspiration. An actor I interviewed in Hong Kong described the sense of freedom and fantasy that she has come to treasure in playing roles that differ from her actual circumstances: "I can play a queen, even though I was born poor. What other profession allows me to do that?" Cyndi, an extra in Hollywood, enjoyed being placed on different films and television shows by the casting agency that is subcontracted by production companies and studios to supply background actors: "I like being an extra because of the fantasy. I get to be a cocktail waitress one day, an OB/GYN nurse the next." The inconsistent nature of the labor sector of extras is precisely what allows Cyndi to role play and temporarily embody different occupations. While she does not encounter the burdens that come with being an actual waitress or nurse, she does live the instability of part-time labor in flexible entertainment. Thus, while the invocations of magic making and fantasy creation that permeate industry discourse in both sites must be critically read, we have to acknowledge that some media workers enjoy creating these spectacles and make the most of the conditions in which they help craft them. As an actress in Hollywood who has worked in both film and television told me,

> You can play anyone. There is a weird . . . even though it is your actual body, if you allow yourself to be this character, it is so freeing because it's not you, but it is you! The more the character is not like you, the more freeing it is. When I played an eco-terrorist murderer on [a police procedural TV drama], driving a getaway car, shooting someone between the eyes, my adrenaline was pumping. When would I ever do this? The freeness of it all! But it is temporary, there aren't real bullets in the gun.

With affective labor, "the body and the mind are simultaneously engaged . . . reason and passion, intelligence and feeling, are employed together" (Hardt 2007: xi). This description also sums up the work of Steadicam operators. The Steadicam camera, used in Hollywood and Hong Kong, is meant to intensify and personalize the audience's experience of the action in a shot. Weighing approximately 50 pounds, the camera is worn as a harness strapped to the operator's body. Its operator mimics the movements of the actors as they move. Steadicam's operation is admiringly described by one cinematographer as "a body art," with training needed in how to shift one's body correctly, even with the stabilizing forces built into this apparatus. A Steadicam operator described to me the muscle control he struggled to maintain over the camera, and explained that the camera is an extension of his own body:

> I even have to use my stomach muscles. There's no body part I don't use! It's part of what makes it so appealing, that everything is involved . . . you can almost communicate your thoughts and they'll be visible on screen. It's really a transcendental experience.

The operator even custom-designed a lighter, back-mounted harness of stiff carbon fiber for his body to facilitate further integration between him and his machine, which he spoke of as a treasured augmentation of himself. His comments, especially his reference to the camera as a body art, recall anthropologist Dorinne Kondo's ethnographic research on the techniques of Japanese artisans such as woodworkers. In her analysis of how these artisans fashioned a sense of self through the crafting of their work, Kondo quotes from colleague Matthews Hamabata's fieldnotes to point out that they possessed a "love of machinery as some kind of spiritual extension of themselves" rather than seeing the machine as an "instrument of alienation" (Kondo 1990: 245). The bond this operator expressed between himself and his camera can thus be understood as a positive foray into laboring between worlds.

Performance and Spirit Possession

While sitting in the warmth of a cafe in Kowloon on a cool weekday afternoon in 2006, a stunt choreographer named Jack sipped coffee and described the time he encountered a ghost on a film production site. Jack explained that he had been working through the night on a grueling outdoor film shoot in the New Territories of Hong Kong, a common occurrence in the film industry given the space afforded by the rural areas and fast-paced filming schedules that entail late-night filming. It was, as he described it, a film with "dark themes." As with other members of the production crew, Jack was able to catch a few hours of sleep in between filming by napping in his car. At around 4 a.m., he woke up to use the public restrooms in the area. As he entered the stall, he was confronted by the ghost of a very old man, hovering in the air a few feet above the ground. After Jack gasped in shock, the image of the old man disappeared. Jack was stunned yet recovered quickly. After talking to other members of the production when they awoke, Jack discovered that various personnel had also experienced spectral sightings while working on this outdoor film shoot.

Despite these ghostly encounters, Jack and the rest of the production adhered to the rushed production schedule, only taking a few minutes at the beginning of each day of filming to light incense as an offering to the ghosts to keep them at bay, as is common on most Hong Kong film and television productions with the *baai sahn* ritual. Jack's spirit sighting illustrates yet another way in which media workers labor between worlds. He mentioned the dark themes in the storyline of this film project as one of the reasons why spirits are attracted to film sets, yet what emerged as more disturbing to him were the long hours of the production and the rush in which he had to choreograph and perform dangerous stunts while ensuring that the tired members of his stunt crew were alert enough to fully observe safety precautions. Evidently, the labor issues were intertwined with spectral ones.

As I discussed in the previous chapter, ghosts and spirit possessions on Hong Kong film sets must be located within the context of popular Hong Kong religious beliefs about the "unsettled" ghosts of individuals who died without descendants to propitiate them. Spirits are known to visit the living, seeking the food, favors, and entertainment that the living can provide (see Constable 1994; Feuchtwang 2001; Weller 1994a; Wolf 1974). Ghosts are also understood to be "hungry" for not only food but entertainment, and are attracted to the spectacle of performance that opera provides (Constable 1994: 111). It is customary to reserve seats for spectral audience members at Cantonese operas, as I observed at a performance of a Cantonese opera play in Kowloon. Many media workers I interviewed shared their experiences of spirit sightings on film sets in Hong Kong, usually at night and in remote settings. Yet what should we make of spirit *possessions* of media industry workers that occur while filming on the production site? During my time in Hong Kong, reports circulated among media workers and throughout various English- and Chinese-language news media and tabloids of spirit possessions of actors and crew members on Hong Kong films. While some of these stories appeared to be of a sensationalist nature, several informants mentioned to me how a Hong Kong actor they knew was pummeled on his chest during the filming of a supernatural thriller by his female co-star in a spontaneous and unscripted moment. The actress later claimed that she was possessed by a ghost. Another informant, a stunt man named Yeung, explained how a crew member became possessed during a nighttime film shoot near a cemetery for a ghost film.

Here again, popular religious beliefs and the legacy of opera performance traditions intersect with the work of film production, particularly the creation and performance of violence, emblematizing the confrontation between rationalization and the passions of affective labor. The unsettled ghosts who pervade production sites of any kind are understood to be attracted to brutality. Popular genres of gangster and horror films in particular feature stylized renditions of action and conflict. The creation of a violent sequence by crew members such as property masters, makeup artists, and camera operators, which entails the enactment and embodiment of violence by actors and stunt workers, provides a riveting spectacle for not only living audience members but occasionally spectral ones as well. Yet it must be pointed out that it is not only spectral constraints with which media workers in both Hong Kong and Hollywood must contend: industrial concerns that emerge from specific sociocultural contexts also shape the labor that they perform, and "take hold" of media workers. Spirit possessions on Hong Kong film sets have been described by some informants as a way to relieve stressful relations between people who work long hours in frequently intimate and sometimes uncomfortable physical conditions. Privacy for principal creative personnel while filming is uncommon. Budgets are devoted largely to technical and logistical needs rather than what are seen as personal luxuries by many Hong Kong film producers and directors, such as trailers for actors or even separate rooms. In outdoor filming sites the production must also deal with gawkers and sometimes harassment from criminals. When filming in rural areas such as the New Territories, production personnel must consult with village elders prior to filming to check that the content of the film or television program is inoffensive to the village community and that the production schedule is not intrusive. Sometimes the production must also offer gifts to the villagers for granting their permission to film.

As Mankekar and Gupta described, the call center agents they observed had to work around the clock, which disturbed their natural body rhythms and metabolism, interfering with their health and, for women, their reproductive functions (Mankekar and Gupta 2016: 16). In the case of both Yeung and the actor who was attacked by his possessed female co-star, the film projects entailed large amounts of capital and production schedules that allowed for far too few hours for turnaround (on some days, only an hour or two of rest for the cast and crew). The time discipline of the production schedule is such that media workers frequently refer to film shoots as "guerilla style." Filming is an expensive, complicated venture, requiring investments and resources and usually very little time in which to bring everyone involved in filming together. I asked a Hong Kong filmmaker why it was, back when the industry produced hundreds of films a year, that the lead actor's character was sometimes the actor's actual name. He answered that one of the reasons was that given the multiple film projects the actors had to juggle and the rush in which they were made, it was sometimes easier for the actors to remember. Another interviewee confirmed this, indicating that creative decisions are sometimes determined by the logistics of hectic production schedules.

Film crews in Hong Kong have even been expected to labor through typhoon conditions on outdoor shoots, sometimes abandoning work only when the government weather service finally enforces the mandatory Signal 8 typhoon warning that makes it illegal to keep employees at work. "We were desperate to finish the shoot," a stunt coordinator recounted to me about one such shoot, "so we just kept working through the Signal 8." Some informants, such as another stunt coordinator, explained spirit possessions and spirit-caused accidents on film sets as a tactic of "saving face," a way of alleviating blame and finger pointing in a relatively small industry where many people hope to repeatedly work together on successive film projects. Filmmaking must also be understood as a socially ambiguous practice in Hong Kong that invites ethically questionable behaviors, which include physical coercion, as also seen in Hollywood and Bollywood (Ganti 2004; Moldea 1987). Socially provocative and in some cases private behaviors such as sexual intercourse and dying are enacted for public consumption on a global market, and individuals involved in this type of work have historically been stigmatized, particularly women. There is no uniform or easy answer regarding spirit possessions. But their occurance, and the rituals and reactions around them, reflect the various strains that such employment engenders, despite the desirability of work. The stories, and the conditions in which they make them, can take hold of their spirits.

Conclusion

Performance requires engaging the humanity of actors and the production personnel, yet the machine-like conditions in which commercial film/television media work often demands a robotic approach to the work. As I argue throughout this chapter, the labor of conjuring illusions and fictions, especially ones that resonate with real events in people's lives, does not leave the personnel untouched. As Kondo attests of the artisanal workers she observed in Japan, "[W]ork and personhood are inextricable from one another. In transforming the material world, my informants also transformed themselves" (Kondo 1990: 48). The notion of affective labor illuminates the social processes and permeability of setwork, which occurs in a largely post-Fordist context.

While there are overall differences between the amounts of financing for Hollywood and Hong Kong film and television media, productions within both industries generally rely upon some combination of production companies, studios, private investors, banks, and multinational corporations. Efficient production processes are in place to strictly manage production. Yet, I argue, media workers can become subsumed by the potent themes of the fictional genres they create and enact, which are difficult to reconcile amid the processes of rationalization. The presumed secularity of these industries is challenged by accounts not only of "enchantment" by personnel who are caught up in industry narratives of magic and glamour, but of hauntings and possessions.

CHAPTER 7

Camera/Chimera

Setwork and the Ethics of Soul Capture

[When filming] I'll notice you if you're in my eyeline, you
can't ignore what is there. If I try to ignore you in my pe-
ripheral vision, you'll read that on camera. That's the scary
aspect of the camera, you can't hide anything from it. *You
can't mask anything, it sees everything. It reads your soul. It
reads into you.*

—SHARON, Hollywood actress

....

Echoing other actors, directors, and camera operators, Sharon describes the film camera as an invasive technology. Cameras play an
active role in an already hazardous workplace, inviting our examination of how media personnel understand these objects. The comment of
this actress, who works in an industry that touts the latest in motion picture science, harkens back to the early days of still photography technology, when, for decades after its invention, indigenous peoples feared still
photography for its uncanny ability to "capture the soul." Even urban
dwellers in 1950s Hong Kong held to this belief, as photographer Ho Fan
recounted of the butcher who wanted his spirit back after Fan photo-
graphed him. As Susan Sontag poignantly noted, "To photograph people
is to violate them . . . *it turns people into objects that can be symbolically
possessed* . . . to take a photograph is to participate in another person's
mortality, vulnerability, mutability" (Sontag 1977: 14–15, italics added).

While showing me his motion camera collection at his production
office, a veteran Hong Kong producer and cinematographer commented
on the dynamic filming process for media workers, and in particular
camera operators: "Something of you goes out of you and into the camera."
His comment illuminates how these machines intimately seize the labor—
indeed, the bodies—of a range of media workers. Entertainment

industries have long capitalized on the staging of spectacular images, raising the issue of media ethics as the behaviors surrounding cameras in these commercial settings reveal the conflicted meanings we impose upon these machines. Given anthropology's history of studying the social relations around objects that hold meaning for us (Appadurai 1988; Mauss 2000[1954]), we need to unpack some of the motion picture camera's meanings for personnel in the commercial production process. Media anthropologists have documented how indigenous peoples have transformed their subjectivities through their direct use of video camera technology in largely noncommercial sites, in some cases appropriating the camera and turning it on themselves as a means of empowerment (see Ginsburg 1994; Heider 2006[1976]; Ruby 1991; Turner 1992). More recently, anthropologists have looked at how cameras embedded in mobile telephony intensify the circulation of images of daily life, social activism, law enforcement, and surveillance (Gursel 2013; Horst and Miller 2006). That people in the entertainment industries also harbor complex feelings toward camera technology and their operators may be less obvious, yet relevant to understanding media labor and ethics nevertheless. We may also see that linear narratives about modernity and machines become unsettled in what many people assume to be disenchanted industrial activity.

The camera is an evocative apparatus around which all activity on the production floor is centered. The camera is understood by many media workers as an active entity that catches hold of something of them in the production process, and that its acquisitive and transformative capability, feared in pre-industrial communities, remains the source of its power in late capitalist societies. Across various cultures, people have expressed astonishment and unease about the motion picture camera's uncanny ability to capture some perceived core or essence of a person and reproduce bodies—a risk that has not abated over time (Zhen 2005: 159, 163–169). It was (and still is, to some degree) considered inauspicious and disrespectful to photograph a dead body in Hong Kong, and, as I've discussed, filming a death scene for a movie remains provocative. "Soul capture" camera and computer technology has proliferated within the commercial motion picture and television industries.[1] Thus, perhaps it is not surprising that there are lingering beliefs—even fears—among some contemporary media workers in commercial production sites that the camera actively possesses an aspect of the provocative imagery it has seen and filmed, in some cases even transmitting a force back onto those in its proximity. In these transmissions, cameras are more than a mechanical device to transform a movie script into profit-driving imagery; a camera can reorder events and people and diminish or enhance the bodies of those in its wake.

In this chapter I discuss an ethnographic vignette about a film production's camera being overtaken by the ghost of a dead man within the broader context of media personnel's attitudes toward cameras. These experiences demonstrate how the camera is a silent yet salient object in the spectacle-ization and commodification of performance and imagery. In exploring the myriad meanings of camera technologies to those on the commercial production floor (a weapon, a labor surveillance device, a window to the audience), I posit that the camera is an ethically charged force on film and television sets, a provocateur as well as a protector of workers, demanding enormous attention and labor from them. The camera is an active, even predatory presence, in some cases extracting physical and psychic energies from those working in relation to it.

My chapter title invokes the chimerical nature of motion picture and television camera technology as the camera represents the multiple meanings of a chimera. First, the camera is an instrument assembled of disparate parts (a lens, a shutter, aperture, etc.) that represents a presence larger and more powerful than the sum of its parts. In this sense, chimera recalls assemblage. Second, posing a fearsome material and metaphorical presence on the production floor, the camera is also a fantastical object. It facilitates the unleashing of affective states and distributes meanings among those who work in its immediate vicinity, raising ontological issues for media workers. With their cameras, media personnel mediate weighty human experiences such as death, in scripted and unscripted ways. These affective forms of labor and meaning-making on the production floor filter through to the final product. Throughout this book, I stress that it is not just the final audience "out there" who are transported in some way by the images and textual themes but also the *immediate* audience of media workers on set.. Hence, the camera possesses a potentially monstrous character, arising from its capacity to loom over and capture an essence for posterity, stealing one's soul, to catalyze conditions that threaten to disrupt and destabilize these workers' social relations and worlds. The camera is an apparatus whose controlling presence, as with a nightmarish monster, persists in the imagination of those around it even after its recording function ceases.

A Spirited Camera: Protector or Provocateur?

While discussing the role of the camera on film sets in a cafe in Hong Kong, a filmmaker named Andy threw up his hands, laughed, and said,

> It's the crucible! Everyone becomes so conscious of the camera. It looks like a funnel, and everything is funneled through it. It sucks everything into it, to the back of the camera.

Andy's description of the camera as an instrument "sucking" everything into it is not an overly exaggerated description of the ambivalent nature of this technology.

Describing an occasion in which he was transported by the capabilities as well as the responses of camera technology, Andy recalled a film he had directed. One of the plotlines follows the tempestuous relationship between a working-class husband and wife who live in a high-rise building in a public housing estate—a reality for many Hong Kong people. Andy was on set for the filming of this sequence in an actual apartment building. There were a series of shots in which the couple fight violently and the husband threatens to kill himself by jumping out of the window as a way for him to escape his desperate financial straits. In a city famed for its densely packed, urban high-rise apartment buildings, suicide by jumping is a not uncommon form of self-inflicted death.

Yet in the middle of filming one of the shots in this scene, an event occurred that would lead Andy to confront the uncanny consequences of cameras. A crew member quietly motioned Andy to one of the windows in the apartment, alerting him to the fact that, off camera, a man had in actuality just committed suicide by jumping out of the window of an apartment building opposite theirs. Andy quickly looked out the window and saw the body and blood on the ground. Since in the script of this film the male character threatens suicide by jumping out of a window, in a cost- and time-efficient effort to capture realistic footage for a possible sequence in the film, Andy quickly reached for the second camera on the set with which to shoot the immediate aftermath of the actual jump. He filmed the first moments after the jump in which the body was splayed out on the ground and a crowd gathering around, and a few minutes after that the arrival of an ambulance. Significantly, Andy and his camera also captured that liminal moment in which the unknown man transitioned from a "person" into a body: a corpse. It is in such an event as this that we see how starkly media personnel labor between worlds.

Andy later explained that he shot the suicide in an expedient manner to capture realistic footage for a possible, alternative sequence in the film since the male character threatened suicide by jumping out of a window. It is fairly common in Hong Kong film production to improvise with impromptu shots or added dialogue. After filming was completed for the scripted shots, Andy told a colleague that he had just filmed what he referred to as a "fresh" suicide; his colleage responded, *"Ho Lan Tzang!"* ("That's fucking great!"). A "fresh" death was seen as a serendipitous event that allowed the filmmakers to further bridge the perceived gap between the "real" and the "reel" by capturing realistic B-roll (background footage that filmmakers acquire as a supplement to scripted imagery in order to provide themselves with more options in the editing phase).

Yet later that day, after filming the suicide, the camera that Andy had used to film the "fresh" death unexpectedly broke. It was puzzling to the crew because, as Andy recounted,

> The camera just sort of slipped out of the hand of the camera guy—it was strange how it broke. Because of the weight of the camera, it shouldn't have broken so hard. The lens was crushed after the suicide. It remained a fuzzy picture afterwards.

In Hong Kong, photographing or filming the deceased is still regarded with some unease, and this protocol is particularly articulated in the film community. Thus, when Andy told the producer of the film about filming a "real" suicide and the subsequent broken camera lens, the producer became worried about what he perceived as a spiritual transgression. Presumably, the deceased man did not intend to have his final moment of mortality immortalized for a commercial film. The film's producer was concerned with maintaining a film shoot free from logistical, financial, and supernatural complications, and he told Andy, "I heard that you shot some 'dirty' stuff. It's because you filmed the dead man." He asked Andy to erase the footage and burn incense. Shrugging sheepishly as he recounted this episode to me, Andy said that he immediately "got rid of the footage" and lit incense and burned paper money to appease what he described as the angry spirit of the recently deceased man, and any other lingering spirits who might be offended at his affront.

In a bid for authenticity, Andy and his colleagues had intentionally set out to make a film that showed the gritty underside of Hong Kong. Yet, actual events trumped the staged violence. I asked Andy to explain what was going through his mind when he grabbed the camera and filmed the suicide. He said,

> I thought, "Shit! Is this gonna turn out well? It must be a sign. Just do it, and worry about it later. I mean, it's a fresh corpse!!" I was on a

> momentum. Everything, the atmosphere, was heightened. It [the sui-
> cide] was so similar to what we were doing—it was a natural reaction. If
> I was just sitting there in my own apartment, and someone jumped, I
> wouldn't shoot it.

Andy's reference to the suicide as a sign reveals how off-camera contingencies are converted into fodder for fictionalized accounts of reality. The
"natural" reaction that Andy spoke of reveals how the industrial attempts
to produce fiction are in some cases endeavors to achieve authenticity, no
matter how grisly or ethically questionable. Andy attributed his ethical
transgression to the filmmaking process, which became symbolized by the
camera. The camera in this sense is a provocateur, enabling not only Andy's
voyeurism but the violation of the deceased man. Without a camera at
hand, Andy could not reproduce so graphically such a visceral experience;
nor, perhaps, would he be compelled to do so. Many ordinary people take
"selfies" with their camera phones in all kinds of provocative situations for
personal, not professional, reasons, without questioning all the ethical implications, at least at the moment the photo's taken. In filming the deceased
man, Andy saw the potential for spectacle, which leads to profit, illustrating
how closely the two are entwined in the film industry. Filming an actual
death with the intention to intercut it into the feature film was naturalized
as the cinematic impulse for authenticity. The intention to pass off documentary footage as fictional was acknowledged as unethical later, through
the producer's interpretation of why the camera lens cracked.

The camera thus played multiple roles: a proxy for commercial audiences as well as an accomplice in the commodification of the spectacle of
suicide. Borrowing from Actor Network Theory (ANT), nonhuman objects are understood to possess agency.[2] As actants, camera technology
constitute performative objects that "participate in the generation of information, of power relations, of subjectivities and objectivities" (Law and
Hetherington 2002: 37). ANT helps us see precise production "networks"—
combinations and recombinations of relations between a variety of human
actors and nonhuman objects and forces (Law 1999). As Andy explained,
the camera is an agent in the production process: provocateur *and* protector for the personnel. He reflected,

> The camera was a buffer, it captured the ghost. The camera buffered the
> misfortunes that would befall us. It captured a misfortune. In Hong
> Kong, if you have bad luck, you buy fish. When a fish dies, it buffers a
> bad future for you. The camera buffered bad fortune for us. Like the fish,
> it took the blow. It's now a cursed camera.

When I asked Andy what or who delivered this blow that damaged the lens, he answered, "It was the ghost [of the dead man]. He was saying, 'You shouldn't have shot me like this'." On Andy's film set, the supernatural reprimand was directed at the instrument that had enabled and mediated the transgression. The spectral struggles to find expression through the very technology that has abetted in its exploitation. Yet because of the symbiotic relationship between the camera and Andy, spectral rage is also conveyed to the filmmakers, indicating their accountability in dealing with contingencies. Thus, we see that the camera and its various parts entrap and transmit spectral rage back onto the production team. An unintended observation of a suicide with the naked eye of a bystander is not equivalent to the deliberate decision to film and then sell it on the market as spectacular imagery. That the camera's lens was so damaged and blurry afterward can be understood as the camera becoming internally destroyed by what it witnessed.

Andy's interpretation of the spectral rebuke for "shooting" the deceased man (Andy used the English-language jargon of "shooting") reads as a double entendre of how the camera can function as a weapon. In Andy's story, then, we can interpret death occurring on two levels—first, self-initiated by the man who jumped off the building; second, a "shooting" committed by a camera in combination with the artistic and financial aspirations and constraints in which such technology is used. Extending Susan Sontag's writings on still photography to filmmaking, the camera can violate its subjects "by having knowledge of them they can never have" (Sontag 1977: 14). This power differential between the seer and the seen casts those who are filmed into "objects that can be symbolically possessed," with the camera ultimately committing an act of "soft murder"— even of someone already dead (Sontag 1977: 14–15). The camera is complicit in blurring the worlds between which media personnel work.

During Andy's film shoot the camera becomes a vehicle for both transgressing *and* implementing ethical conduct. Thus we see that the camera is an ambivalent force in the filming process; chimera-like, the camera, as with the goldfish that Andy mentioned, provoked supernatural forces, yet it also protected the film crew from further injury. In this and other Hong Kong film productions, spectral forces, to varying degrees, are invoked by producers and directors to set ethical guidelines by which the film community must operate, reminding them that transgressions of a spiritual-moral nature may meet with retribution. Capturing the moment in which a man *moved between worlds* via camera technology—without his permission and with the intention to sensationalize the spectacle—is a stark example of the efforts to which filmmakers go for authenticity and profitability. This encounter also underscores the interdependence of filmmaker and camera. ANT stresses the transformative power of the human actors such as Andy and that other actor of "radical indeterminacy," the deceased man (Callon 1999: 181) and of nonhuman actants (the camera, which acts as both provocateur and protector for the film crew). The hybrid participants of the filmmaking experience thus come into sharp relief: an entanglement of actors and actants engaged in dynamic, shifting processes such that cameras and filmmakers together mediate confrontations with "reality," ethics, and their vulnerability in dealing with contingencies. In Andy's vignette we also see a form of memorialization that exploits the image of a random deceased man whose use and exchange value in this visual economy could possibly come to measure more in death than in life, hinging on its spectacularization. But any profits from such imagery would go to the production company or studio and distributor, not the family of the deceased man. Eventually the illicit footage was erased and, although the ritual economy is not commensurate with the political economy, the dead man's spirit received a belated payment from Andy in the form of special-purpose votive money and incense burned as an offering to him. What bears noting is some of the media workers' thrill in looking at and, indeed, helping to compose such images—a sort of professionalized and even institutionalized scopophilia—and how that is an integral component in the production of commercial entertainment. Imagery of death and dying has historically served as a form of entertainment not just in Hollywood and Hong Kong action and horror films, but in various sociocultural contexts. As noted by Jay Ruby in his study on late 19th-century American postmortem photography, some viewers and photographers found "pleasure" in capturing images of death (Ruby 1995: 6) as a way to remember the dearly departed.

Hong Kong media workers are certainly not unique when it comes to dubious practices on set: ethics have also been an issue for decades in Hollywood. Actors have complained about directors who have been known to continue filming when actors are accidentally injured or in pain during a scene, to ostensibly be used as "authentic" and/or supplemental footage (such as Ellen Burstyn during filming of *The Exorcist* and P. J. Soles in *Carrie*). In the early 1930s, child welfare workers were on set, but as former child star Shirley Temple recalled in her autobiography, the directors sometimes separated them from the youngsters they were there to protect, and used harsh physical discipline to manipulate the children for filming. But as Andy's situation reinforces, media workers, much like paying audiences, are spectators. As Gunning writes of late 19th- and early 20th-century American cinema and Chris Berry and Mary Farquhar write of contemporaneous Chinese cinema, "attractions" such as magic, optical tricks, and thrills were popular features. Berry and Farquhar even note the Chinese "peep shows" that were filmed, whose format beckoned a voyeuristic viewer to partake of provocative images (Berry and Farquhar 2005: 28). This legacy, in which media workers partake of the spectacle even while filming it, remains evident in the production of contemporary entertainment imagery.

Andy and his camera also reveal how "real" tragedies are repurposed for social fictions as a consequence of concerns about time and cost. Andy's sensitivity to the industrial pressures of working quickly, using whatever means at hand to widen the production's repertoire of provocative images by turning the camera on "real" events, backfired in this case, since the lens break resulted in losing a day of filming. They wanted to use both cameras for simultaneous filming later that day, but since they were unable to replace the broken camera on that same day and thus had to work with only one camera. Therefore this transgression resulted in Andy reconsidering his future labor practices (specifically, what spontaneous filming he would undertake) and increasing his cosmological practices on other production sites. Andy's experience with the camera points to how media workers labor between worlds: to film "reality" is to explore a realm that is somewhere between fiction and nonfiction, and in this case, between life and death.

"Camera Ready": Transitions and Transformations

Camera technology is a compelling force, and even when it is not recording imagery and is not in visible proximity to media workers, its signification seeps into how media workers in both Hollywood and Hong Kong relate to one another. Media personnel located anywhere in relation to the realm of the camera—investors, directors, producers, and production crews—respond to what they imagine this machine to represent: a mirror, an invasive technology, a conduit to potential audiences and markets. As an actor in Hollywood said of her relationship to the camera: "It's interesting because you can't truly ever forget about it because it's your window to your audience. So you have to be able to convey through it."

As Andy's vignette demonstrated, the camera also evokes and captures the labor that is performed in its vicinity. I introduce the Hollywood industry term "camera ready" here to discuss how I observed the camera impacting the labor and social relations on Hollywood film sets for a range of media workers. Being "camera ready" is Hollywood industry on-set jargon that means an actor is physically presentable to appear on screen (having undergone wardrobe and cosmetic changes and dressed with the appropriate props). This entails preparing for the scrutiny of one's labor, whether one's labor is in front of the camera (such as an actor) or behind the camera (such as the members of the wardrobe, property, or makeup departments). In this section I illustrate how the camera starts to take hold of a range of media workers before filming actually starts.

Media workers mediate in the immediate production site, simultaneously producing and receiving images. The quality of "to-be-looked-at-ness" that feminist film scholar Laura Mulvey famously describes as orienting the male gaze toward the female image on the screen (Mulvey 2000[1975]: 40) is already a thriving dynamic *behind* the screen on the production sites of commercial media production, and is directed by workers of all genders and sexual orientations toward actors on the premises. It is the task of craft and technical workers to constantly evaluate how everything *looks*. This includes constant touchups of the actors' makeup or readjusting of props such as backpacks or computers. Particularly on union and big-budget productions in Hollywood, attention to detail is thorough: I would regularly observe craft workers scrutinizing every aspect of an actor's appearance, for these things could be read on screen. These media workers must maintain a particular and consistent vision, and in doing so they internalize the gaze of the camera.

The increasingly intimate gaze of camera technology requires actors in particular to undergo temporary physical and affective transformations. For instance, while observing many of the actors enter the hair and makeup trailer early in the morning, I would notice that the persona with which they would enter would undergo a change as they were cosmetically transformed. While their appearance was in the process of transitioning, many would study their lines to memorize for the day's shoot, with the assistant directors periodically checking in to see if the actors were "camera ready." This was for many the start of when their persona became a blend of their "real" self and their character. Being "camera ready" for some actors meant more than just cosmetic applications; it meant donning their character and assuming different body language and posture, contorting facial muscles, altering their voice in pitch or accent: in some cases, thoroughly changing their demeanor. Because of the intimate labor involved, these shifts also impacted those who managed their appearance (such as members of the wardrobe, makeup, and hair departments) as well as the technicians (camera crew, electricians, carpenters, and sound technicians) and the director. Some of these workers described having to deal with shifting personas from actors. Of course, where there are are cameras, there are lights. This actor speaks of the unnatural and anomalous conditions of performing affect under technical constraints; in other words, the ways in which camera technology in combination with lighting, dictates how "reality" is captured:

> It's not normal. In real life, I'm not having to worry about if I'm crying and moved out of my light, if I've moved off my mark, am I not in front of the camera, am I in my partner's shadow? If I'm having a fight in real life with my boyfriend I don't have to worry about my placement, if I'm standing in a shadow.

The camera represents an audience lying in wait to consume the imagery in front of it, and its innovations also require that technical workers be "camera ready." A makeup artist on the set of a television show that I observed commented on how technological innovations posed new risks and anxieties for those who work behind the camera as well as those who work in front of it. With the switch to high-definition television (HDTV) for many television programs and films, the increased resolution of the picture evokes new concerns about the scrutiny of the camera. The ocular perception and precision of this new technology means that blemishes and details of the appearance of the actors and the background previously not visible are now laid bare. Directors of photography, lighting technicians, editors, makeup artists, set dressers, and actors work to optimize this microscopic gaze. They are assisted by post production artists who perform digital "enhancement," as well as another and more invasive option for actors: surgery. Nevertheless, as much effort as possible is made on the set, and workers must be seen as doing so. After observing a makeup artist touch up one of the principal actors for a TV show filmed in HDTV, I asked him how he dealt with the technology. He sighed and said,

> With the harsh light needed for Hi-Def, it makes every little line and blemish stand out on the actors' face. It's more work for us, and more exposure for the actors. We try to make it up to them with close-ups using dark shadows, soft light, or silk scarves over the camera when possible.

Many of the makeup artists on this television program watched tapes of the show to study how their work looks on film. Both on screen and off, craft and technical workers must refine their labor techniques as they innovate, attending to the worries and insecurities of actors while working at breakneck speed. The technical workers in particular (such as the camera operator, the director of photography, the assistant camerapersons, and the lighting crew) are frequently perceived as the bridge to that final audience. A camera operator told me,

> You become instant friends with the subject when you have a camera on your shoulder. There is an instant rapport with the actor. They're all so conscious about how they look. Their energy is going towards you—they have a relationship with the camera. People put their trust in you to make them look good and their performance shine. People are without a doubt very nice to me.

The power of the camera transfers to those who direct and operate them. On various film and television sets in Hollywood and Hong Kong the camera operators were popular with the actors. On one television set in Hollywood in particular the cast made an effort to regularly socialize with the camera operator and other camera crew as well as the other image personnel on and off the set. The environment of those who mediate images that are transmitted to commercial audiences is itself inundated with an abundance of images. On film and television sets, the presence of cameras and TV monitors imposed an ocular mode of discipline that records and regulates the behavior of media workers—a two-way instrument of surveillance of labor practices. Similar to the role of the computer as an "electronic panopticon" among data processors in the work environment of offshore informatics that Carla Freeman observed, the camera monitors personnel (Freeman 2000). On one of the Hollywood TV shows I observed, whichever camera was in use was generally still hooked up to the television monitors even when not recording a specific scene, thus transmitting framed images of the labor, socializing, and break time back onto the set. Positioned at various places on the set, the monitors resembled a set of mirrors in a fun house, projecting distorted images of the workplace to the media workers. The constant yet partial surveillance provided for some media workers a sense of scopic pleasure. The sense of vision is a heightened one in this type of production site, and seeing themselves and others on screen, captured by the camera plugged into the monitors even when not filming, was enjoyable for many of the media workers. At the same time, the camera and the monitors served as a reminder that their behavior could be critiqued and constrained by others, thus revealing the ocular mode of discipline on such sites. They could be seen to be relaxing when they should be working.

I turn now to how shifts in technology can impact labor practices and power relations in the Hollywood workplace. Since the director is considered the first in command on a film set (and second to producers on a television set), on many Hollywood film and television sets the regimented labor divisions dictate that the camera operator and the actors are not initially supposed to consult with one another. Often at the beginning of a project, camera operators in Hollywood lack speaking rights to the actors. The camera operator is supposed to receive instructions and make comments to the director and/or the director of photography, who sits alongside the director and also watches the filming from afar. Yet in some cases, knowing that the director is watching the filmed scene in a different room or from many yards away results in a shift in how actors respond to camera operators and their technology, as a more intimate relationship between the camera operator (and in some cases the camera assistant) and the actors develops, despite the (in)formal hierarchy.[3] On network TV sets in particular, which film for approximately nine months a year, as the camera operator quoted above said, they become quite friendly with the actors. Another camera operator describes the complex on-set relationships between himself as the holder of the camera, the actors, directors, and others:

> Sometimes the actors come to me instead of the director, especially if they don't like what the director tells them, and I'm uncomfortable sometimes with this dynamic. There is a director–DP relationship. There is an unspoken actor–DP relationship. You usually as DP or camera operator go through the director first if you need to give instruction to an actor, but then after a week or so you may talk to the actor directly or wait for the director to tell you to tell the actor. But with certain directors, I would never address the actors directly. Some directors are control freaks, you can't talk to the actors but there is an unspoken relationship. When I let them know if there is an unflattering shot or ask them to do something, they are very thankful, very grateful.

Combined with the camera's physical proximity to the actors and the director's distance from the immediate site of filming, the camera operator and the actors in some cases form an alliance. Thus, as the technological capacities of the camera evolve, so the social relations in this work environment also shift.

One of the most striking examples of emergent relationships and experiences on commercial film and television sets is Steadicam technology. Steadicam operators, who literally wear the camera on their body, are freed from the presence of a director hovering beside them and are enabled to enter into more intimate relations with actors. There is a dynamic relationship between the images the Steadicam operator observes, his response, and how he in turn manipulates his body and machinery.

Steadicam is designed to facilitate an affective relationship between camera technology, its operators, professional actors, and imagery. As a world-renowned Steadicam operator named Lenny told me,

> There can be, and often is, a more intimate connection between cameras and actors. I think that if you are good at Steadicam you respond to what actors are doing in an immediate and personal way. I act on behalf of the audience. I *am* the audience they are playing to. Especially when they improvise lines, as some directors like Scorsese allow them to do. If they say something dubious, I may just start to move in a little bit, lean in a little bit. There are body cues we have that can be communicated with Steadicam that resembles the instinctive response of a person listening in on a conversation.

As Lenny thoughtfully articulates, the particular gaze afforded by Steadicam heightens affective possibilities for audiences as well as its operators, who partake in a dynamic process with those in its field of action, especially actors. What emerges between the performance of the actor and the camera movement reveals that setwork is a highly important component of film-making. The development and popularity of such technology also means a lack of adherence to scripted material and predetermined camera moves, and a rise in spontaneity and agency on the part of media workers.

Conclusion

In this chapter, I examined how cameras shape labor practices on commercial film and television sets in Hollywood and Hong Kong. I have attempted to demonstrate the material and symbolic significance of cameras as an orienting force on production sites for media workers in both Hollywood and Hong Kong. The cameras' potential to entrap something of those who work with them renders the filming process not just uncanny, but chimerical. There is also the contradictory aspect to camera technologies in the production process: we commonly think of film and television media as granting media personnel, especially actors and stunt workers, immortality, yet the camera, as Sontag points out, can confer mortality. Andy's episode also demonstrates how cameras "make us" do things and instigate activity, and that the ethics of pointing and shooting even in a scripted, staged context can be breached. In his case, the "real" violence eclipsed the staged violence. It becomes evident that camera technology used in specific cultural and industrial settings brings forth complicated relationships and ontological terrain for media workers. Staged violence, death and dying, and physical intimacy are provocative imagery that commercial film and television rely upon for profit. Cameras can take on sinister connotations and capabilities, and the fact that these concerns persist reveal that the rationalization process of production and the scientific, secular ethos of modernity have not entirely triumphed. The notion of the camera as a chimera thus reminds us that capturing images via camera technology can haunt media workers. In our current era, when bystanders can capture people's "natural" behavior on camera phones without their consent and footage goes viral with all sorts of personal, political, and professional consequences, examining professionals who work in scripted, staged contexts provides another perspective. Studies of people whose livelihood revolves around cameras (literally and figuratively) provide a useful avenue into media ethics, as their deliberate engagement with cameras to create "real" dramatic images for fictional purposes shows us the interactive relationship and distributed accountability between a seemingly inanimate object and a person in the pursuit of industrial spectacle. Andy's story also depicts the seduction of spontaneity in our use of camera technology, whether for the big screen or for selfies. A multivalent object, the camera captures the various stakes in what it means to work at the interstices of mortality and immortality.

In his consideration of anthropology and time, Tom Ingold reminds us that "the world stands still for no one, least of all for the artist or the anthropologist, and the latter's description, like the former's depiction, can do no more than catch a fleeting moment in a never-ending process" (Ingold 2011: 232). This book has attempted to convey some of the concerns and dreams, ambitions and anxieties that people in Hollywood and Hong Kong who create commercial film and television bring to their work, as well as the meanings that emerge from their work process. Today, the dynamics on film and television sets remain very similar, but the broader landscapes in which they occur have undergone some shifts—and will continue to do so. Below, I discuss a few of those current developments.

Hong Kong

Since I conducted research in Hong Kong, the anxieties that some of the media personnel expressed have reverberated throughout the city. In September 2014, the Occupy movement in Hong Kong burst forth onto the streets. And as I write this now, more than a year after Occupy ended, protesters and riot police have just clashed on the streets of Mongkok, a sign of continued sociopolitical unrest. The street protests of late 2014, which started out as Occupy Central and became known as the Umbrella Revolution, or Movement, received worldwide attention for the images of the protesters (many of them young people who came of age after Hong Kong's

1997 return to China). Protesters used their ubiquitous umbrellas in the rainy city in self-defense against tear gas and pepper spray. As Vivienne Chow and Ng Kang-chung noted in a *South China Morning Post* article on October 24, 2014, members of Hong Kong's entertainment industries who expressed sympathy or solidarity for the protestors were reportedly criticized in China's media and by mainland fans. The protests were prompted in part by Beijing's refusal to grant full universal suffrage for Hong Kong's chief executive election in 2017 and the Legislative Council elections in 2020.[1] However, it is important to point out that within Hong Kong, many people did not support the 2014 protests for various reasons, whether they identify as pro-Beijing or not. The political upheaval of the past year has been a divisive issue within Hong Kong society, as people retain cultural, familial, and sentimental ties and loyalties to China, and many businesses and industries in the territory rely upon mainland Chinese investment and tourism as well as cross-border ventures.

Signs of Life

A year before the world was inundated with images of Hong Kong people protesting in the streets about the lack of universal suffrage, thousands of Hong Kong people took to the streets to protest the paucity of good television in Hong Kong. Sparking that protest was the Hong Kong government's decision to deny a TV license to entrepreneur Ricky Wong, who had proposed a free-to-air television channel called HKTV that many in the Hong Kong public hoped would diversify Hong Kong television. However, local websites and internet television are broadening the range of choices for Hong Kong viewers, and the forums for local cultural expression. For instance, the social media platform and site Most TV offers political and social satire on issues in the territory. The developments in what is available on people's TV screens can potentially mean shifts in film production, too. The U.S.-based Netflix was made available in Hong Kong in January 2016, and as Vivienne Chow reported in a *South China Morning Post* article on January 28, 2016, the streaming content provider is interested in developing original Hong Kong content with local Hong Kong filmmakers. If this content is made available to users in other regions, could Netflix eventually replace international film festivals as a far-reaching venue for local filmmakers?

The pronouncements of death and dying in the industry continue as informants complain of the industry being "really dead." Currently, many of them and their colleagues increasingly work in film (and television) in China or on co-productions with China; some of them do so happily, excited to pursue opportunities there, others with more ambivalence and even sadness. Some personnel work in other parts of the world, too. A number of them have left film and television altogether due to the lack of local work. On July 22, 2014, Hong Kong's *South China Morning Post* ran an article titled "Stuntmen a Dying Breed in Hong Kong, Says Daredevil Expert, as Hollywood Comes Calling." Bruce Law, the "daredevil" stunt man and director, commented to Yvonne Teh that China has grown its own stunt worker base, and only "about 50" stunt workers are left in Hong Kong. The Hong Kong-based Law now works mostly across the border in China and in Hollywood. While the number of locally produced films fluctuates slightly, the dominance of foreign film releases in Hong Kong is confirmed in Table Epilogue.1.

The majority of top-grossing films in Hong Kong are Hollywood blockbusters. According to Box Office Mojo, Hollywood productions accounted for eight of the 10 top-grossing films in Hong Kong in 2014; corresponding figures for 2013, 2012, and 2011 were seven, 10, and seven (Box Office Mojo 2011–2014). Hong Kong production thus continues to be squeezed not just by China, but by Hollywood.

Yet while the output of the Hong Kong film industry continues to decrease, new directions and developments show promise. Following Mirana Szeto and Yun-chung Chen's articulation of a "third way" to make films in which filmmakers use big-budget film profits to fund smaller-budget films (Szeto and Chen 2013), Yiu-wai Chu posits that popular crime and gangster genres, made with fresh perspectives garnered from new resources and experiences (including co-productions), can help push Hong Kong filmmakers "beyond the 'big-budget Mainlandized inauthentic' versus 'small-budget local authentic' dichotomy," a plurality that he maintains is crucial for the rejuvenation of Hong Kong film (Chu 2015: 119). Chu sees this potential in the 2012 films *Cold War* and *Motorway*. The government has also made some overtures. In 2007, the Film Development Council was

Table Epilogue. 1 **Local Films Released in Comparison to Foreign Films Released in Hong Kong**

	2012	2013	2014
Number of local films released	52	43	51
Number of foreign films released	249	267	259

Source: HKTDC Research 2014.

founded with the aim of "sustainable development" of the Hong Kong film industry by advising the Secretary for Commerce and Economic Development on the policy, strategy, and institutional arrangement for the film industry. Its Film Development Fund Scheme for Financing Film Production has received 78 applications since its founding and will hopefully rejuvenate the industry; however, training and jobs also need to be accessible to a younger generation of filmmakers. In 2009, Hong Kong Baptist University's Academy of Film received government and industry support.

There is a growing collection of films about local identity and the city's future from filmmakers such as Fruit Chan, Pang Ho-Cheung, and Christopher Doyle. These films are directed toward Hong Kong audiences, resisting the lure (and demands) of the mainland market. The Umbrella protests spawned local artwork and reflected a desire for more local and Cantonese-language cultural productions, which is also apparent in newer work. The low-budget 2015 film *Ten Years*, a collection of short films directed by five filmmakers, has received international attention in its depiction of a subordinated Hong Kong identity under China. After the film was heavily criticized by state-controlled media in China, it was pulled from theaters in Hong Kong in early 2016, yet shown in public screenings around the city organized by community groups due to growing public interest. Unexpectedly, the film won Best Film at the Hong Kong Film Awards in April 2016. Chinese media outlets had refused to broadcast the film awards in China due to the film's being nominated. The film features stories about Cantonese language loss and protests against mainland Chinese authority. The latter story culminated in a local Hong Kong activist's self-immolation outside the British consulate, an on-screen depiction that seemed to draw inspiration partly from actual protesters who identify as localists and choose to fly the former colonial flag at various protests. I observed the presence of the colonial flag myself during a visit in the summer of 2014 on the June 4 holiday (the commemoration of Tiananmen Square). The protesters, both on screen and off, saw China as encroaching on Hong Kong's autonomy, democracy, and free press, not respecting the 1984 Sino-British Joint Declaration in which Hong Kong's way of life was codified to be preserved until 2047. Underscoring the political risks of making such a film, one of the directors told CNN that some actors at the auditions and during production expressed nervousness over the politically sensitive material in the script, noting that "in the production process, our hearts were not free" (Griffiths 2016).

Given Western media's extensive coverage of Hong Kong's Occupy protests, there may be international interest in Hong Kong films that offer the perspective of local sovereignty and suffrage. However, Hollywood's investments from, and involvement with, Chinese conglomerates both in China and in Los Angeles (such as Alibaba's investment in Paramount Pictures, Dalian Wanda's acquisition of the Los Angeles-based Legendary

Photo Epilogue. 1 The Historic Grauman's Chinese Theater on Hollywood Boulevard is Now Owned by a Chinese Multinational Electronics Company, TCL (*Credit: Author*).

Entertainment production company as well as Hollywood's historic Grauman's Chinese Theater, now owned by an actual Chinese multinational company, TCL [Photo Epilogue.1], and Disney's investment in a Shanghai amusement park which U.S. President Barak Obama praised as a kind of joint alliance) means it is unlikely that American studios and media conglomerates will want to seriously disturb their relationship with China. Hollywood's 2012 remake of *Red Dawn*, for instance, changed the villains from Chinese to North Korean, reflecting a clear business agenda of caution toward China.

But longstanding cultural practices also continue to sustain local cinema. During the Hungry Ghost Festival in the seventh month of the lunar calendar (*Yue Laan Jit*), ghost films are commonly released. For the 2014 Hungry Ghost Festival a film called *Hungry Ghost Ritual* was released, a story about a Cantonese opera troupe that leaves empty seats at its performances for lingering ghosts (as opera troupes actually do at the festival), only to become haunted by their spectral spectators. *Yue Laan Jit*, as discussed earlier, is the time when ghosts are believed to walk along the living, demanding food and entertainment and causing mischief, and this holiday is very publicly observed in Hong Kong. A co-production with a Malaysian company, the Hong Kong-based film remains local in that it was filmed in Hong Kong, in Cantonese; it follows in the internationally renowned Hong Kong horror film tradition; and it draws upon a Cantonese-language art form: opera. *Hungry Ghost Ritual* thus illustrates that Hong Kong films continue to emerge from and reflect local cultural practices.

Revisiting the Media Assemblage: From "Extinction" to Exceptionality

"Win a Trip to Hong Kong For the *Transformers: Age of Extinction* Premiere!" screamed the headline on the website for KROQ, Los Angeles' premier rock radio station on June 15, 2014. On June 19, 2014, the Hollywood blockbuster *Transformers* held its world premiere in Hong Kong with its star Mark Wahlberg attending (Photo Epilogue.2) and Transformer Optimus Prime stationed nearby at the Harbour (Photo Epilogue.3). I was visiting Hong Kong and it was the first time the city had ever hosted the world premiere for a Hollywood film co-produced with China. *Transformers: Age of Extinction* is the fourth installment in the sci-fi action *Transformers* series; it was filmed on location in Hong Kong and China as well as all over the United States, another example of the media assemblages in which media industries and personnel participate.

Photo Epilogue. 2 Hollywood Actor Mark Wahlberg, Star of *Transformers: Age of Extinction*, at the Film's Premiere in Hong Kong (*Credit: Author*).

Photo Epilogue. 3 Optimus Prime Guards Hong Kong's Victoria Harbour for the *Transformers* Film Premiere (*Credit: Author*).

The *Transformers* director, Michael Bay, hadn't been able to resist the dazzling neon and soaring skyscrapers Hong Kong offers. The city is a popular locale for small-scale productions in the Asian region such as the Bollywood television show that unobtrusively filmed earlier this year at Central Pier on Hong Kong Island (Photo Epilogue.4). But the entire city of Hong Kong is served up as one big film set for American billion-dollar films as well. Even though China is increasingly included as a location site for Hollywood films as a tactic to draw in mainland audiences and revenue, U.S.-based filmmakers remain enticed by Hong Kong's spectacular skyline and vibrant street life, as seen in *The Dark Knight, Black Hat,* and *Contagion.* Hollywood tentpole films—the films that sustain Hollywood media studios and conglomerates—are increasingly filmed overseas, absorbing global landmarks to encompass global box-office receipts. Robert Sickles defines Hollywood's tentpole films as a studio's "centerpiece" that can "spread out over various other subsidiary companies in the form of ancillary products, such as video games, toys, DVDs, theme park rides, and so on" (Sickles 2010: 79).

The city government's cooperation with an American and Chinese coproduction and their provision of a local crew underscore the kind of transnational and regional encounters in which Hollywood and Hong Kong continue to engage. Local industry personnel are able to continue to work, albeit in reduced numbers and on nonlocal films, and the city itself retains its cinematic visibility, even if in the service of Hollywood dominance. Cheuk Pak-tong, the director of the Academy of Film at Hong Kong Baptist University, was quoted as saying that the premiere of *Transformers 4* in Hong Kong "will do nothing to reboot the local movie-making industry," in an article by Hilary Wong of *The Standard* on June 18, 2014. Cheuk's prediction seems accurate, as being a site of exhibition does not ensure increased production. Cinematically, *Transformers* represented the sense of doom hanging over various sectors within Hong Kong. Havoc is wreaked on the city, and one of the most explosive film scenes is the image of Hong Kong's harbor under attack—a Hollywood–China rendering of the city's demise, which, given the fears of both Hollywood's assault on the local film market and mainland Chinese encroachment, carries some resonance.

Local dynamics also pervaded this transnational production process when the director, Michael Bay, was attacked by low-level triad members while filming. Bay wrote on his blog after the attack on October 17, 2013, that it took "fifteen Hong Kong cops in riot gear to deal with these punks," one of whom bit the toe of a guard. Part of the lure of this former

Photo Epilogue. 4 A Bollywood Television Show Films Unobtrusively at Hong Kong Central Pier *(Credit: Author).*

colony for such high-profile Anglo-American visitors is its reputation for law and order. The Film Services Office in particular seeks to reassure foreign crews that film shoots in the frenetically paced city will occur without incident. Yet this incident underscores that foreign film productions are not insulated from local dynamics (and may in fact trigger such reactions).

Hong Kong's selection as the film premiere site also reveals another political dimension of that assemblage. Although China was originally chosen to host the film premiere, its visa requirements for foreigners apparently forced the Hollywood studio to shift its opening to Hong Kong, as Western media could not easily stay in China to cover the opening. Evidently, Hollywood still needs Hong Kong both on screen and off for its tentpole expansionist policy. Hong Kong's political exceptionality to China (see Ong 2006) is played out on the world stage in its selection as the alternative premiere site. Therefore, the city further retains its relevance for Hollywood through media events such as film premieres. Despite all the market opportunities that China represents to Hollywood, it is the "open" Anglo-American political and financial system of Hong Kong—a holdover of its colonial era—that helps to keep the city a participant in the workings of Hollywood and the larger American entertainment complex.

Hollywood

Rejuvenation?

Death scenes on screen are often followed by signs of life and renewal. Recalling Marshall Berman's invocation of Marx, the industrial structures that appear to be solid are "made to be broken tomorrow, smashed or shredded or pulverized or dissolved, so they can be recycled or replaced next week, and the whole process can go on again and again, hopefully forever, in ever more profitable forms" (Berman 1982: 99). In Hollywood, the film and television production company at which I interned has since closed, but several members have regrouped to form a newer film production company, which in recent years has made several high-profile films. Other informants have gone on to work on new projects. However, some informants have not been able to find work at all and are struggling to find new career paths.

Media conglomerates have certainly survived. In fact, as the author of *The Hollywood Economist 2.0*, Edward Jay Epstein, noted in 2012, despite claims of being in turmoil, the Hollywood studios actually posted record profits that year. American television, seen by many as in decline a few years ago, has become a major profit provider for studios, which produce content for network and cable channels. Epstein cites other ways in which Hollywood studios have been swelling their profits: licensing to new media, ramping up video on demand, reducing star salaries, and taking larger cuts of blockbusters that play in foreign markets (Epstein 2012). Traditional networks face competition from digital companies and streaming entertainment such as Amazon, Netflix, and Hulu, as well as the older premium pay channels, all of which combine film talent with that of television.

Regarding the decline in local production, in 2004, California held about 65 percent of the film and television jobs in the United States; by 2012, that number had declined to 52 percent, with New York, Louisiana, and other states taking up the rest. The California Film and Television Tax Credit Program 2.0, which Governor Jerry Brown signed into law in 2014, is an updated, five-year program that provides annual funding of $330 million to film and television programs that film in California to combat the more competitive tax credits and subsidies offered in other states and countries. The City of Los Angeles' official film office, FilmL.A., reported on January 19, 2016, that on-location filming in Greater Los Angeles had increased 1.3 percent in 2015 in shoot days, due to a boost in scripted television production, as well as the state's revised tax-credit program (FilmL.A. 2016).

However, while celebratory reports currently emerge from Hollywood that Los Angeles-based television production jobs are returning, film production, on the other hand, especially for big-budget, tentpole films, faces challenges in keeping production in state. Contrary to popular and industry assumptions about China, India, and other developing parts of the world grabbing these opportunities to the detriment of the United States, a report by the California State legislature points out that some of California's biggest competitors are actually Canada and the United Kingdom: "In addition to offering generous film and television production subsidies, Canada and the United Kingdom also possess high-quality soundstages, experienced crews, and post-production facilities with many specialized suppliers and vendors located near their major production centers" (Taylor 2014).

The California Film and Television Tax Credit Program 2.0 credit allocation applies only to the first $100 million in qualified expenditures for feature films (http://www.film.ca.gov/Incentives.htm), whereas many of the globally popular superhero films have for years boasted budgets well over that. So, for instance, 2015 tentpole films *Star Wars: The Force Awakens* filmed some scenes in the United States, but the majority of them were shot in Ireland, the United Kingdom, and Iceland, while *Mad Max: Fury Road* filmed in Namibia, South Africa, and Australia, according to IMDb. Others, including *Avengers: Age of Ultron* and *Fantastic Four*, were also filmed mostly out of California and out of the country, including Canada and the United Kingdom.

The perception that California, and Los Angeles in particular, is losing its historical hold on film production has continued to gain momentum over recent years. In what they warn can result in a "race to the bottom" between states to offer the most tax credits and subsidies, the California Legislative Analyst's Office issued a 2014 report in which they provided "preliminary observations regarding tax credits" for California's motion picture industry (which includes commercials and music videos) (Taylor 2014). The report was issued in light of the proposed changes to legislation that resulted in the California Film and Television Tax Credit Program 2.0. Significantly, however, the report pointed out that the motion picture industry may no longer be a profitable investment for the state. The film tax credit does not, as industry groups claim, "pay for itself," since for every $1 spent, the state receives only 65 cents in taxes (Taylor 2014). The report also cautions that between 1997 and 2012, "the motion picture industry grew at an average annual rate of 1.5 percent, while the overall economy grew at an average annual rate of 2.3 percent" (Taylor 2014). In considering the number of films annually submitted to the Motion Picture Association of America (MPAA) for rating, "film production appears to have peaked in 2003 with 949 films rated by the MPAA," whereas starting in 2009, between 700 and 800 films a year were submitted. The report also warns that such state subsidies unfairly favor one industry over other industries, and that industrial decline may be inevitable despite subsidies, the effectiveness of which is difficult to measure given insufficient data.

Although the Tax Credit Program 2.0 was signed into effect, boosting state subsidies, this report's findings (and its sober tone) remind the industry that state government support cannot be taken for granted, even for what has long been a Los Angeles-based industry and institution. Will the current tax credit program be renewed in 2021? How will other state industries be faring at that point? Regarding the reported increased jobs in television production, what are their conditions? How consistent will part-time, short-term work be? The report does suggest that state subsidization should continue to matter because Hollywood is part of the state's "brand" and therefore a lure for tourism and investment, as well as a partner to the hi-tech industry and a source of considerable American soft power. However, its concerns signal a possible decline, or even end, in sight. By acknowledging the endless competition, strain on workers, and decrease in environmental standards, as well as their findings above, the California Legislative Analyst's office builds a strong case for delinking film and television production from state support—an official stance that may be surprising to many Los Angeles-based media personnel. While corporate offshoring is nothing new for Hollywood, the state government's decline in subsidies, combined with China's growing expansion of Hollywood production, could one day portend something approaching the *Transformers 4* "age of extinction" for Los Angeles-based big-budget film production. The premise of deterritorialization, of media production becoming unmoored from historic place-based sites at the behest of government, remains a potential reality for Hong Kong; arguably, it is not entirely ruled out for Hollywood as well.

Stealing Shots

Safety risks continue to be an issue on film and television sets, especially on location, where oversight is reputedly less stringent. Recall the classic 1917 silent film image mentioned in the Introduction of a woman tied to the tracks of an oncoming train to be saved at the last minute, the seminal image that offered viewers a cinema of attractions. A hundred years later, in an incident not intended for the camera, Sarah Jones, a 27-year-old camera assistant, was killed on the train tracks of a bridge 25 feet above the water during the filming of the "runaway production" *Midnight Rider* in Georgia. Jones's on-set death on February 20, 2014, caused shockwaves in Hollywood and calls for increased set safety. This sad episode encapsulates the themes of this book: risk, death, and prayer on set to forestall danger.

The script, based on the autobiography of singer Gregg Allman, called for a dream sequence to be filmed with a metal-framed hospital bed on a train track; it became a real-life nightmare when an oncoming train came with less time to clear the track than the crew had been warned. The bed's metal parts, struck by the 57-m.p.h. train, pushed Jones into the path of the train, killing her instantly. The director of the film, Randall Miller; his producing partner (his wife); and the film's executive producer were sued; in addition to Jones's parents, a makeup artist and hairstylist pursued charges for their injuries. The director, Miller, is currently serving his two-year jail term for criminal trespass and felony involuntary manslaughter in the on-set death of Jones, the first of its kind for a Hollywood director. In addition to eight years of probation, the judge's sentence bars Miller from serving as director, first assistant director, or safety supervisor on any film production.

In the aftermath of the accident, the Department of Labor's Occupational Health and Safety Administration's investigation uncovered that crew members had not been informed about an email from the railroad owner, CSX, "denying them permission to shoot on the train trestle in rural Georgia, as at least 20 members piled onto the tracks 25 to 30 feet above the water under dangerous conditions led by director Randall Miller," noted Anita Busch and Jen Yamato for Deadline website on October 30, 2014. This reflects the threats typically encountered in offshoring in other industries and other parts of the world: less regulation and lower safety standards amid hasty work schedules. The director claimed that he had been told that the train's whistle would signal that they would have 60 seconds to move the bed and the crew safely from the tracks. However, the time from the whistle was only 26 seconds. Among the many concerns is that the director believed that even *60 seconds* was adequate time for the cast and crew to safely leave a live track. The hairstylist, Joyce Gilliard, whose arm was badly fractured and who witnessed Jones get killed up close, recalls that when the crew were told they'd have only one minute to clear the track on the trestle for an oncoming train, people expressed nervousness. Gilliard and others on set gathered in an impromptu prayer circle, praying, "Lord, please protect us on these tracks . . . Surround us with your angels and help us, Lord," as Scott Johnson reported for *The Hollywood Reporter* on March 4, 2014. Clearly, that risks continue to be addressed not just with secular measures (which were inadequate that day) but also spiritual ones—in the actual space of filming, not in private off-hours, away from the set—reveals how multifaceted a cultural process media production remains.

According to Gilliard, the producers "wanted to get the shot, so whatever it took to get the shot is what they did . . . The entire crew was put in a situation where we all had to basically run for our lives" (Dorian, Putrino, and Valiente 2014). That the endangered crew included the director himself recalls Andy's being so caught up in the pursuit of shock-and-awe cinema that he shot the aftermath of a suicide for his film. In these various examples of what Hollywood personnel refer to as "stealing shots," we see how, in the moment of creating powerful images, commonsensical and ethical decisions are sometimes cast aside. Joyce Gilliard has spoken of waking at night from pain in her arm and nightmares of Jones's death. Discussion and debate have exploded among Hollywood industry members about the risky practice of "stealing shots," compounded by the concern that low-budget productions filmed in rural parts of the country, away from the "headquarters" of Hollywood, with less experienced local crew members, are prone to increased negligence and risk taking. What makes a producer, a director, and an executive producer put themselves and others in such danger on a live train track? Is it just to pay the bills, as some suggest? To dazzle one's peers and superiors, and hope to yield enormous profits? To tantalize audiences with dark visions, and display their heroics at playing creator and destroyer while audiences remain safe at home? Production personnel become caught up in carrying out the tasks for which they have been hired, and the pressure to meet a deadline. But there is also, as we have seen, that shared desire to come close to the "attractions," to the shocking and awesome phenomena that such visual and visceral entertainment relies upon. In the affective labor on a set, people such as Randall Miller seem to become "possessed" by the energy and intensity of their work. There is clearly an industrial—and internalized—fascination for as-realistic-as-possible footage of often fantastical scenarios (see Martin 2012).

Sarah Jones's death was especially tragic given the dearth of women working and being promoted within camera departments. Responses to Jones's death from industry members included a public service announcement and a Facebook community page with over 73,000 likes, as well as walkathon fundraisers and the creation of a free app for set safety. Over a year later, the "Slates for Sarah" initiative still features camera slates (clapperboards) dedicated to her on film and television sets throughout Hollywood. That a fantasy sequence turned into such a real-life nightmare for members of the production underscores the dreams and dangers of filmmaking.

NOTES
....

Introduction

1. Extras are nonspeaking actors who fill a scene; "background artist" is the term many extras use to refer to themselves.

2. I use "personnel" and "workers" interchangeably to include everyone physically involved on film and television sets, from camera operators to actors to directors to members of the wardrobe department. Above-the-line workers are typically producers, writers, directors, and some principal actors who are "highly paid via individual negotiation and contract," while below-the-line workers include the "hourly employees in the craft or manual sectors whose wages and extensive proliferation of job descriptions are set by union contract or nonunion negotiation" (Caldwell 2008: 377). I will point out informal hierarchies on Hollywood and Hong Kong sets, as industry categories of "above-the-line" and "below-the-line" do not always determine the actual power dynamics on set, especially in Hong Kong, where unions are weak and job descriptions are not as fixed. Regarding Hollywood, a makeup artist, for instance, can, due to his or her physical and emotional proximity to a principal actor, wield influence regarding that actor's filming conditions and contractual demands.

3. Dr. Joseph Bosco of the Anthropology Department at Chinese University of Hong Kong has also been interviewed by Hong Kong's RTHK Radio 3 program about ghosts and the supernatural in Hong Kong.

4. Hong Kong's film industry has long been referred to by media workers, government institutions, scholars, and journalists as the "Hollywood of the East" for its high commercial output, numbering in the hundreds in the

1980s and early 1990s (Dannen 1997: 1; Fu 2000: 200; Stokes and Hoover 1999: 17; Teo 2005: 192). The term is sometimes used as a casual shorthand (as with Bollywood and Nollywood), yet it is problematic as it glosses over the specific histories and contours of both industries, and casts Hollywood as a timeless universal standard. Nevertheless, more than a few of my informants nostalgically laid claim to it. I deploy the term as a way to signal it as a common reference point for those mentioned above and not to uncritically reproduce the term's inaccuracies.

5. Soundstages are soundproof and in Hollywood range from 10,000 to 30,000 square feet (Scott 2005: 82).

6. Susan Seizer's thoughtful ethnography of Special Drama stage actresses in Tamilnadu, India, who enact intimate emotions in public performance spaces helped develop this insight (Seizer 2000).

7. The mark is the location on the set where the actor must start or finish; it is usually marked by a piece of neon-colored tape applied by the film crew.

8. Also, in Hong Kong many actors I spoke with were unfamiliar with Lee Strasberg's Method acting.

9. Fordism refers to the mass production of standardized products for mass consumption, as envisioned by Henry Ford in the 1910s. At his car factories, large workforces worked the assembly lines where "scientific management of all facets of corporate activity," including but not limited to production, "became the hallmark of bureaucratic corporate rationality" (Harvey 1991: 134). However, the physical concentration of (white, male) workers in factory spaces facilitated their organization into unions. Fordism would go global, adapted by markets around the world. Starting in the early 1970s, Fordism gave way to what geographer David Harvey calls the regime of flexible accumulation, which in contrast to the "rigidity" of Fordism promoted adaptability (Harvey 1991: 142). Flexible accumulation refers to not only a change in production but "new ways of providing financial services, new markets, and, above all, greatly intensified rates of commercial, technological, and organizational innovation" (Harvey 1991: 147). Flexible specialization—firms that cater to niche markets and specific and changing tastes—is an outgrowth of this post-Fordist regime and reflects the pressure of innovation. The shift to flexible accumulation, urged by corporations' reduced profit margins, engenders increased job insecurity for employees who are hired on an as-needed basis. Workers in flexible production have been increasingly subcontracted as part-time and temporary, with a loss of insurance and pensions. The workforce becomes more fractured and inconsistent, which hampers their ability to organize labor and collectively bargain (Harvey 1991: 151). In the developing world as well, subcontracted

workers in offshore factories are typically exploited with "extremely low pay and negligible job security," particularly female workers (Harvey 1991: 153). See Chapter 1 for the configurations of Fordism and post-Fordism in Hollywood and Hong Kong.

10. The *mahurat* includes the breaking of a coconut and the "rotational display of an oil lamp" to the film camera (Ganti 2012: 248).

11. I thank an anonymous reviewer for emphasizing this point.

12. See Buyandelgeriyn 2007; Comaroff and Comaroff 1999, 2000; Geschiere 1997; Hickel 2014; Johnson 2012; Kendall 1996; Kwon 2007; Niehaus 2002; Ong 1987; Taylor 2007; Weller 1994a.

13. Witches (migrant workers from other African countries) are thought to deploy zombies to work for them, a labor system that disrupts existing social and family relations (Hickel 2014).

14. Conferences such as the Fulbright Symposium entitled "Hong Kong/ Hollywood at the Borders" that I attended at Hong Kong University in 2004, in which various papers were devoted to the convergences between the two industrial sites and the permeability of national and regional boundaries, illustrate this emergence. Another example are books such as *Hong Kong Film, Hollywood, and the New Global Cinema: No Film Is an Island* (Marchetti and Kam 2007). Conference panels at other media conferences on transnational media flows and various publications also have examined links between Hollywood and Hong Kong.

15. With its rigorous attention to the movement of peoples and objects through its hallmark methodology of ethnographic fieldwork, anthropology has provided valuable contributions to the study of transnational film/TV media flows (see Appadurai 1996; Hannerz 1996; Schein 2002, 2004; Yang 1997, 2004).

16. Mei Zhan's focus on the "interactive processes" that emerge between two medical traditions provides a fruitful analysis of uneven flows in her ethnographic study of the transnational movement of traditional Chinese medicine (Zhan 2001: 454).

17. In 2010, shortly after my fieldwork, the nonwhite demographics were 12.6 percent black, 16.3 percent Latino, and 4.8 percent Asian, totaling over one third of the U.S. population. For empirical work on the intersection of race and media in Hollywood productions, and specifically the systemic racism in casting and stereotyped roles, see Kristen J. Warner's *The Cultural Politics of Colorblind TV Casting* (2015) and Nancy Wang Yuen's *Reel Inequality: Hollywood Actors and Racism* (2016).

18. "Westerner" is a multivalent term that refers to people of varying racial backgrounds who hail from a variety of geographic locations such as Australia, Canada, Russia, Morocco, Mexico, and Italy.

19. Allen Scott quotes the SIC as employment being above 130,000 in 2002 (Scott 2005: 122). In 2008, John Caldwell cites 250,000 workers as directly employed by the film and television industries (Caldwell 2008: 7).
20. This was an unpaid internship, the type that Hollywood companies typically expect for newcomers to the industry who want to work in production or development, subsidized with a generous supply of office snacks and coffee. Many college students receive course credit for an internship in lieu of payment (which has the unfortunate consequence of limiting low-income students from accessing industry training and networking and/or can put them in financial debt).

Chapter 1

1. http://www.thedailybeast.com/articles/2014/12/17/exclusive-sony-emails -allege-u-s-govt-official-ok-d-controversial-ending-to-the-interview.html
2. For industrial histories of Hollywood see Caldwell 2008; Gomery 2008; and Scott 2005. For Hong Kong, see Curtin 2007; Davis and Yeh 2009; Fu and Desser 2002; Ma 1999; Stokes and Hoover 1999; and Szeto and Chen 2013.
3. Alan Scott and John T. Caldwell point out that in Hollywood's case, its Fordist mode of production lacked the auto industry's degree of product standardization (Curtin 2007: 13; Scott 2005: 40).
4. The exception for Hong Kong is its period of occupation under Japan in 1941 to 1945, in which commercial filmmaking temporarily ceased, but it resumed when Hong Kong returned to British rule (Fu 2000).
5. For more on production processes and labor of the Hong Kong TV industry see Chow and Ma 2008; Ma 1999; Zhou 2014; for the Hollywood TV industry see Caldwell 2008; Lotz 2007; Scott 2005.
6. "In the Asian region, Castells argues that developmental states mainly depend on links with indigenous business firms and actors to form distinct regional networks that are separable from networks of greater extension" (Ong 2005: 338).
7. Govil argues that Indian conglomerates' acquisition of Western brands (such as Jaguar, Land Rover, and now DreamWorks) is symptomatic of India's attempts to overcome its developing world status by leveraging its corporate capital, while the benefit to DreamWorks of receiving the Indian capital injection is the severance of its ties to its corporate parent Viacom.

Chapter 2

1. Gunning explicates that his usage of "attractions" comes from Sergei Eisenstein's use of the term to describe his theatrical approach in which

spectators should be overwhelmed by "sensual or psychological impact" (Eisenstein, "How I Became A Film Director," in *Notes of a Film Director* [Moscow: Foreign Language Publishing House, n.d.], p. 16).

2. Mayer demonstrates how straight male videographers for *Girls Gone Wild* become affectively and sexually aroused (yet conflicted) through their interactions with the young women they film (Mayer 2008).

Chapter 4

1. Daughters and sisters sometimes were trained to perform in Cantonese Opera and transitioned to film and television work, but these numbers are much fewer (and were unavailable). I interviewed a couple of stunt workers whose sisters were trained by family members in Cantonese Opera, but these women did not go on to work in film and television.

2. This includes Laikwan Pang's 2001 article "Death and Hong Kong Cinema," Ackbar Abbas' 1997 analysis of Hong Kong's "culture of disappearance," and discourse on cinematic imagery of crisis and expiration as well as industrial decline (Cheung and Chu 2004; Marchetti 2000; Pang 2007; Szeto and Chen 2013; Williams 2000).

3. See Rey Chow's critique of the British colonial government's push to accelerate democratic measures through the Hong Kong government (Chow 1998; see also So 2004: 229–230).

Chapter 5

1. See Robert Weller for further discussion on the appeal of ghosts for entrepreneurial and sometimes dubious individuals in Taiwan (Weller 1994a).

2. These Hong Kong films include *You Shoot, I Shoot* by Pang Ho-Cheung and *Viva Erotica* by Derek Yee. Gangsters are portrayed as alternately bullying, financing, and protecting film industry workers.

3. It should be noted that some film workers in other commercial film industries, as with capitalist industries elsewhere, engage in some combination of supernatural and religious practices as part of the production process (see also Ganti 2004).

4. My choice of pseudonym mirrors many participants' adoption of an English-language name, reflecting the diasporic experiences of Hong Kong film personnel and the territory's British colonial past.

5. Hong Kong film industry guilds and craft associations such as the Hong Kong Stunt Man Association may provide financial help for injured members, but this is informal assistance and may not cover long-term needs.

6. The article "Spirits Heed Casting Calls" in *The Straits Times* attributes an altercation between co-stars to mischievous spirits to whom the actors had not offered enough incense.

7. Dual endings were offered in *Infernal Affairs* since in the original ending the gangster went unpunished for killing the undercover cop. An alternate ending, in which the gangster is apprehended by the police, was filmed for audiences in China.

8. Beliefs in ghosts, gods, or crime is not new to China; rather, the ghost appeasement and graft manifested differently in different time periods.

Chapter 6

1. Laura Grindstaff (2002) and David Hesmondhalgh and Sarah Baker (2008) offer rich ethnographic studies of the management of emotions by talk show producers and talent show researchers in reality television formats.

2. Affective labor is frequently used in discussions of gendered care and nursing, in which is it often glossed as "intimate labor," as well as service and media industries that strive to produce a certain reaction among consumers. Hardt also notes that he uses affective labor to link up feminist writing on labor to the work of Italian and French economists and labor sociologists for what they describe as cognitive labor (Hardt 2007: xi).

Chapter 7

1. DreamWorks Animation's DreamLab and USC's Institute for Creative Technologies have developed virtual human and CGI capabilities that achieve this kind of capture. They were preceded by other groups who were explicitly seeking to "capture the soul." Image Metrics, for instance, emerged out of image analysis for medical research and development at the University of Manchester, England, and allowed technicians to lift the coordinates of miniscule muscular movements from the face of a human actor (such as inner lip muscles or the way in which an eye dilates in response to fear) onto a digital face, thus "capturing the soul" of the human actor, as described by the creators and users of this technology and film industry professionals. The "soul transference" between a human actor and a virtual or human film character, alive or dead, meant that Image Metrics could reanimate movie stars from the past (Waxman 2006).

2. The use of the word "actor" in ANT is not to be confused with the term indicating a professional of the stage or screen. ANT is derived from STS (science and technology studies).

3. The divisions are generally much less institutionalized on Hong Kong film and television sets.

Epilogue

1. The stark socioeconomic disparity in Hong Kong also received international media coverage; Liyan Chen reported for *Forbes* on October 8, 2014, that in 2011 the city held a Gini coefficient of .537 and that its real estate prices are among the highest in the world.

REFERENCES CITED

....

Abbas, Ackbar. 1997. *Hong Kong: Culture and the Politics of Disappearance.* Minneapolis: University of Minnesota Press.

Abu-Lughod, Lila. 1995. "The Objects of Soap Opera: Egyptian Television Serials and the Cultural Politics of Modernity." In *Worlds Apart: Modernity Through the Prism of the Local,* edited by Daniel Miller, pp. 190–210. London: Routledge.

Abu-Lughod, Lila. 2005. *Dramas of Nationhood: The Politics of Television in Egypt.* Chicago: University of Chicago Press.

Altman, Rick. 2007. *Silent Film Sound.* New York: Columbia University Press.

Appadurai, Arjun. 1988. *The Social Life of Things: Commodities in Cultural Perspective.* Cambridge, UK: Cambridge University Press.

Appadurai, Arjun. 1996. *Modernity at Large: Cultural Dimensions of Globalization.* Minneapolis: University of Minnesota Press.

Balio, Tino. 1993. *History of the American Cinema, Volume Five: Grand Design: Hollywood as a Modern Business Enterprise, 1930–1939.* New York: Charles Scribner's Sons.

Bautista, Julius. 2015. "Export-Quality Martyrs: Roman Catholicism and Transnational Labor in the Philippines." *Cultural Anthropology* 30(3): 424–447.

Benjamin, Walter. 1968. "The Work of Art in the Age of Mechanical Reproduction." In *Illuminations,* edited by Hannah Arendt. Harry Zohn, translator. New York: Schocken Books.

Berger, Suzanne, and Richard K. Lester. 1997. "Challenges to Hong Kong Industry." In *Made By Hong Kong,* edited by Suzanne Berger and Richard K. Lester, pp. 59–96. Hong Kong: Oxford University Press.

Berman, Marshall. 1982. *All That Is Solid Melts Into Air: The Experience of Modernity.* New York: Penguin Books.

Bernal, Victoria. 2005. "Eritrea On-line: Diaspora, Cyberspace, and the Public Sphere." *American Ethnologist* 32(4): 660–675.

Berry, Chris, and Mary Farquhar. 2005. "Shadow Opera: Towards a New Archaeology of the Chinese Cinema." In *Chinese Language Film: Historiography, Poetics, Politics*, edited by Sheldon H. Lu and Emilie Yueh-yu Yeh, pp. 27–51. Honolulu: University of Hawaii Press.

Bhabha, Homi K. 1994. *The Location of Culture*. London: Routledge.

Boellstorff, Tom, Bonnie Nardi, Celia Pearce, and T. L. Taylor. 2012. *Ethnography and Virtual Worlds: A Handbook of Method*. Princeton, NJ: Princeton University Press.

Bordwell, David. 2000. *Planet Hong Kong: Popular Cinema and the Art of Entertainment*. Cambridge, MA: Harvard University Press.

Bordwell, David, Janet Staiger, and Kristen Thompson. 1985. *The Classical Hollywood Cinema: Film Style and Mode of Production to 1960*. New York: Routledge.

Bosco, Joseph. 2003. "The Supernatural in Hong Kong Young People's Ghost Stories." *Anthropological Forum* 13(2): 141–149.

Box Office Mojo. 2010–2014. "Hong Kong Yearly Box Office." Accessed February 1, 2016. http://www.boxofficemojo.com/intl/hongkong/yearly/?yr=2014&p= .htm.

Butsch, Richard. 2000. *The Making of American Audiences from Stage to Television, 1750–1990*. New York: Cambridge University Press.

Buyandelgeriyn, Manduhai. 2007. "Dealing With Uncertainty: Shamans, Marginal Capitalism, and the Remaking of History in Postsocialist Mongolia." *American Ethnologist* 34(1): 127–147.

Caldwell, John T. 1995. *Televisuality: Style, Crisis, and Authority in American Television*. New Brunswick, NJ: Rutgers University Press.

Caldwell, John T. 2008. *Production Culture: Industrial Reflexivity and Critical Practice in Film and Television*. Durham, NC: Duke University Press.

Callon, Michel. 1999. "Actor-Network Theory: The Market Test." In *Actor-Network Theory and After*, edited by John Law and John Hassard, pp. 181–195. Oxford: Blackwell.

Castells, Manuel. 1996. *The Rise of the Network Society: The Information Age: Economy, Society and Culture,* Volume I. Oxford: Blackwell.

Castells, Manuel. 1998. *End of Millennium: The Information Age: Economy, Society and Culture*, Volume III. Oxford: Blackwell.

Castells, Manuel. 2000. *The Information Age: Economy, Society and Culture*, Volume I: End of Millenium, 2nd Edition. Oxford: Blackwell.

Chan, Joseph M., Anthony Y. H. Fung, and Chun Hung Ng. 2010. *Policies for the Sustainable Development of the Hong Kong Film Industry*. Hong Kong Institute of Asia-Pacific Studies. Hong Kong: The Chinese University of Hong Kong.

Chan, Sau Y. 1993. "The Offering to the White Tiger in Cantonese Opera." *Journal of the Hong Kong Branch of the Royal Asiatic Society* 30: 169–179.

Cheung, Esther M. K., and Yiu-Wai Chu. 2004. *Between Home and World: A Reader in Hong Kong Cinema.* Hong Kong: Oxford University Press.

Cheung, Esther M. K., Gina Marchetti and Tan See-Kam. 2010. Hong Kong Screenscapes: From the New Wave to the Digital Frontier. Hong Kong: Hong Kong University Press.

Chiu, Stephen, K. C. Ho, and Tai-Lok Lui. 1997. *City-States in the Global Economy.* Boulder, CO: Westview.

Choi, Wai Kit. 2007. "(Post)coloniality as a Chinese State of Exception." *Postcolonial Studies* 10(4): 391–411.

Chow, Carol, and Eric Ma. 2008. "Rescaling the Local and the National: Trans-border Production of Hong Kong TV Dramas in Mainland China." In *TV Drama in China*, edited by Ying Zhu, Michael Keane, and Ruoyun Bai, pp. 201–215. Hong Kong: Hong Kong University Press.

Chow, Rey. 1998. "King Kong in Hong Kong: Watching the 'Handover' From the USA." *Social Text* 55: 93–108.

Choy, Timothy K. 2005. "Articulated Knowledges: Environmental Forms After Universality's Demise." *American Anthropologist* 107(1): 5–18.

Chu, Yiu Kong. 2000. *The Triads as Business.* London: Routledge.

Chu, Yiu-wai Stephen. 2015. "Toward a New Hong Kong Cinema: Beyond Mainland Hong Kong Co-productions." *Journal of Chinese Cinemas* 9(2): 111–124.

Clough, Patricia Ticineto. 2007. Introduction. In *The Affective Turn: Theorizing the Social*, edited by Patricia Ticineto Clough and Jean Halley, pp. 1–33. Durham, NC: Duke University Press.

Comaroff, Jean, and John Comaroff. 1999. "Occult Economies and the Violence of Abstraction: Notes From the South African Postcolony." *American Ethnologist* 26(2): 279–303.

Comaroff, Jean, and John Comaroff. 2000. "Millenial Capitalism: First Thoughts on Second Coming." *Public Culture* 12(2): 291–343.

Constable, Nicole. 1994. *Christian Souls and Chinese Spirits: A Hakka Community in Hong Kong.* Berkeley: University of California Press.

Crawford, Barclay, and Kelly Chan. 2007. "Crowds Flock to Greet Batman: Fans Throng Central as Lead Characters Suit Up For Action and Cameras Roll." *South China Morning Post*, November 10.

Curtin, Michael. 1999. "Industry on Fire: The Cultural Economy of Hong Kong Media." *Post Script* 19(1): 28–51.

Curtin, Michael. 2007. *Playing to the World's Biggest Audience: The Globalization of Chinese Film and TV.* Berkeley: University of California Press.

Curtin, Michael and Kevin Sanson. 2016. *Precarious Creativity: Global Media, Local Labor.* Berkeley: University of California Press.

D'Acci, Julie. 1994. *Defining Women: Television and the Case of Cagney and Lacey.* Chapel Hill: University of North Carolina Press.

Dannen, Fredric. 1997. *Hong Kong Babylon: An Insider's Guide to the Hollywood of the East.* New York: Hyperion.

Davidson, Drew. 2010. *Cross-Media Communications: An Introduction to the Art of Creating Integrative Media Experiences*. Pittsburgh: ETC Press.

Davis, Darrell W., and Emilie Yueh-yu Yeh. 2001. "Warning! Category III: The Other Hong Kong Cinema." *Film Quarterly* 54(4): 12–26.

Davis, Darrell W., and Emilie Yueh-yu Yeh. 2009. *East Asian Screen Industries*. London: British Film Institute.

Desser, David. 2000. "The Kung Fu Craze: Hong Kong Cinema's First American Reception." In *The Cinema of Hong Kong: History, Arts, Identity*, edited by Poshek Fu and David Desser, pp. 19–43. Cambridge, UK: Cambridge University Press.

Dorian, Marc, Lauren Putrino, and Alexa Valiente. 2014. "'Midnight Rider' Hairstylist Describes When Train Hit Her, Killed Fellow Crew Member." *ABC News* Website, October 31. http://www.chicagomanualofstyle.org/tools_citationguide.html.

Dornfeld, Barry. 1998. *Producing Public Television, Producing Public Culture*. Princeton, NJ: Princeton University Press.

Douglas, Mary. 1966. *Purity and Danger: An Analysis of Concept of Pollution and Taboo*. London: Routledge Classics.

Eisenstein, Sergei. 1988. "The Montage of Attractions." In *S. M. Eisenstein: Selected Works, Vol. 1, Writings, 1922–1934*, edited and translated by Richard Taylor. London: British Film Institute.

Eisenstein, Sergei. 2003. *Notes of a Film Director*. Moscow: Foreign Language Publishing House.

Elsaesser, Thomas. 1990. "Early Cinema: From Linear History to Mass Media Archaeology." In *Early Cinema: Space, Frame, Narrative*, edited by Thomas Elsaesser, pp. 1–10. London: British Film Institute.

Epstein, Edward Jay. 2012. *The Hollywood Economist 2.0: The Hidden Financial Reality Behind the Movies*. Brooklyn, NY: Melville House.

Faier, Lieba, and Lisa Rofel. 2014. "Ethnographies of Encounter." *Annual Review of Anthropology* 43(1): 363–377.

Feuchtwang, Stephen. 1974. *An Anthropological Analysis of Chinese Geomancy*. Vientiane, Laos: Vithagna.

Feuchtwang, Stephen. 2001. *The Imperial Metaphor: Popular Religion in China*. London: Routledge.

FilmL.A. 2016. "Television Projects, Tax Credits Bring Production to Los Angeles in 2015." Report by FilmL.A. Research for FilmL.A., Inc. http://www.filmla.com/uploads/News%20Release%2001-19-16_1453230319.pdf.

FilmL.A. Research. 2014. "Filming On Location in Los Angeles 1993–2013." Report by FilmL.A. Research for FilmL.A., Inc. http://www.filmla.com/uploads/Filming-On-Location-Los-Angeles-1993-2013_1389748368.pdf.

Fonoroff, Paul. 1988. "A Brief History of Hong Kong Cinema." *Renditions* 29–30: 293–308.

Fore, Steve. 1994. "Golden Harvest Films and the Hong Kong Movie Industry in the Realm of Globalization." *The Velvet Light Trap* 34: 40–58.

Freeman, Carla. 2000. *High Tech and High Heels in the Global Economy: Women, Work, and Pink-Collar Identities in the Caribbean.* Durham, NC: Duke University Press.

Friedman, Milton. 2006. "Hong Kong Wrong." *Wall Street Journal*, October 6. http://www.wsj.com/articles/SB116009800068684505.

Fu, Poshek. 2002. "Between Nationalism and Colonialism: Mainland Emigres, Marginal Culture, and Hong Kong Cinema 1937–1941." In *The Cinema of Hong Kong: History, Arts, Identity*, edited by Poshek Fu and David Desser, pp. 199–226. Cambridge, UK: Cambridge University Press.

Fu, Poshek, and David Desser. 2002. Introduction. In *The Cinema of Hong Kong: History, Arts, Identity*, edited by Poshek Fu and David Desser, pp. 1–16. Cambridge, UK: Cambridge University Press.

Ganti, Tejaswini. 2000. "Casting Culture: The Social Life of Hindi Film Production in Contemporary India." Ph.D. diss., New York University.

Ganti, Tejaswini. 2002. "'And Yet My Heart is Still Indian': The Bombay Film Industry and the (H)Indianization of Hollywood." In *Media Worlds: Anthropology on New Terrain*, edited by Faye D. Ginsburg, Lila Abu-Lughod, and Brian Larkin, pp. 281–300. Berkeley: University of California Press.

Ganti, Tejaswini. 2004. *Bollywood: A Guidebook to Popular Hindi Cinema.* New York: Routledge Press.

Ganti, Tejaswini. 2012a. *Producing Bollywood: Inside the Contemporary Hindi Film Industry.* Durham, NC: Duke University Press.

Ganti, Tejaswini. 2012b. "Sentiments of Disdain and Practices of Distinction: Boundary-Work, Subjectivity, and Value in the Hindi Film Industry." *The Anthropological Quarterly* 85(1): 5–43.

Geertz, Clifford. 1973. "Deep Play: Notes on the Balinese Cockfight." In *The Interpretation of Cultures*, pp. 412–454. New York: Basic Books.

Gergen, Kenneth. 1992. *The Saturated Self: Dilemmas of Identity in Contemporary Life.* Basic Books.

Geschiere, Peter. 1997. *The Modernity of Witchcraft: Politics and the Occult in Postcolonial Africa.* Translated by Peter Geschiere and Janet Roitman. Charlottesville: University of Virginia Press.

Ginsburg, Faye. 1994. "Culture and Media: A Mild Polemic." *Anthropology Today* 10(2): 5–15.

Gitlin, Todd. 1983. *Inside Prime Time.* New York: Pantheon.

Gomery, Douglas. 2008. *The Hollywood Studio System: A History.* London: British Film Institute.

Gordon, Colin. 1991. "Governmental Rationality: An Introduction." In *The Foucault Effect: Studies in Governmentality*, edited by Graham Burchell, Colin Gordon, and Peter Miller, pp. 1–52. Chicago: University of Chicago Press.

Govil, Nitin. 2009. "Wind(fall) from the East." *Television & New Media* 10(1): 63–65.

Grewal, Inderpal, and Caren Kaplan. 2005. *An Introduction to Women's Studies: Gender in a Transnational World*, edited by Inderpal Grewal and Caren Kaplan. New York: McGraw-Hill Higher Education. Second Edition.

Griffiths, James. 2016. "'Ten Years': Dark Vision of Hong Kong's Future Proves Surprise Box Office Hit." *CNN*, January 21. http://edition.cnn.com/2016/01/20/asia/hong-kong-ten-years-future/.

Grindstaff, Laura. 2002. *The Money Shot: Trash, Class, and the Making of TV Talk Shows*. Chicago: University of Chicago Press.

Gunning, Tom. 1990. "The Cinema of Attractions: Early Film, Its Spectator, and the Avant-Garde." In *Early Cinema: Space, Frame, Narrative*, edited by Thomas Elsaesser, pp. 56–62. London: British Film Institute.

Gunning, Tom. 1995a. "An Aesthetic of Astonishment: Early Film and the [In]Credulous Spectator." In *Viewing Positions*, edited by Linda Williams, pp. 114–133. New Brunswick, NJ: Rutgers.

Gunning, Tom. 1995b. "Phantom Images and Modern Manifestations: Spirit Photography, Magic Theater, Trick Films, and Photography's Uncanny." In *Fugitive Images: From Photography to Video*, edited by Patrice Petro, pp. 42–71. Bloomington: Indiana University Press.

Gunning, Tom. 1998. "Early American Film." In *The Oxford Guide to Film Studies*, edited by John Hill and Pamela Church Gibson, pp. 255–271. Oxford: Oxford University Press.

Gursel, Zeynep. 2013. "A Challenge for Visual Journalism: Rendering the Labor Behind News Images Visible." *Anthropology Now*. http://anthronow.com/reach/a-challenge-for-visual-journalism-rendering-the-labor-behind-news-images-visible.

Hardt, Michael. 1999. "Affective Labor." *Boundary* 26(2): 89–100.

Hardt, Michael. 2007. Foreword. In *The Affective Turn: Theorizing the Social*, edited by Patricia Ticineto Clough and Jean Halley, pp. ix–xiii. Durham, NC: Duke University Press.

Hardt, Michael, and Antonio Negri. 2001. *Empire*. Cambridge, MA: Harvard University Press.

Harvey, David. 1991. *The Condition of Postmodernity*. Oxford: Blackwell.

Heider, Karl G. 2006 [1976]. *Ethnographic Film*. 2nd edition. Austin: University of Texas Press.

Hesmondhalgh, David. 2007. *The Cultural Industries*. 2nd edition. London: Sage Publications.

Hesmondhalgh, David, and Sarah Baker. 2008. "Creative Work and Emotional Labour in the Television Industry." *Theory, Culture and Society* 25(7–8): 97–118.

Hesmondhalgh, David, and Sarah Baker. 2011. *Creative Labour*. Abingdon and New York: Routledge.

Hesmondhalgh, David, and Sarah Baker. 2013. *Creative Labour: Media Work in Three Cultural Industries*. doi: 10.4324/9780203855881

Hickel, Jason. 2014. "'Xenophobia' in South Africa: Order, Chaos and the Moral Economy of Witchcraft." *Cultural Anthropology* 29(1): 103–127.

Ho, Vicci. 2007. "Hong Kong Crazy for *Batman*: Dark Knight Takes Hold of City." *Variety International*. November 11. http://www.variety.com/article/VR1117975751.html?categoryId=19&cs=1.

Hochschild, Arlie Russell. 1983. *The Managed Heart: Commercialization of Human Feeling*. Berkeley: University of California Press.

Hong Kong Employment and Statistics Section. 2004–2007. "Quarterly Report of Employment and Vacancies Statistics." Census and Statistics Department.

Hong Kong Film Archives. 2008. "Hong Kong Filmography 1913–2006." Hong Kong: Hong Kong Film Archives Research Section.

Hong Kong Trade Development Council. 2004. "Revitalize Hong Kong's Manufacturing By Leveraging CEPA." Report for HKTDC Research. http://economists-pick-research.hktdc.com/business-news/article/Economic-Forum/Revitalize-Hong-Kong-s-Manufacturing-by-Leveraging-CEPA/ef/en/1/1X000000/1X00EB4Z.htm.

Hong Kong Trade Development Council. 2005. "Hong Kong's Media Entertainment Industry: Prospects & Challenges." Hong Kong: Hong Kong Trade Development Council Research Department.

Hong Kong Trade Development Council. 2015. "Film Entertainment Industry in Hong Kong." Report for HKTDC Research. http://hong-kong-economy research.hktdc.com/business-news/article/Hong-Kong-Industry-Profiles/Film-Entertainment-Industry-in-Hong-Kong/hkip/en/1/1X000000/1X0018PN.htm.

Horkheimer, Max, and Theodor W. Adorno. 2002. *Dialectic of Enlightenment: Philosophical Fragments*. Edited by Gunzelin Schmid Noerr and translated by Edmund Jephcott. Palo Alto, CA: Stanford University Press.

Horne, Gerald. 2001. *Class Struggle In Hollywood, 1930–1950: Moguls, Mobsters, Stars, Reds, and Trade Unionists*. Austin: University of Texas Press.

Horst, Heather, and Daniel Miller. 2006. *The Cell Phone: An Anthropology of Communication*. London: Bloomsbury Academic.

Hozic, Aida. 1999. "Uncle Sam Goes to Siliwood: Of Landscapes, Spielberg and Hegemony." *Review of International Political Economy* 6(3): 289–312.

Hozic, Aida. 2001. *Hollyworld: Space, Power, and Fantasy in the American Economy*. Ithaca, NY: Cornell University Press.

Inda, Jonathan X., and Renato Rosaldo. 2007. "Tracking Global Flows." In *The Anthropology of Globalization: A Reader*, edited by Jonathan X. Inda and Renato Rosaldo, pp. 3–46. 2nd edition. Malden, MA: Blackwell Publishing.

Ingold, Tim. 2011. *Being Alive: Essays on Movement, Knowledge and Description*. London: Routledge.

Jarvie, Ian C. 1977. *Window on Hong Kong: A Sociological Study of the Hong Kong Film Industry and its Audience*. Hong Kong: Centre of Asian Studies, University of Hong Kong.

Jenkins, Henry. 1992. *Textual Poachers: Television Fans and Participatory Culture*. New York: Routledge.

Johnson, Andrew. 2012. "Naming Chaos: Accidents, Precariousness and the Spirits of Wildness in Urban Thai Spirits Cults." *American Ethnologist* 39(4): 766–778.

Kar, Law. 2000. "The American Connection in Early Hong Kong Cinema." In *The Cinema of Hong Kong: History, Arts, Identity*, edited by Poshek Fu and David Desser, pp. 44–70. Cambridge, UK: Cambridge University Press.

Kendall, Laurel. 1996. "Korean Shamans and the Spirits of Capitalism." *American Anthropologist* 83(3): 512–527.

Klowden, Kevin, Anusuya Chatterjee, and Candice Flor Hynek. 2010. "Film Flight: Lost Production and Its Economic Impact on California." Report by the Milken Institute California Center. http://assets1b.milkeninstitute. org/assets/Publication/ResearchReport/PDF/FilmFlight.pdf.

Kondo, Dorinne. 1990. *Crafting Selves: Power, Gender, and Discourses of Identity in a Japanese Workplace*. Chicago: University of Chicago Press.

Kondo, Dorinne. 1997. *About Face: Performing Race in Fashion and Theatre*. New York: Routledge.

Kraicer, Shelly. 2001. "Interview: Johnnie To and Wai Ka-fai." *Senses of Cinema* 18 http://sensesofcinema.com/2001/feature-articles/to_and_ka-fai/.

Kwon, Heonik. 2007. "The Dollarization of Vietnamese Ghost Money." *Journal of the Royal Anthropological Institute* 13: 73–90.

Larkin, Brian. 1997. "Indian Films and Nigerian Lovers: Media and the Creation of Parallel Modernities." *Africa: Journal of the International African Institute* 67(3): 406–440.

Larkin, Brian. 2003. "Itineraries of Indian Cinema: African Videos, Bollywood and Global Media." In *Multiculturalism, Postcolonialism and Transnational Media*, edited by Ella Shohat and Robert Stam, pp. 170–192. New Brunswick, NJ: Rutgers University Press.

Lauzen, Martha M. 2009. "The Celluloid Ceiling II: Production Design, Production Management, Sound Design, Key Grips, and Gaffers." Report for SDSU's Center for the Study of Women in Television and Film. http:// womenintvfilm.sdsu.edu/files/2008%20Celluloid%20Ceiling%20II.pdf.

Lauzen, Martha M. 2015a. "Boxed In: Portrayals of Female Characters and Employment of Behind-the-Scenes Women in 2014–2015 in Primetime Television." Report for SDSU's Center for the Study of Women in Television and Film. http://womenintvfilm.sdsu.edu/files/2014-15_Boxed_In_Report.pdf.

Lauzen, Martha M. 2015b. "Women and the Big Picture: Behind-the-Scenes Employment on the Top 700 Films of 2014." Report for SDSU's Center for the Study of Women in Television and Film. http://womenintvfilm.sdsu. edu/files/2014_Women_and_the_Big_Picture_Report.pdf.

Law, John. 1999. "After ANT: Complexity, Naming and Topology." In *Actor Network Theory and After*, edited by John Law and John Hassard, pp. 1–14. Oxford: Blackwell Publishers.

Law, John, and Kevin Hetherington. 2002. "Materialities, Spacialities, Globalities." In *Knowledge, Space, Economy*, edited by John Bryson, P. W. Daniels, Nick Henry, and Jane Pollard, pp. 34–49. London: Routledge.

Lee, Ching Kwan. 1998. *Gender and the South China Miracle: Two Worlds of Factory Women*. Berkeley: University of California Press.

Lenoir, Timothy, and Henry Lowood. 2005. "Theaters of War: The Military Entertainment Complex." In *Collection, Laboratory, Theater: Scenes of Knowledge in the 17th Century*, edited by Helmar Schramm, Ludger Schwarte, and Jan Lazardzig, pp. 427–456. Berlin: Walter de Gruyter.

Levine, Elana. 2001. "Toward a Paradigm for Media Production Research: Behind the Scenes at *General Hospital*." *Critical Studies in Media Communication* 18(1): 66–82.

Liu, Tik-sang. 2003. "A Nameless but Active Religion: An Anthropologist's View of Local Religion in Hong Kong and Macau." In *Religion in China Today. The China Quarterly Special Issues New Series*, No. 3, edited by Daniel L. Overmyer, pp. 67–88. Cambridge, UK: Cambridge University Press.

Lotz, Amanda D. 2007. *The Television Will Be Revolutionized*. New York: New York University Press.

Lotz, Amanda D. 2009. "Industry-Level Studies and the Contributions of Gitlin's Inside Prime Time." In *Production Studies: Cultural Studies of Media Industries*, edited by Vicki Mayer, Miranda J. Banks, and John T. Caldwell, pp. 25–38. London: Routledge.

Lu, Sheldon H. 2000. "Filming Diaspora and Identity: Hong Kong and 1997." In *The Cinema of Hong Kong: History, Arts, Identity*, edited by Poshek Fu and David Desser, pp. 273–288. Cambridge, UK: Cambridge University Press.

Ma, Eric Kit-wai. 1999. *Culture, Politics, and Television in Hong Kong*. London: Routledge.

Malinowski, Bronislaw. 1984 [1922]. *Argonauts of the Western Pacific*. Prospect Heights, IL: Waveland Press, Inc.

Mankekar, Purnima. 1999. *Screening Culture, Viewing Politics: An Ethnography of Television, Womanhood, and Nation in Postcolonial India*. Durham, NC: Duke University Press.

Mankekar, Purnima, and Akhil Gupta. 2016. "Intimate Encounters: Affective Labor in Call Centers." *Positions* 24(1): 17–43.

Marchetti Gina. 2000. "Buying American, Consuming Hong Kong: Cultural Commerce, Fantasies of Identity, and the Cinema." In *The Cinema of Hong Kong: History, Arts, Identity*, edited by Poshek Fu and David Desser, pp. 289–313. Cambridge, UK: Cambridge University Press.

Marchetti, Gina, and Tan See Kam. 2007. *Hong Kong Film, Hollywood, and the New Global Cinema: No Film Is an Island*. London: Routledge.

Marcus, George. 1995. "Ethnography in/of the World System: the Emergence of Multi-Sited Ethnography." *Annual Review of Anthropology* 24: 95–117.

Martin, Emily. 1995. *Flexible Bodies*. Boston: Beacon Press. Revised Edition.

Martin, Sylvia J. 2012. "Stunt Workers and Spectacle: Ethnography of Physical Risk in Hollywood and Hong Kong." In *Film and Risk*, edited by Mette Hjort, pp. 97–114. Detroit: Wayne State University Press.

Martin, Sylvia J. 2013. "Transformations and Tactics: The Production Culture of the Hong Kong Film Industry." In *The International Encyclopedia of Media Studies: Media Production*, Volume 2, edited by Vicki Mayer. West Sussex: Wiley-Blackwell.

Marx, Karl. 1992 [1867]. *Capital: Volume I: A Critique of Political Economy*, translated by Ben Fowkes. London: Penguin Classics.

Massumi, Brian. 2002. *Parables for the Virtual: Movement, Affect, Sensation*. Durham, NC: Duke University Press.

Masters, Kim. 2016. "Steven Spielberg on Dreamworks' Past, Amblin's Present, and His Own Future." *The Hollywood Reporter*, June 15. http://www.hollywoodreporter.com/features/steven-spielberg-dreamworks-past-amblins-902544

Matthews, Gordon, Eric Ma, and Tai-Lok Lui. 2008. *Hong Kong, China: Learning to Belong to a Nation*. London: Routledge.

Mauss, Marcel. 2000 [1954]. *The Gift: The Form and Reason for Exchange in Archaic Societies*. New York: W. W. Norton & Company Inc.

Mayer, Vicki. 2008. "Guys Gone Wild? Soft Core Video Professionalism and New Realities in Television Production." *Cinema Journal* 47(2): 97–116.

Mayer, Vicki. 2009. "Bringing the Social Back In: Studies of Production Cultures and Social Theory." In *Production Studies: Cultural Studies of Media Industries*, edited by Vicki Mayer, Miranda J. Banks, and John T. Caldwell, pp. 15–24. London: Routledge.

Mayer, Vicki. 2011. *Below the Line: Producers and Production Studies in the New Television Economy*. Durham, NC: Duke University Press.

Mayer, Vicki, Miranda J. Banks, and John T. Caldwell. 2009. Introduction: Production Studies: Roots and Routes. In *Production Studies: Cultural Studies of Media Industries*, edited by Vicki Mayer, Miranda J. Banks, and John T. Caldwell, pp. 1–12. London: Routledge.

Mayer, Vicki, and Tanya Goldman. 2010. "Hollywood Handouts: Tax Credits in the Age of Economic Crisis." *Jumpcut: A Review of Contemporary Media* 52: 17–43.

Mazzarella, William. 2009. "Affect: What Is It Good For?" In *Enchantments of Modernity: Empire, Nation, Globalization*, edited by Saurabh Dube, pp. 291–309. London: Routledge.

Meyer, Birgit, and Peter Geschiere. 1999. Introduction. In *Globalization and Identity: Dialectics of Flow and Closure*, edited by Birgit Meyer and Peter Geschiere, pp. 1–16. Oxford: Blackwell.

Miller, Daniel, and Don Slater. 2000. *The Internet: An Ethnographic Approach*. Oxford: Berg.

Miller, Toby, Nitin Govil, John McMurria, Richard Maxwell, and Ting Wang. 2005. *Global Hollywood 2*. London: British Film Institute.

Moldea, Dan E. 1987. *Dark Victory, Ronald Reagan, MCA and the Mob.* New York: Viking Penguin.

Moore, Henrietta, and Todd Sanders. 2002. *Magical Interpretations, Material Realities: Modernity, Witchcraft and the Occult in Postcolonial Africa,* edited by Henrietta Moore and Todd Sanders. London: Routledge.

Morris, Meaghan. 2005. "Introduction: Hong Kong Connections." In *Hong Kong Connections: Transnational Imagination in Action Cinema,* edited by Meaghan Morris, Siu Leung Li, and Stephen Chan Ching-kiu, pp. 1–18. Durham, NC: Duke University Press.

Morris, Meaghan, Siu Leung Li, and Stephen Chan Ching-kiu. *Hong Kong Connections: Transnational Imagination in Action Cinema.* Durham, NC: Duke University Press.

Muehlebach, Andrea. 2011. "On Affective Labor in Post-Fordist Italy." *Cultural Anthropology* 26(1): 59–82.

Mulvey, Laura. 2000 [1975]. "Visual Pleasure and Narrative Cinema." In *Feminism and Film,* edited by E. Ann Kaplan, pp. 34–47. Oxford: Oxford University Press.

Murray, Dian H. and Qin Baoqi. 1994. *The Origins of the Tiandihui: The Chinese Triads in Legend and History.* Stanford: Stanford University Press.

Myers, Fred R. 2002. *Painting Culture: The Making of an Aboriginal High Art.* Durham, NC: Duke University Press.

Nader, Laura. 1972. "Up the Anthropologist: Perspectives Gained From Studying Up." In *Reinventing Anthropology,* edited by Dell Hymes, pp. 284–311. New York: Pantheon Books.

Naficy, Hamid. 2001. *An Accented Cinema: Exilic and Diasporic Filmmaking.* Princeton, NJ: Princeton University Press.

Neff, Gina, Elizabeth Wissinger, and Sharon Zukin. 2005. "Entrepreneurial Labor Among Cultural Producers: 'Cool' Jobs in 'Hot' Industries." *Social Semiotics* 15: 307–334.

Ngo, Tak-Wing. 1999b. "Industrial History and the Artifice of Laissez-Faire Colonialism." In *Hong Kong's History: State and Society Under Colonial Rule,* edited by Tak-Wing Ngo, pp. 119–140. London: Routledge.

Niehaus, Isak. 2002. "Witchcraft in Anthropological Perspective." In *Talking About People: Readings in Contemporary Cultural Anthropology,* edited by William Haviland, Robert Gordon, and Luis Vivanco, pp. 225–229. New York: McGraw-Hill Education.

Nye, Joseph S. 2004. *Soft Power: The Means to Success in World Politics.* Washington, DC: Public Affairs.

Ong, Aihwa. 1987. *Spirits of Resistance and Capitalist Discipline: Factory Women in Malaysia.* Albany: State University of New York Press.

Ong, Aihwa. 1999. *Flexible Citizenship: The Cultural Logics of Transnationality.* Durham, NC: Duke University Press.

Ong, Aihwa. 2005. "Ecologies of Expertise: Assembling Flows, Managing Citizenship." In *Global Assemblages: Technology, Politics, and Ethics as*

Anthropological Problems, edited by Aihwa Ong and Stephen J. Collier, pp. 337–353. Malden, MA: Blackwell Publishing.

Ong, Aihwa. 2006. *Neoliberalism as Exception: Mutations in Citizenship and Sovereignty*. Durham, NC: Duke University Press.

Ong, Aihwa, and Stephen Collier. 2005. Introduction. In *Global Assemblages: Technology, Politics, and Ethics as Anthropological Problems*, edited by Aihwa Ong and Stephen J. Collier, pp. 3–21. Malden, MA: Blackwell Publishing.

Ortner, Sherry. 2009. "Studying Sideways: Ethnographic Access in Hollywood." In *Production Studies: Cultural Studies of Media Industries*, edited by Vicki Mayer, Miranda J. Banks, and John T. Caldwell, pp. 175–189. London: Routledge.

Ortner, Sherry. 2013. *Not Hollywood: Independent Film at the Twilight of the American Dream*. Durham, NC: Duke University Press.

Pandian, Anand. 2015. *Reel World: An Anthropology of Creation*. Durham, NC: Duke University Press.

Pang, Laikwan. 2001. "Death and Hong Kong Cinema." *Quarterly Review of Film and Video* 18(1): 15–29.

Pang, Laikwan. 2005. "Post-1997 Hong Kong Masculinity." In *Masculinities and Hong Kong Cinema*, edited by Laikwan Pang and Day Wong, pp. 35–56. Hong Kong: Hong Kong University Press.

Pang, Laikwan. 2007. "Postcolonial Hong Kong Cinema: Utilitarianism and (Trans)local." *Postcolonial Studies* 10(4): 413–430.

Piore, Michael J., and Charles F. Sabel. 1984. *The Second Industrial Divide: Possibilities for Prosperity*. New York: Basic Books.

Powdermaker, Hortense. 1951. *Hollywood the Dream Factory: An Anthropologist Looks at the Movie-Makers*. Boston: Little, Brown and Company.

Powdermaker, Hortense. 1967. *Stranger and Friend: The Way of an Anthropologist*. New York: W.W. Norton and Company.

Pun, Ngai and Ka-Ming Wu. 2004. "Lived Citizenship and Lower-Class Chinese Migrant Women: A Global City Without its People." In Remaking Citizenship in Hong Kong: Community, Nation and the Global City, edited by Agnes S. Ku and Ngai Pun, pp. 125–138. London: RoutledgeCurzon.

Rodriguez, Hector. 1999. "Organizational Hegemony in the Hong Kong Cinema." *Post Script* 19(1): 107–119.

Rosten, Leo C. 1941. *Hollywood: The Movie Colony, the Movie Makers*. New York: Harcourt Brace.

Ruby, Jay. 1991. "Speaking For, Speaking About, Speaking With, or Speaking Alongside—An Anthropological and Documentary Dilemma." *Visual Anthropology Review* 7(2): 50–67.

Ruby, Jay. 1995. *Secure the Shadow: Death and Photography in America*. Cambridge, MA: MIT Press.

Sassen, Saskia. 2000. *Cities in a World Economy*. Thousand Oaks, CA: Pine Forge Press.

Sassen, Saskia. 2001. *The Global City: New York, London, Tokyo*. 2nd edition. Princeton, NJ: Princeton University Press.

Schechner, Richard. 2002. *Performance Studies: An Introduction*. 2nd edition. New York: Routledge.

Schein, Louisa. 2002. "Mapping Hmong Media in Diasporic Space." In *Media Worlds: Anthropology on New Terrain*, edited by Faye Ginsburg, Lila Abu-Lughod, and Brian Larkin, pp. 229–244. Berkeley: University of California Press.

Schein, Louisa. 2004. "Homeland Beauty: Transnational Longing and Hmong American Video." *Journal of Asian Studies* 63(2): 433–463.

Scott, Allen J. 2005. *On Hollywood: The Place, The Industry*. Princeton, NJ: Princeton University Press.

Seizer, Susan. 2000. "Roadwork: Offstage with Special Drama Actresses in Tamilnadu, South India." *Cultural Anthropology* 15(2): 225–238.

Sickles, Robert C. 2010. *American Film in the Digital Age*. Santa Barbara, CA: Praeger.

Singer, Ben. 2001. *Melodrama and Modernity: Early Sensational Cinema and Its Contexts*. New York: Columbia University Press.

Sinn, Elizabeth. 1989. *Power and Charity: The Early History of the Tung Wah Hospital, Hong Kong*. Hong Kong: Oxford University Press.

Smith, Stacy L., Marc Choueiti, and Katherine Pieper. 2015. "Inequality in 700 Popular Films: Examining Portrayals of Gender, Race, and LGBT Status from 2007 to 2014." Report by USC Annenberg's Media, Diversity & Social Change Initiative. http://annenberg.usc.edu/pages/~/media/MDSCI/Inequality%20in%20700%20Popular%20Films%2081415.ashx.

So, Alvin. 2004. "Hong Kong's Pathway to Becoming a Global City." In *World Cities Beyond the West: Globalization, Development, and Inequality*, edited by Josef Gugler, pp. 212–239. Cambridge, UK: Cambridge University Press.

Sontag, Susan. 1977. *On Photography*. New York: Farrar, Straus, and Giroux.

Spitulnik, Debra. 2002. "Mobile Machines and Fluid Audiences: Rethinking Reception Through Zambian Radio Culture." In *Media Worlds: Anthropology on New Terrain*, edited by Faye Ginsburg, Lila Abu-Lughod, and Brian Larkin, pp. 337–354. Berkeley: University of California Press.

Stokes, Lisa Odham, and Michael Hoover. 1999. *City on Fire: Hong Kong Cinema*. London: Verso.

Storper, Michael. 1994. "The Transition to Flexible Specialization in the U.S. Film Industry: External Economies, the Division of Labor, and the Crossing of Industrial Divides." In *Post-Fordism: A Reader*, edited by Ash Amin, pp. 195–226. London: Blackwell.

Strathern, Marilyn. 1995. "The Relation: Issues in Complexity and Scale." *Prickly Pear Pamphlet No. 6*. Cambridge, UK: Prickly Pear Press.

Strauss, Claudia. 2014. "Unemployment and Divine Plans." *Anthropology News* 55: 16–23. doi: 10.1111/j.1556-3502.2014.55802.x.

Sullivan, John L. 2009. "Leo C. Rosten's Hollywood: Power, Status and the Primacy of Economic and Social Networks in Cultural Production." In *Production Studies: Cultural Studies of Media Industries*, edited by Vicki Mayer, Miranda J. Banks, and John T. Caldwell, pp. 39–53. London: Routledge.

Sutton, Matthew A. 2009. *Aimee Semple McPherson and the Resurrection of Christian America*. Cambridge, MA: Harvard University Press.

Szeto, Mirana M., and Yun-chung Chen. 2013. "To Work or Not to Work: The Dilemma of Hong Kong Film Labor in the Age of Mainlandization." *Jumpcut* 55 http://ejumpcut.org/archive/jc55.2013/SzetoChenHongKong/.

Taussig, Mike. 1980. *The Devil and Commodity Fetishism in South America*. Chapel Hill: University of North Carolina Press.

Taylor, Mac. 2014. "Film and Television Production: Overview of Motion Picture Industry and State Tax Credits." A Legislative Analyst's Office Report. http://www.lao.ca.gov/reports/2014/finance/tax-credit/film-tv-credit-043014.pdf.

Taylor, Philip. 2007. *Modernity and Re-enchantment: Religion in Post-revolutionary Vietnam*. Lanham: Lexington Books.

Teo, Stephen. 2000. "The 1970s: Movement and Transition." In *The Cinema of Hong Kong: History, Arts, Identity*, edited by Poshek Fu and David Desser, pp. 90–112. Cambridge, UK: Cambridge University Press.

Teo, Stephen. 2005. "Wuxia Redux: Crouching Tiger, Hidden Dragon as a Model of Late Transnational Production." In *Hong Kong Connections: Transnational Imagination in Action Cinema*, edited by Meaghan Morris, Siu Leung Li, and Stephen Chan Ching-kiu, pp. 191–204. Durham, NC: Duke University Press.

Teo, Stephen. 2008. "Promise and Perhaps Love: Pan-Asian Production and the Hong Kong-China Interrelationship." *Inter-Asia Cultural Studies* 9(3): 341–358.

Teo, Stephen. 2009. "Hong Kong Cinema in the 21st Century." *The Diplomat* May/June. http://www.the-diplomat.com/article.aspx?aeid=13481.

Tinic, Serra. 2005. *On Location: Canada's Television Industry in a Global Market*. Toronto: University of Toronto Press.

Traweek, Sharon. 1988. *Beamtimes and Lifetimes: The World of High Energy Physicists*. Cambridge, MS: Harvard University Press.

Turkle, Sherry. 1984. *The Second Self: Computers and the Human Spirit*. New York: Simon and Schuster.

Turner, Terence. 1992. "Defiant Images: The Kayapo Appropriation of Video." *Anthropology Today* 8: 5–15.

Turner, Victor. 1995 [1969]. *The Ritual Process: Structure and Anti-Structure* (Lewis Henry Morgan Lectures). Piscataway, New Jersey: Aldine Transaction.

Turner, Victor. 1985. *The Anthropology of Performance*. New York: PAJ Publications.

Turner, Victor. 1986. *On the Edge of the Bush: Anthropology as Experience*. Tucson: University of Arizona Press.

Vitalis, Robert. 2000. "American Ambassador in Technicolor and Cinemascope: Hollywood and Revolution on the Nile." In *Mass Mediations: New Approaches to Popular Culture in the Middle East and Beyond*, edited by Walter Armbrust, pp. 269–291. Berkeley: University of California Press.

Ward, Barbara. 1979. "Not Merely Players: Drama, Art, and Ritual in Traditional China." *Man* 14(1): 18–39.

Warner, Kristen J. 2015. *The Cultural Politics of Colorblind TV Casting*. New York: Routledge.

Waxman, Sharon. 2006. "Cyberface: New Technology That Captures the Soul." *Los Angeles Times*, October 15.

Weller, Robert. 1994a. "Capitalism, Community, and the Rise of Amoral Cults in Taiwan." In *Asian Visions of Authority: Religion and the Modern States of East and Southeast Asia*, edited by Charles F. Keyes, Laurel Kendall, and Helen Hardacre, pp. 141–164. Honolulu: University of Hawaii Press.

Weller, Robert. 1994b. *Resistance, Chaos and Control in China: Taiping Rebels, Taiwanese Ghosts and Tiananmen*. Macmillan Press and University of Washington Press.

Weller, Robert. 2000. "Living at the Edge: Religion, Capitalism, and the End of the Nation-State in Taiwan." *Public Culture* 3: 477–498.

Wilkinson-Weber, Clare. 2004. "Behind the Seams: Designers and Tailors in the Hindi Film Industry." *Visual Anthropology Review* 20(2): 3–21.

Wilkinson-Weber, Clare. 2012. "An Anthropologist Among the Actors." *Ethnography* 13(2): 144–161.

Williams, Tony. 2000. "Space, Place and Spectacle: The Crisis Cinema of John Woo." In *The Cinema of Hong Kong: History, Arts, Identity*, edited by Poshek Fu and David Desser, pp. 137–157. Cambridge, UK: Cambridge University Press.

Wolf, Arthur. 1974. "Gods, Ghosts, and Ancestors." In *Religion and Ritual in Chinese Society*, edited by Arthur Wolf, pp. 131–182. Stanford, CA: Stanford University Press.

Yang, Mayfair Mei Hui. 1997. "Mass Media and Transnational Subjectivity in Shanghai: Notes on (Re)cosmopolitanism in a Chinese Metropolis." In *Ungrounded Empires: The Cultural Politics of Modern Chinese Transnationalism*, edited by Aihwa Ong and Donald Nonini, pp. 287–322. New York: Routledge.

Yang, Mayfair Mei Hui. 2004. "Goddess Across the Taiwan Strait: Matrifocal Ritual Space, Nation-State, and Satellite Television Footprints." *Public Culture* 16(2): 209–238.

Yanagisako, Sylvia J. 2002. *Producing Culture and Capital: Family Firms in Italy*. Princeton, NJ: Princeton University Press.

Yelvington, Kevin A. 1995. *Producing Power: Gender, Ethnicity, and Class in a Caribbean Workplace*. Philadelphia: Temple University Press.

Yeh, Yueh-yu Emilie, and Darrell W. Davis. 2002. "Japan Hongscreen: Pan-Asian Cinemas and Flexible Accumulation." In *Historical Journal of Film, Radio, and Television* 22(1): 62–82.

Yeh, Yueh-yu Emilie, and Darrell W. Davis. 2008. "Re-nationalizing China's Film Industry: Case Study on the China Film Group and Film Marketization." *Journal of Chinese Cinemas* 2(1): 37–51.

Yuen, Nancy Wang. 2016. *Reel Inequality: Hollywood Actors and Racism.* New Brunswick, NJ: Rutgers University Press.

Yung, Sai-Shing. 2005. "Moving Body: The Interactions Between Chinese Opera and Action Cinema." In *Hong Kong Connections: Transnational Imagination in Action Cinema*, edited by Meaghan Morris, Siu Leung Li, and Stephen Chan Ching-kiu, pp. 21–34. Durham, NC: Duke University Press.

Zaloom, Caitlin. 2006. *Out of the Pits: Traders and Technology from Chicago to London.* Chicago: University of Chicago Press.

Zhan, Mei. 2001. "Does It Take A Miracle? Negotiating Knowledges, Identities and Communities of Traditional Chinese Medicine." *Cultural Anthropology* 16(4): 453–480.

Zhen, Zhang. 2005. *An Amorous History of the Silver Screen: Shanghai Cinema, 1896–1937.* Chicago: University of Chicago Press.

Zhou, Lulu. 2014. "Mainland Chinese Fans, Hong Kong Television Stars, and the Transborder Cultural Consumption." PhD diss., The Chinese University of Hong Kong.

Zizek, Slavoj. 2002. *Welcome to the Desert of the Real: Five Essays on September 11 and Related Dates.* London and New York: Verso.

INDEX

Page numbers in italics indicate photographs and illustrations.

I

Indian entertainment conglomerates, 56, 200n7
Ingold, Tom, 182
intellectual property rights, 55
Interview, The, 39

J

Jillson, Joyce, 20
Jones, Sarah, 194–96

K

Kang-chung, Ng, 183
Kar, Law, 24, 43, 47
"King Kong in Hong Kong: Watching the 'Handover' from the US" (Chow), 109
Kondo, Dorinne, 160, 162–63, 166
kung fu, 107
Kung Fu Hustle, 61
Kwan Man-Ching, Moon, 58–59

L

labor. *See also* affective labor; media personnel; unions
divisions on Hong Kong production sets, 202n3
emotional, 154, 155
flexibility, 49–55
Hollywood, Hong Kong media industries and, 42–43, 46–55, 97
practices and camera technology, 178–79, 180, 202n3
transnational, 99
WGA strike of 2007, 88, 95, *96,* 97
lai see (lucky money), 2–3, *126, 128, 136*
Lake Hollywood, *44*
Lauzen, Martha M., 94
Law, Bruce, 184
Law Lok Sam, 2–3
Lee, Bruce, 5, 24, 59
statue, *59*
Lester, Richard, 114

live entertainment, early. *See also* variety theaters
audience of, 77–78
local production. *See also* Hollywood local production
Hong Kong local production, 184, 184t, 187, 189–91, *190*
transnational flows of, 99
loss, as media production theme, 11–12
Lucas, George, 38–39
Lung-won, Bak, 18

M

Ma, Eric Kit-wai, 8, 29, 53
magic shows, 70
mahurat (astrologically-timed ceremony), 199n10
makeup artists, 68, 72–73
male domination, of media production, 26, 68–69, 142, 159. *See also* gender discrimination
Malinowski, Bronislaw, 6, 7
Mankekar, Purnima, 153, 154, 155
martial arts films, 59
Mayer, Vicki, 5, 8, 13, 28, 78, 92, 201n2
McPherson, Aimee Semple, 20
media assemblages
Cantonese opera troupes and, 58–59
Hollywood television production and, 91
Hong Kong media personnel in Hollywood and, 88, 98–104
joint productions and collaborations, 55–62, 187
media personnel and, 25, 57–61
overview, 24–25, 33, 55–56
stunt workers, martial arts and, 59
media conglomerates
Hollywood studio, 28, 191–92
Indian entertainment, 56, 200n7